DISINTEGRATION
OR
TRANSFORMATION?

THE CRISIS OF THE STATE IN
ADVANCED INDUSTRIAL SOCIETIES

Patrick McCarthy and Erik Jones

EDITORS

St. Martin's Press

DISINTEGRATION OR TRANSFORMATION?
THE CRISIS OF THE STATE IN ADVANCED INDUSTRIAL SOCIETIES
Copyright © 1995 by Patrick McCarthy and Erik Jones
All rights reserved. Printed in the United States of America.
No part of this book may be used or reproduced in any manner whatsoever
without written permission except in the case of brief quotations embodied
in critical articles or reviews. For information, address St. Martin's Press,
Scholarly & Reference Division, 175 Fifth Avenue, New York, N.Y. 10010

ISBN 0-312-12199-7

Library of Congress Cataloging-in-Publication Data

Disintegration or transformation? : the crisis of the state in
  advanced industrial societies / Patrick McCarthy and Erik Jones,
  editors. — 1st ed.
        p.   cm.
    Includes bibliographical references and index.
    ISBN 0-312-12199-7 (alk. paper)
      1. State, The—Case studies. 2. Political cultures—Case studies.
I. McCarthy, Patrick, 1941-   . II. Jones, Erik.
JC131.D57   1995
320.1'09'049—dc20   95-37477
                                                                  CIP

INTERIOR DESIGN BY DIGITAL TYPE & DESIGN

First Edition: December 1995
10   9   8   7   6   5   4   3   2   1

CONTENTS

To the city of Bologna,
and all the friends we have made there.

PREFACE

As junior editor of this collection, the task of preparing the manuscript to send to the publisher somehow inexorably found its way to me. Even worse, I think it was my idea. Nevertheless, having the final word gives me the chance to give credit where deserved and to express my gratitude to the two people who inspired this collection, Patrick McCarthy, my co-editor, and David Calleo, my dissertation supervisor.

The idea of writing about the state, as opposed to a particular region or country, emerged out of the many similarities between Professor McCarthy's recent work on *tangentopoli* (bribe-city) in Italy and Professor Calleo's work on *The Bankrupting of America*. Conversations with Gregory Marchildon about my own dissertation on Belgium brought out the obvious comparison with Canada. And previous work on France, by Julius Friend, and on Germany, by Dana Allin, gave added depth to the still-vague picture.

Our study only came into focus, however, when we called upon Sergio Fabbrini to provide a different perspective on Italy and when we asked Michael Green to share his insights on Japan. Professor McCarthy agreed to shift his attention to the UK, his country of birth, and suddenly we had a chain of similarities that reached across cultures, nationalities, and governmental structures.

The present volume is the result, with its thematic introduction and national case studies. Where possible, Professor McCarthy and I have tried to start the process of in-depth comparison. More often, however, we have restricted ourselves to developing the themes we believe to be common to the "crisis of the state in advanced industrial societies," and we have asked our colleagues to consider the same themes in drafting their own contributions.

On Professor McCarthy's behalf, I would like to use these concluding paragraphs to acknowledge a primary debt to our contributors, whose timeliness was the essential ingredient in our work. In addition, I would like to thank the Political Studies Association for allowing us to reproduce (in updated form) Professor Calleo's essay on the United States. The essay originally appeared in the 1994 special edition of *Political Studies* under the title: "America's Federal Nation State: A Crisis of Post-Imperial Viability?"

Credit is also due to our respective institutions—the Bologna Center of the Johns Hopkins University (Bologna, Italy) and the Centre for European Policy Studies (Brussels, Belgium) for allowing us to take the time to prepare this volume. Bologna Center director Robert Evans and CEPS director Peter Ludlow deserve particular gratitude for generously making available the logistical support necessary to coordinate a project that spans the Atlantic. Our thanks go also to CEPS librarian Françoise de Rose for tracking down and confirming numerous bibliographic references.

From St. Martin's, Simon Winder and Michael Flamini provided useful editorial guidance. And, on the more technical side, Sarah Picchi provided the advice and encouragement necessary to ensure that what we have written is actually what we meant to say. Her help in this regard is deeply appreciated. Obviously any remaining errors are our own.

The final words of gratitude belong to Veronica Pye and Kate McCarthy, who allowed their husband and father to be highjacked by a former student who simply won't seem to go away.

ERIK JONES
Brussels
June 1995

·1·

The Crisis of the State in Advanced Industrial Societies

Patrick McCarthy and Erik Jones

This book is about change. It is also about the nation-state, its transformation or disintegration. By looking at a sample of advanced industrial societies we hope to understand better what is happening to the state in periods of upheaval. Even within the range of countries that may be considered industrially advanced the diversity is striking; to venture outside of this group would be impossible in a book of this length. The Central European states—such as Poland, the Czech Republic, and Hungary —not only face exacerbated forms of many of the problems discussed in this book, but must also wrestle with their Communist past. Even within the European Union the variety of problems is striking as Ireland still ponders its unity and grapples with the issue of Catholicism and laicization. The latter is a question that France resolved a century ago, only to have it re-posed in a new form by Moslem immigrants.

However, the essential tasks that a state faces are universal, and they remain what they have been since democracy took shape. A state is legitimate if it adequately represents those who live within its boundaries and if it is competent in caring for their interests. These matters are less simple than they seem. In what sense did the Thatcher government "represent" Britain when it won the support of only 44 percent of the electorate? Does the level of efficiency in Italian public services constitute "competence"? In

Charles de Gaulle's eyes the test of competence was a state's ability to protect its citizens against attack from outside. The state also claims a domestic monopoly of the legitimate use of force.[1] But in Italy the state's monopoly of violence is challenged by the Mafia, which, significantly, tries to negotiate with the state as an equal and perceives itself as a state.[2]

In addition, the state has another set of tasks, which it shares with the nation, with its regions, with its religions, with the various corps of civil society, and with the family. It is supposed to offer its citizens an identity, an image of themselves of which they can be proud and that helps them to perform their duties as citizens.[3] To turn this concept around, states where large numbers of people refrain from voting, avoid paying taxes, and pollute the environment are not providing such an identity. This is also a more complex matter than it seems for democratic states must not demand to monopolize identity, and yet sharp clashes with other kinds of identity weaken the state, as for example, the Italian state has been damaged by the Vatican's claim on the allegiance of its citizens.[4]

All of these problems are posed today in forms dictated by world time. But although these forms constitute the main theme of this chapter, individual states do not deal with them in the same manner. National time persists, interwoven with, but separate from, world time. The global economy imposes a move toward free trade and a reduction of state intervention, but Britain and France set about meeting these requirements in very different ways. Each country is shaped by its national past, by liberalism and dirigisme respectively.[5] Membership of regional blocs such as the European Union (EU) does not obliterate national time, rather each nation-state tries to impose its culture on the bloc—France's EU is nationalist, Britain's is Atlanticist, and Germany's is federalist. The following chapters demonstrate that each state has its own crisis, although many share the same symptoms.

Conversely this does not mean that Britain and Germany will survive unscathed and remain faithful to a frequently invented image of their past. Innumerable observers have foreseen the demise of the nation-state. Some fifteen years ago Jean-François Lyotard argued that power was slipping from national elites, trained in national education systems, to an international technical-scientific elite associated with multinational corporations. The nation-state was a creation of modernity, but postmodern structures are global.[6]

Certainly the state is faced with an array of international rivals. Multinational corporations, which relocate wherever conditions are best and which force the states to compete for their favors by offering infrastructure and skilled labor, are merely one example.[7] Others are trading blocs such as the North Atlantic Free Trade Association (NAFTA), politico-economic confederations like the EU, and rich clubs like the Group of Seven (G7). Only they are large enough to bargain in such fora as the General Agreement on Trade and Tariffs (GATT). The world economy has dwarfed the nation-state. The international assembly line and the movement of capital by computer networks have perforated national frontiers.

To complete the discomfiture of the state, so the argument runs, the global meshes with the local: For example, linguistic divisions acquire renewed salience in Belgium and Canada. Regional movements undermine the state from within as prosperous regions believe they can bargain better in international fora without poorer regions to weaken them.[8] Such movements have shifted from "have-nots" seeking a larger slice of the national cake—Wallonia, Wales, or Brittany—to "haves" like Baden-Württemburg, Lombardy, and Catalonia which seek a Europe of the regions.[9] Even more insidious is the tendency of civil society in advanced countries to reject the pedagogical role of the state and to make decisions about vital matters—such as sexuality, birth, and death—on its own.[10]

Stranded between the tendency to band together and the temptation to disintegrate, the nation-states are prey to anomie.[11] One manifestation is political corruption, as demonstrated by Japan and Italy. Whether the corruption explodes because national political systems have lost their role and parties have lost their sense of mission, or whether the corruption is old but is only now revealed because the state has been stripped of its sacred aura does not matter in this context. National institutions are losing their legitimacy. The tribulations of Princess Diana are caused by a press that no longer sees a need to protect the monarchy. It is not merely that Rupert Murdoch's communications group is worldwide and hence indifferent to the fate of the British state. The readers of the *Sun* and the *News of the World* do not need a traditional monarchy to reinforce their identity: they have not ceased to feel British.

AND YET THE STATE REMAINS

There is abundant evidence that within the European Union people consider themselves to be Dutch or Spanish rather than European.[12] Popular patriotism is rampant and institutional decline may strengthen it. In Italy Silvio Berlusconi used the success of his soccer team, AC Milan, in the European Champions Cup as a weapon in his election victory. Significantly he fused AC Milan with the national team, calling his campaign workers "the Blues," which is Italy's color, rather than "the Red and Blacks," after the Milan shirts. Soccer united the Italian nation when its political and economic elites were discredited by the Clean Hands investigation.[13]

So the need for the nation-state is still felt. It is the bulwark that distinguishes Norwegians from the European Union. It is the engine that elevated Bill Clinton to the presidency and then deprived him of a Congressional majority, all in the hope that the U.S. government will turn inward and concentrate on the ills of the nation rather than those of the world. And it is the wave of protest evident in the Maastricht referenda held in Denmark and France where voters demonstrated that they expected the Danish and French governments to defend them against faceless Brussels technocrats. In France the "no" campaign was led by Philippe Séguin who consciously cast himself in the tradition of popular Gaullism or Bonapartism. Two thirds of the Gaullist party followed Séguin rather than its leader, Jacques Chirac, who called for a "yes" vote. Moreover there is an organic link between the 49 percent "no" vote, which included blue-collar workers protesting against the unemployment associated with the Internal Market, as well as farmers voting against cuts in the Common Agricultural Policy subsidies, and the Gaullist Party's victory in the 1993 elections to the French Parliament. The Gaullists won because they were identified with defense of the French state.

This leads us closer to the core of the crisis. Despite the Gaullist victory, Edouard Balladur's new government continued the François Mitterrand policy of a strong franc and a close tie with Germany. Séguin and Chirac—in a more guarded way—called for a reduction of interest rates to combat unemployment at the cost of letting the franc decline and weakening the alliance with Germany. Yet Balladur did not heed them even during the currency crisis of August 1993. He adhered to his "internationalist" policy, and Chirac did not press. This indicates that the "nationalist" option is unreal in an international economy, and yet the government has paid a price, which in turn provoked Chirac to renew his attack by calling for a referendum on monetary union.

The price has come in two forms, the first of which is a strengthening of protest movements. Most of them are on the Right—Le Pen's Front national is the reincarnation of a long French tradition of extreme nationalism, while Philippe de Villiers's movement is a more polite version of it. However Bernard Tapie's supporters are situated on the Center-Left. This is less common because, if there is a market for protest against the many manifestations of internationalism, then the radical Right has an advantage. But the Lega

Nord was an unhappy member of Silvio Berlusconi's coalition in part because its culture has a left-wing component: it defended the trade unions when they organized a general strike against the budget that it had helped draft. Such incoherence is characteristic of a period where rapid change has undermined traditional forms of political allegiance and social categories.

Thus it becomes more difficult for the state to arbitrate among blocs of voters, explaining to some that their interests cannot fully be met. This spans the second difficulty: when groups take their demands to the street, governments are obliged to chose between repression and concession. The Balladur government backed down in the face of farmers and fishermen, while, in a potentially more important situation, it retreated from a plan to reduce the minimum wage for young people. Since high wage costs and rigidity in the labor market are two of the reasons cited for French unemployment, one might argue that the government was prevented by protest from taking action to solve a problem that is discrediting the nation-state.

A vicious circle had been set up, another phase of which is that weak governments are less able to win concessions in international fora, which further weakens their legitimacy. The crisis of the nation-state plays itself out: Centrist governments are condemned to internationalism because the national option is no longer valid. Beneath this lies an organic link between national coherence and international integration. Only well-integrated nations have the strength to integrate with the larger world.[14] The logic here is formalized in the concept of two-level games, where national leaders negotiate collectively with each other and separately with their own electorates.[15] If governments can no longer claim the support of their electorates, the international bargaining process breaks down; hence the reliance in the United States on so-called "fast-track" negotiations, and the troubled GATT ratification in the U.S. Senate.

Similarly, a national government's inability to shape international events vitiates its authority at home, exposing it to rhetorical protest that does not seek to replace it but that feeds on its misfortunes.[16] The Austrian elections of October 1994 afford an example. The governing coalition of the Socialist and People's Parties has seen its vote decline in eight years from 84 percent to 63 percent. It could no longer ensure the two-thirds majority that was needed for the constitutional reforms to allow Austria to enter the EU. Meanwhile the right-wing protest party, led by Jörg Haider, jumped from 16.6 percent to 23 percent.

In a familiar development two small parties—the Liberals and the Greens—also benefitted from the losses of the government coalition.

Fragmentation is another aspect of the ills that afflict national political systems as voters, who are freed from ideological and class bonds, express ever more "local" identities as hunters and fishermen or supporters of the motor car. The danger is that the national government will be unable either to represent or to act for such a plethora of interest groups, many of them unreal because they are no more than fictitious incarnations of alienation: here it may be useful to consider the symbolism, supporters, and, above all, political power of the U.S. National Rifle Association (NRA).

As the state's authority is weakened, so it is unable to deal with the all-too-real issue of the underclass that is formed by high unemployment, declining social services, immigration, and prejudice against immigrants. The riots in Brixton, Toxteth, Bristol, and elsewhere, which marked the Thatcher years, are being matched by the violence in Mantes and Dreux on the outskirts of Paris or at Ostia near Rome. To American observers these seem minor, which is precisely why they are worrying: their potential for matching the racial tensions of Los Angeles is great. The development of a permanent underclass, culturally as well as financially deprived, challenges the solidarity of the nation as well as the very notion of citizenship.

In our context it is only one, albeit the most grave, example of the nation-state's declining ability to represent and display competence, much less to inspire. However examples of states that have improved their performance are not lacking. Italy might not seem a plausible example since in the Autumn of 1994 the Berlusconi government was striving to monopolize television, which it used as a means of manipulating the public; it actively discouraged citizenship by offering generous amnesties for non-payment of taxes and infringements of the building code, while Berlusconi himself showed no sense of the need to separate his economic interests from that of Italy. Yet Italians have shown their desire for citizenship in the anti-Mafia movement and in initiatives such as the "fax people's" demonstration of support for the Milan magistrates.

More important, since 1992 Italy has made a bid to reform the state in part to enable it to play its role in the international arena. Support by the Employers Association for electoral reform in the 1991 and 1993 referenda was inspired by the belief that Italy needed a more responsible political system and improved public services, if it were to compete in the Internal Market. The form that the crisis of the state has taken in Italy results in part from an effort to modernize. A political class that used social services for clientelistic ends and that levied a bribe-tax on public contracts became intolerable to the civil society of Northern Italy. Laicization and the end of the Cold War removed the reasons to vote for the Christian Democrats who had set up a regime based on systemic clientelism in the 1950s. Thus the very factors that were supposedly working to undermine the nation-state created in Italy the conditions for its, admittedly as yet unsuccessful, transformation.

German history since reunification offers a mixed, but not unimpressive performance by a nation-state. Helmut Kohl's government has been criticized for its refusal to pay for the conversion of the Eastern economy by tax increases, which had the effect of compelling the Bundesbank to raise interest rates in order to check the inflation created by government borrowing. This damaged the other EU economies, even if they were able to increase their exports to Germany in the first two years after reunification. Germany gradually made concessions to its neighbors and at Maastricht agreed to monetary union, long a French goal, and did not press for a federalist Europe, to which France objected. More recently Germany has also agreed to the use of its armed forces in peacekeeping missions, in response to pressure from its North Atlantic Treaty Organization (NATO) partners. In the October 1994 elections the center-right Kohl government won a narrow victory as the center-left Social Democrats gained votes, and yet the radical right Republikaner failed to obtain representation in parliament.

Finally, there is the United States, where voters returned a Republican Congress for only the second time since the end of World War II. Although this changeover in party control of the legislature threatens to deadlock the final two years of the Clinton administration, and possibly even heralds a (partial) retreat to isolationism, the electorate has shown that it will not accept a continuance of "business as usual" from either of the two main parties. Moreover, the obvious potency of the electoral process has sapped support from some reform measures (like term limitations on legislators) while strengthening the appeal of others (like a constitutional amendment for balancing the federal budget).

THE BARGAINING STATE

These examples indicate how nation-states must be transformed if they are to continue performing their traditional tasks. In the age of the global economy they must become bargaining states.[17] Sovereignty in monetary matters, for example, has been lost for most countries by abandonment of currency controls and the improved technology of capital markets. A certain degree of power may be recovered by states willing to pool sovereignty, to negotiate more efficiently, and so on.[18] A variant is that an electorate may be persuaded to accept sacrifices, if they are presented as the price of increased influence in international fora. Irish governments have tried over the last fifteen years to make austerity palatable by depicting it as the prerequisite for remaining in the EU, a source of agricultural subsidies and regional aid as well as an organization that offers Ireland relief from the stifling embrace of Great Britain.[19]

The limits of such blandishments are clear, but nation-states must, if they are to flourish, make the changes in their political culture, economies, and societies that the global economy demands. The abandonment of overly nationalist policies is only one such change. As the Berlusconi government discovered, international markets are quick to punish financial laxity: the price of ignoring a government debt that stands at around 120 percent of GDP takes the form of a declining lira and higher interest rates on government bonds. From this viewpoint it is inaccurate to speak of less public intervention in the economy. Even in the area of industrial policy governments have indeed largely given up nationalizations and direct subsidies. Still, there is much that national governments can do to improve infrastructure and to create skilled labor. Success in such areas allows a state to influence the global economy: the quality of German labor allows it to dominate the international trade in machine tools, making it a model for other countries.

FROM KEYNESIANISM, THROUGH MONETARISM, TOWARD WHAT?

Yet here precisely is the gravest threat to the national state: In the 1950s its role was "happy," it provided its gratified citizens with social services and demand-led growth. Now the state imposes austerity, it cuts back welfare, and it declares that hitherto unacceptable levels of unemployment are "structural." Since all these unhappy things are done in the name of international competitiveness, the state seems nothing more than the handmaiden of the almighty global economy. In fact the new period challenges the state to adapt. We must now examine specific aspects of the interaction between various states and world time.

The open economy has replaced the closed blocs of the Cold War. It is hard to imagine that one might regret the passage of the Cold War, with its static ideologies, its Orwellian hate sessions, and its intolerance of nonconformity. Nor was it kind to the nation-state: de Gaulle argued that it locked the old nations of Western Europe into a bloc dominated by the

United States and he sought to improve relations with the Soviet Union in order to gain greater leverage for France.

Yet the Cold War also assigned tasks and hence legitimacy to the states within the Western Alliance, and the loss of these tasks has caused upheaval. This is most obviously true of the United States, which for forty years lived out the leading role as champion of freedom. The end of the Cold War caused a debate where the Bush administration tried to prolong the role by casting the United States as the global superpower. But despite Saddam Hussein's help, George Bush failed because running the Western Alliance had helped undermine the U.S. economy.[20] Since Bush's fall from grace, the U.S. economy has improved, although whether it is because of Bill Clinton's policies is dubious, particularly as his administration has been forced to conduct a more active foreign policy than it at first intended.[21] The shifts of roles and the general problem of withdrawing from a position of hegemony to one of shared leadership have troubled the U.S. state but have not crippled it.

The end of American hegemony has provoked rethinking among the allies. Japan has been forced to take stock of its position, which can no longer be one of a protectorate allowed to concentrate on economic development. Japan's success in this sphere has led to clashes with its former protector and the need to redefine the functions of the Japanese state. It must be more active in the foreign and security sphere and more open economically. It may well be that such changes will in turn open Japanese society and undermine a political system based on one-party rule and riddled with corruption. Such a process can hardly not be painful but it is likely to expand rather than contract the state's power.

The West European states are hesitating between realizing de Gaulle's vision of independence from the American protectorate and allowing themselves to be overwhelmed by their economic difficulties. Rapid development of the Maastricht plan for a common foreign and security policy and the expansion of the West European Union's role would not only prevent future tragedies such as Bosnia, but would strengthen the independence of the EU confederation and hence of its member states. Nevertheless, the practical and financial challenges to developing a true European defense identity are legion, and made all the more difficult as European electorates cling to their "peace dividends" in order to soften the impact of fiscal austerity.

So far we have argued that the advanced industrial states will gain power from the removal of the Soviet threat and the straitjacket of the Western Alliance. However the argument has been made that the Cold War gave a deeper meaning to the life of states. Values emerged through the struggle between the capitalist democracies and the Communist bloc, and victory in the struggle became a goal that endowed history with significance. The Cold War belonged to the period that began with the Enlightenment and the collapse of Communism marks the end of that period.[22] With the end of the Cold War, goals and values disappeared and the world is "deprived of sense." In turn this vitiates the life of the states accustomed to projecting their "sense" against the outside world. Now, lacking antithesis and adversaries, and finding outside itself only other versions of itself engaged in the global economy, the state can no longer create meaning.[23]

If, by meaning, one understands a total or teleological meaning, this view is certainly correct. Moreover the contemporary state is not the grand, independent force that it may have been—or at least pretended to be—when it was able to send its citizens to die in hundreds of thousands in 1914. However, one might suggest that the very bargaining process creates a kind of value. Could not states, like propositions, acquire substance through what Lyotard calls "communicational interaction."[24] If states remain, as we have argued, very different, then surely their attempt to reach agreements could become a moral struggle to create a more harmonious order. Of course this depends on how one understands "globalization."

Until now we have avoided the term that has come to mean something different from, and more than, the global economy. Globalization also comprises the impact of information technology, the rise of an epistemic elite and a qualitative change in the human condition. Thus it can be affirmed that the Major government, which came to power after 1989, has more in common with the Balladur government than with the Thatcher government that preceded it in Britain.[25] Clearly our emphasis on national political culture does not allow us to accept this, but more is involved. The assertion that the human condition has changed leads to the depiction of globalization as a nightmare because deprived of sense, or as a utopia where the military and economic clashes of previous history are resolved.[26] However, in our view no such transformation has taken place. States—albeit much altered—their struggles, their occasional victories, and their lapses into original sin, still constitute normality.[27]

For this reason we limit ourselves to the term "the global economy," which describes a centuries-old process that sped up after the Second World War, and has accelerated again with the collapse of Communism. In one sense this term too is inaccurate, for the economy, or at least the prosperity it brings, is not global. Africa risks being excluded except for its Southern tip, while Eastern Europe is half-in and half-out. The new economy is marked by an enormous expansion of the market and hence also of its logic, but this in no sense means that the market can replace states, or even confederations of states and international organizations like the United Nations (UN) or the G7—organizations that are no stronger than the states that compose them. The market cannot police itself: the example of the environment is only one case where limits must be set on the circulation of market values. The tenet that "the polluter pays" is inadequate because there are occasions when pollution must be prevented.

The threat to the state is really a threat to one kind of state, which was linked with an earlier stage of economic development and which we might term the Keynesian state. The postwar use of John Maynard Keynes's thought turned into a fully-fledged design for a state with its particular economic and social policies and its political actors. It operated within the context of the Fordist economy and an international order dominated by the United States. Its chief characteristic was a certain kind of interventionism. Although it might tolerate nationalizations, the Keynesian state did not consider them necessary, and it did not share the Socialist belief in public ownership. It did, however, believe in shaping the economy by fiscal and monetary policy and in particular it believed that economic growth could be created through demand management.

It thus offered a solution to the mass unemployment of the 1930s and it was one cause—but only one and in itself an insufficient cause—of the high growth of the 1950s and 1960s. Politically the Keynesian state was reformist and conciliatory: Class conflicts could be resolved by steady economic growth, trade unions became important political actors, politics were centrist, governments were dominated by Social and Christian Democrats. With the fruits of growth the welfare state was built. Societies grew more democratic, although it was clear as early as the 1950s that social inequality was blurred rather than abolished.

The contrast with the 1930s was so great that the Keynesian state seemed impregnable. Yet it was dependent on the international order; on the ability and willingness of the United States to guarantee stability, whether monetary or military, and on the profitability of the Fordist industries—steel, coal, cars—that were the engines of full employment. Once these two pillars were shaken in the 1970s, the edifice of the Keynesian state began to crumble. It also contained internal contradictions: continuous expansion of demand created inflation that could be reduced only by unpopular contraction of demand. More important, the state's interventionist role grew too profusely and it lost its ability to arbitrate and to look beyond the short term.

All this is well known, but another theme has been less stressed although it emerges clearly from the comparative studies of this book. The Keynesian state was not a separate construction but was grafted onto the existing state structures, which were quite varied.[28] Thus the German state inherited a distrust of inflation that left it suspicious of Keynesianism. The French state integrated Keynesianism into its powerful, centralized dirigisme, Belgium and the Netherlands adapted it to their corporatist organization, while in Britain Keynesianism was a temporary palliative for the problems of a historically stagnant state. In consequence, not only were some states—such as Germany—better equipped to confront the crumbling of Keynesianism in the 1970s, but in no case did this mean the end of the state itself. Rather one form that various states had adopted would be replaced by another, it too grafted onto the traditional state.

In retrospect it is clear that neo-liberal talk of doing away with the state was misleading.[29] Neo-liberals wished to do away with the Keynesian state and to replace it with their own—for lack of a better term—"monetarist" state. Even had they wished to banish the state, they could not have done so because they needed it to destroy the old political actors. Margaret Thatcher strengthened the police, toughened her party and gained a reputation for not changing her mind before she did battle with the coal miners in 1984. Where Edward Heath had stumbled into conflict with them and never gave up hope of an agreement, Thatcher saw Arthur Scargill as a second Leopoldo Galtieri. Similarly Ronald Reagan dispatched the air-traffic controllers.

What then were the outlines of the new "monetarist" state? To begin with, it was assertive in foreign policy: Reagan criticized not only Jimmy Carter but also Henry Kissinger for appearing weak in the face of the Soviets, while one may safely say that previous British governments would not have gone to war over the Falklands. The state wished to convey to its own citizens that it possessed an authority that it would use both on their behalf and against them. The key tenet was the state's partial withdrawal from the economic sphere. It would stabilize domestic prices but it would not guarantee full employment, mediate wage disputes, or bail out lame-duck industries. The state's role was thus to set the market working again, free of the encumbrances it had accumulated. Yet this was not really a withdrawal because in order to rein in domestic inflation, the state had to control interest rates, which in turn helped determine the level of economic activity. Moreover by holding down inflation, the state made implicit political choices; first, between inflation and unemployment—which the state denied by declaring all unemployment structural, and therefore unrelated to the level of economic activity; and second, by allowing unemployment to grow, it chose to weaken trade unions and to increase the share of value-added that went to business.[30]

Where the Keynesian state sought consensus, the monetarist state was combative. A segment of the population was to become worse off and social disorder—Brixton, Toxteth—would increase. Hence the need for a strong law and order stance. Cuts in welfare spending represented a decline in statism, but along with them went an increased role for the state in the control of immigration. The political balance of the state shifted to the Right: In Britain and Germany, home of Europe's largest Social Democratic parties, the Left lost power in 1979 and 1982 respectively and the Right began a period in office that is still in progress.

The monetarist state was grafted on to the various state traditions and assumed national forms. In Germany, where the Bundesbank defeated the unions easily in 1975, the transition was easy. The political form it took was the *Wende* of 1982, in which the Free Democrats changed coalition partners. In the United States, conversely, the political change from Carter to Reagan was made with the sound of trumpets, but in fact the economic austerity that the monetarist state is supposed to guarantee never followed. Throughout Reagan's two terms in office, the American habit of running deficits grew stronger.[31]

France offers a complex example because the transformation of the state was underwritten by the Left and because it involved changing the traditional dirigisme. Overburdened after the second oil crisis, the state reacted in three ways. It withdrew from some functions and pushed civil society to replace it: Finance Minister Pierre Bérégovoy, encouraged companies to raise money on capital markets instead of borrowing from nationalized banks. The state took a tougher line with its own employees, holding down wage increases in the public sector. It launched into international bargaining, accepting the discipline of the European Monetary System (EMS) and the hegemony of the Deutschemark but initiating a new drive toward European unity which would give the French state more influence over Germany and, via the EC, over the world economy.[32]

Finally, in the corporatist states like Belgium and the Netherlands, the Right reactivated the mechanisms for price-wage bargaining, and harnessed them to the task of disinflation. There the trade unions could not be destroyed because their discipline was essential to the success of government austerity measures and wage controls. But by preserving the trade unions, the Right also preserved its political alternative, enabling the electorates of both countries to shift back to the Center-Left by the end of the 1980s.[33]

In the last decade states have continued to evolve, maintaining the broad outlines of the monetarist model but also modifying it. On the whole, trade unions remain weak and central banks strong, but the welfare state, while subject to cuts out of economic necessity, has retained its legitimacy. The shift from Margaret Thatcher to John Major marks a softening of the belligerence that the Conservatives had considered necessary to break with Keynesianism. Canada and Belgium have drawn closer to splitting on linguistic lines out of a combination of economic strains and more self-assertive because better-educated cultural communities. However, in both cases sophisticated arrangements are being devised to retain the essential functions of the original states. Out of these experiments there may emerge new kinds of federal, multicultural states.

The greatest threat to all states is high unemployment, which undermines the legitimacy of international bargaining. In the advanced industrial societies unemployment seems likely to endure as it stems at least in part from the world economy. Although the Third World has been a locomotive of the present nascent recovery,[34] it is hard to see how unskilled workers in high-wage countries can survive competition from countries where wages are many times lower. Protectionism is no answer. Increased flexibility in the labor market will help, while improved job training will help still more. But the latter is a long-term solution and Keynes's comment on the long-run is all too relevant.

As well as retaining their welfare states, countries like France and Germany have demonstrated cohesion. The need is to build on existing bases for solidarity and to improve the bonds of citizenship. During his spell as prime minister, Michel Rocard tried to develop national debates on such subjects as social security and unemployment. His experiments did not go far, but it is hard to see how the creation of an underclass can be avoided without a renewed effort of dialogue. The impact of harder world bargaining can only be mitigated by greater national sharing of jobs as well as other scarce resources.

THE NATION, THE STATE, AND THE CITIZEN

One might conclude by reviewing the triad of nation, state, and civil society. Historically, the basis for the nation has been the solidarity derived from a shared historical or cultural heritage. A common language helps, as does a set of mutually acceptable philosophical principles. Once more national solidarity rests on different foundations in different nations. The United States is rooted in the belief that varied cultural heritages can be woven into a new, American identity. Germany has learned that not all people who speak German may be part of a German nation. Ireland still does not know whether its nation includes none of the people of the North, all of them, or just the Catholic community.

The state is best defined as a collection of people who have decided to live together. They have signed a contract to pay their taxes, not to destroy their natural habitat, and to treat one another as equals before the law. If they constitute a nation, then it will probably be easier for them to abide by their contract. However nation-hood is not a prerequisite for state-hood and in a mobile world like ours overemphasis on certain attributes of nationality is undesirable. The notion, presented by Jean-Marie Le Pen, that only people born of parents who are French may constitute part of the French nation[35] may slide over all too rapidly into the notion that other people are not entitle to the protection of the French state even when they have signed the contract and paid their taxes. A recent vote in California to limit social services to the citizenry of the state has already claimed as least one life unnecessarily, and rhetoric used against illegal immigrants has threatened the status of those who immigrated legally as well.

Modern states are very much *Gesellschaften*—societies based on shared self-interest—because the size and anonymity of the economic processes in which they are actors do not permit the close personal ties and acceptance of authority that characterize the *Gemeinschaft,* or "community." This makes it all the more necessary to widen the concept of citizenship and the underlying mutual trust.

Here again the notion that the more sophisticated civil societies of advanced industrial nations can dispense with the state seems wrong. Certainly the current of individualism, which continues to mark such societies, wants to limit the state's authority to intervene in the ever larger sphere that it defines as private. Thus, divorce, contraception, and abortion are all matters to be decided by the individual. But these decisions raise issues of child care and adoption that cannot be handled without the state.

There must be a constant dialogue between civil society and state that is parallel to the dialogue among states at the world level.[36] Here again power flows between the two partners. In environmental issues the impetus to act often comes from groups that emerge out of civil society. They turn to the state to pass legislation and the state dictates "right-to-know" laws that send power back to civil society. The danger here again is that minority groups will be left out of this information flow. The voice of the unemployed and the immigrants must be heard, as must the have-not states at the world level. This is not a claim made out of idealism but rather out of realism. Shutting out the have-nots will not resolve the crisis of the advanced states. Instead, exclusion will only reinforce the vicious circle of incoherence and disintegration, exacerbating the crisis of the state, and inhibiting its necessary transformation.

THE PLAN OF THE BOOK

This broad introduction to the crisis of the state in advanced industrial society is meant to do just that, introduce. The heart of the matter, as we have argued above, is best examined piecemeal—through the various national case studies. Each of the states that we have examined carries within it the seeds of its own crisis. Thus while the symptoms are often the same, this is more because the state has important universal properties than because the states we examined face a common set of problems to be addressed by common solutions.

In the next chapter, David Calleo questions whether the United States is experiencing the symptoms of imperial overstretch and hegemonic decline. His analysis focusses on a state that for too long concerned itself with developments abroad, at the expense of paying closer attention to the requirements for effective governance at home. Now political entrepreneurs must wrestle with dysfunctional institutions in a political marketplace benefitting from more liquidity than discipline.

Michael Green's analysis of the situation in Japan provides an obvious and important contrast. There, national obsession with Japanese "exceptionalism" combined with a characteristically feudal political structures to undermine both the legitimacy of the state and the efficiency of the marketplace. As economic turmoil and political corruption chip away at Japan's sense of its own uniqueness, the state must choose between alternate visions of its future role in the world.

A similar choice has already been faced by Italy, though as Sergio Fabbrini explains, the outcome is as yet unclear. Like Japan, Italy too was ruled by oligarchical groups of economic and political elites whose legitimacy derived from a mixture of clientelism, ideology, and class. Unlike Japan, however, Italy has little sense of its own exceptionalism. Indeed, the uncertainty of Italy's future is very much linked to the ambiguities of Italian nationalism.

On this point, the appropriate European contrast is with France, where, as Julius Friend notes, the pervasiveness of French nationalism leaves little room for a "crisis of the state." To be sure, France is beset by problems that it can address only through difficult adjustments. Nevertheless, the continuity of France as a nation state is without question.

Dana Allin's analysis of Germany highlights the difficulties of state adaptation to a nation enlarged. Like Japan, this Germany must carve out a space for itself in the post–Cold War world. However, the Germans as a nation lack the self-confidence of either the Japanese or the French, and so they face a moral crisis in some ways linked to their fascist past.

Gregory Marchildon deals not with unification but (perhaps) disintegration. His discussion of Canada reveals the tension inherent to competing forms of nationalism and overlapping levels of administrative jurisdiction. Canada's crisis is very much tied to a lack of equilibrium in terms of identity and responsibility, both regional and national.

Canada is not alone, however, in its struggle to satisfy diverse political communities with an increasingly decentralized state apparatus. As Erik Jones illustrates, Belgium also suffers from the coincidence of competing identities and overlapping jurisdictions. However the origins of the Belgian crisis lie not in the problem of regional separation, but rather in the collapse of an ideologically oriented party system—similar to Italy's. For Belgium, decentralization promises to be more a solution than a problem, provided, at least, that Belgians continue to identify with their national state.

Patrick McCarthy's analysis of the British case brings the discussion full circle by returning to its origins in the "melancholy pleasure of decline." It is here that we see the transition from the Keynesian to the monetarist state in its most extreme form, and here also that we observe the state's difficulties fulfilling a role in a world deprived of sense. With an empowered state but without Thatcher's vision, Britain must struggle to redefine itself both at home and abroad.

◆ NOTES TO CHAPTER 1 ◆

1. Discussion of this attribute of the state is commonly linked to Max Weber, who argued that: "A compulsory political association with continuous organization . . . will be called a 'state' if and in so far as its administrative staff successfully upholds a claim to the *monopoly* of the *legitimate* use of physical force in the enforcement of its order" (emphasis in original). See Max Weber, *Theory of Social and Economic Organization*,

translated by A. M. Henderson and Talcott Parsons, edited by Talcott Parsons (New York: Oxford University Press, 1947), p. 154.

2. Salvatore Lupo, *Storia della mafia* (Rome: Donzelli, 1993), p. 165.

3. The state's creation of popular identity is one half of what has come to be known as the "structuration" process in state-society relations: society establishes the state as a set of institutions (structure) that in turn effect societal attitudes, causing institutional change, et cetera. See Anthony Giddens, *Central Problems in Social Theory: Action, Structure and Contradiction in Social Analysis* (Berkeley: University of California Press, 1979).

4. The threat of "other identities" to the legitimacy of the state is a recurrent theme in Seymour Martin Lipset, *Political Man: The Social Bases of Politics* (New York: Doubleday/Anchor, 1963). However, the legitimacy of the state is also threatened by the absence of identity altogether: Hence Lipset's classic essay on "The End of Ideology" (pp. 439-56).

5. See, for example, Peter A. Hall, *Governing the Economy: The Politics of State Intervention in Britain and France* (New York: Oxford University Press, 1986).

6. Jean-François Lyotard, *La condition postmoderne* (Paris: Minuit, 1979).

7. Here the classic treatment is Raymond Vernon, *Sovereignty at Bay: The Multinational Spread of U.S. Enterprises* (London: Penguin, 1971).

8. As one newspaper columnist recently noted: "Nationalism has discovered the world economy and fallen in love with it." See Neal Acherson, *The Independent on Sunday*, 18 September 1994, p. 18.

9. See, for example, Lothar Späth, "Europe's Nation States Are Obsolete," *European Affairs* (March 1990) pp. 9-13. For a more general treatment of "Europe of the Regions," see Paul Romus, *L'Europe regionale* (Brussels: Editions LABOR, 1990).

10. As of this writing, the Netherlands and the U.S. state of Washington have officially declared their acceptance of doctor-assisted suicides in the event of terminal illness.

11. Walter Lippmann referred to anomie as "drift" and, more recently, John Kenneth Galbraith has labelled it "the culture of contentment." See Walter Lippmann, *Drift and Mastery: An Attempt to Diagnose the Current Unrest* (Englewood Cliffs: Prentice Hall, 1961), William E. Leuchtenburgh and Bernard Wisky, eds.; John Kenneth Galbraith, *The Culture of Contentment* (Boston: Houghton-Mifflin, 1992).

12. See Patrick McCarthy, "Help or Hindrance: The European Union in Domestic Politics," *Harvard International Review* 41:3 (Summer 1994), p. 63. For a thorough treatment of the enduring nature of national cultural differences, see Ronald Inglehart, *Culture Shift in Advanced Industrial Society* (Princeton: Princeton University Press, 1990).

13. Patrick McCarthy, "Silvio Berlusconi: la parola crea l'Uomo Politico," *Europa-Europe* 3 (1994), pp. 243-58.

14. Gunnar Myrdal, *An International Economy: Problems and Prospects* (New York: Harper and Brothers, 1956).

15. Simon Bulmer, "The European Council's First Decade: Between Interdependence and Domestic Politics," *Journal of Common Market Studies* 24:2 (1985), pp. 89-104.

16. We would agree with Zaki Laidi—*Le Monde*, 8 November 1994—that "because nationalism is hard . . . nationalist forces tend to exacerbate it."

17. Pierre Rosanvallon, *L'état en France* (Paris: Seuil, 1990), p. 280.

18. Though it has long been a part of the theory of optimum currency areas, this point seems to have been forgotten by opponents of European monetary integration who fail to see in a common currency the means to shield themselves from the broad fluctuations of the dollar. See Ronald I. McKinnon, "Optimum Currency Areas," *American Economic Review* 53:4 (September 1963), pp. 717-25.

19. The Irish experience sparked economists Francesco Giavazzi and Marco Pagano to question whether severe fiscal contractions might promote economic expansion as a

result of favorable changes in international expectations regarding national economic performance. See Francesco Giavazzi and Marco Pagano, "Can Severe Contractions Be Expansionary? Tales of Two Small European Countries," *CEPR Discussion Papers*, 417 (1990).

20. David P. Calleo, *The Bankrupting of America: How the Federal Deficit Is Impoverishing the Nation* (New York: William Morrow, 1992).

21. See John Peterson, "Europe and America in the Clinton Era," *Journal of Common Market Studies* 32:3 (September 1994), pp. 411-26.

22. Such analysis lies at the heart of the "End of History" debate ignited by Francis Fukyama, "The End of History?" *The National Interest* 16 (Summer 1989), pp. 3-18.

23. Zaki Laidi, *Un monde privé de sens* (Paris: Fayard, 1994), p. 23.

24. Lyotard, *La condition postmoderne*, p. 6.

25. Ghita Ionescu, "Turbulence in British Politics: The First Two Years of the Major Government," *Government and Opposition* 29:1 (Winter 1994), pp. 181-90.

26. Jean Baudrillard, *L'illusion de la fin* (Paris: Galilei, 1992) makes fun of both notions, arguing that history offers no possibility of order or project. In our view, Baudrillard's book should be read as a surrealist fable.

27. Thus our argument accepts many of the conclusion of Stanley Hoffmann, "Obstinate or Obsolete?: The Fate of the Nation-State and the Case of Western Europe," in Stanley Hoffmann, ed., *Conditions of World Order* (Boston: Houghton-Mifflin, 1968), pp. 110-63.

28. Peter Hall, ed., *The Power of Economic Ideas* (Princeton: Princeton University Press, 1989).

29. Andrew Gamble, *The Free Economy and the Strong State: The Politics of Thatcherism* (London: Macmillan, 1994).

30. The first claim, that most unemployment is structural, was initially supported by an impressive consensus among mainstream labor economists. See Edmond Malinvaud, *Profitability and Unemployment* (London: Cambridge University Press, 1980). More recently, however, economists have noted that a more moderate approach to disinflation might have mitigated some of the growth in unemployment during the 1980s. See R. Layard, S. Nickell, and R. Jackman, *Unemployment: Macroeconomic Performance and the Labor Market* (Oxford: Oxford University Press, 1991). Left-wing economists adhere to the second claim that austerity measures were intended to break the back of the trade unions, and are supported by the general decline in trade-union activity at the macroeconomic level. See Göran Therborn, *Why Some Peoples Are More Unemployed than Others* (London: Verso, 1986).

31. Calleo, *The Bankrupting of America*.

32. Patrick McCarthy, "France Faces Reality: Rigueur and the Germans," in David P. Calleo and Claudia Morgenstern, eds., *Recasting Europe's Economies: National Strategies in the 1980s* (Lanham: University Press of America, 1989), pp. 25-78.

33. Erik Jones, "Economic Adjustment and the Political Formula: Strategy and Change in Belgium and the Netherlands," doctoral dissertation, Nitze SAIS, 1995.

34. "A Survey of the Global Economy," *The Economist* (1 October 1994), p. 13.

35. Jean-Marie Le Pen, *Français d'abord* (Paris: Carrere-Michel Lafon, 1984), pp. 30-45.

36. International relations theorists have recently adopted this notion in the concept of structuration. See note 3 above, and Alexander E. Wendt, "The Agent-Structure Problem in International Relations," *International Organization* 41:3 (Summer 1987), pp. 225-70; David Dessler, "What's at Stake in the Agent-Structure Debate?" *International Organization* 43:3 (Summer 1989), pp. 441-73.

·2·

America's Federal Nation-State:
A Post-Imperial Crisis?*

David P. Calleo

D oes the end of the Cold War point less to the triumph of one super-power over the other than to the collapse of both? Intriguing symmetries aside, are there serious reasons to see the United States entering its own crisis as a continental nation state?

While the United States is hardly about to follow the Soviet Union into rapid disintegration, it does have problems as a nation-state that are causing serious trouble now and will almost certainly bring great difficulty in the future. America's problems are not, however, the result of ending its hegemonic global role of the Cold War. Rather they result from bad habits picked up while prolonging that role. But are these problems sufficient to raise serious questions about America's continuing viability as a nation state?

Addressing this issue requires some sense of the traditional problems and performance of the American federal state. In the long run, a state's viability is presumably connected with its performance. A state is meant to preserve physical peace and security for its citizens and their property against external or domestic disorder. A state is also meant to foster economic prosperity and security. And a state is supposed to provide its citizens with a source of pride, awe, and idealism—or at least emotional and psychological satisfaction—a function that grows in importance when traditional religions are in relative decline.

*Adapted from my essay, "America's Federal Nation State: A Crisis of Post-Imperial Viability," first published in *Political Studies*, special issue 1994. Original copyright, Political Studies Association. Used with Permission.

Historically, the United States is often thought to have had a relatively easy task meeting these criteria. The point should not be exaggerated. America's Civil War was, after all, a bloodier military struggle than anything else between the Napoleonic Wars and World War I. For Americans, the death and devastation were much worse than in either World War. But the United States has certainly had an easier task than European nation states in providing security from external threats, thanks to its physical isolation from other great powers. Prosperity has also been relatively easy, with an abundance of space and resources, an enterprising population, and market-oriented culture, and a structure of government that encouraged development and did not smother it with controls.

Historically, the United States has not done badly with the third criterion either. The federal nation state was created around its written Constitution, which has endured for two centuries and which many Americans continue to believe embodies the best liberal and constitutional traditions of the Enlightenment. With the terrible exception of the Civil War, pride in the Constitution has been a powerful support to national unity. Americans have also united around the less intellectual satisfactions of their continental "Manifest Destiny." The "American Dream," a vision combining liberty with economic opportunity, enabled the United States to attract and absorb generations of immigrants, whose numbers and vitality helped the new federal state to assume a preeminent position in the world within a mere century and a half. The large and continuously replenished immigrant population naturally posed a particular challenge for American national identity and political consensus. But the United States succeeded in developing a viable sense of nationality, thanks to the vigor of the dominant Anglo-Saxon culture, which had its own very considerable cosmopolitan and regional diversity, along with the prosperity that made the American Dream a concrete myth for the children and grandchildren of European immigrants as well as for the rest of the country. At the same time, America's "melting pot" has not robbed the nation's culture of a rich ethnic diversity that imparts not only vitality and pride, but also a certain comprehensive identity.

After 1945, however, the basic situation of the American state changed profoundly. This was widely seen as a matter of necessity. After two world wars, isolationism no longer seemed a reasonable way to protect national security. Fulfilling the traditional state functions, particularly once the Cold War had started, no longer appeared possible without remaining a global superpower. Fostering global economic interdependence was widely seen as the best way to preserve America's own peace and prosperity. Intercontinental nuclear weapons were soon to cancel America's old geographic invulnerability.

Changing America's role in the world also changed America's self-image. Alongside the traditional pride in constitutional virtue and economic prosperity grew pride in military prowess and political leadership. Manifest Destiny on the North American continent evolved into an "American Century" for the world. American globalism also changed the face of the nation's government and economy. An enormous peacetime military establishment developed together with a very large imperial political elite occupied with managing or analyzing America's international role. The big peacetime military establishment gave new opportunities for significant parts of the aspiring middle class, while the civilian imperial elite absorbed significant portions of traditional social and intellectual elites. Huge military spending reoriented large sections of the American economy and created numerous symbiotic relationships between business and government around the superpower role.

These radical changes were not universally welcomed. Enthusiasm for the superpower role among the public at large was frequently tempered by a somber reckoning of the burdens and hazards of military service, resentment of elites with greatly enhanced power, and suspicion of foreign "free-riding." A considerable part of the intellectual and political elites worried that the world role would distort constitutional, economic, cultural, and social balances, endanger constitutional democracy, blight prosperity, or embroil the nation in grandiose and perhaps unworthy projects abroad, which might prove its moral, economic, and cultural undoing at home.

Diffidence turned into resistance whenever large-scale fighting was required. This became clear in the Korean War, which probably did more than anything else to end the long ascendancy of the Democratic Party. Public resistance exploded during the Vietnam War and once more drove the Democrats from power. Although a professional army quickly replaced the draft army, it would be twenty years before American forces again engaged in any large-scale military conflict. Nor does American diffidence about military involvements since the Gulf War suggest that the lessons of Vietnam have been erased.

Happily for American political consensus, the Cold War, with its nuclear balance of terror, involved very little actual fighting. There was, however, a great deal of expense for the two superpowers. Arguably, that expense ultimately ruined the Soviet system. It certainly caused a great deal of difficulty for the American system. Just how the imperial role has weakened the huge U.S. economy is a complex and contentious subject. Often, apparently successful policies, based on apparent national strength, have nevertheless worked to undermine the springs of national vitality.

Fiscal conditions are a major point of linkage between world role and national decline. By the time of the Reagan administration (1981-1988), as the Soviet Union was entering its death throes, America's long-gathering fiscal disorder was entering a new dimension. By the mid 1980s, annual federal deficits, already at double-digit levels in the 1970s, jumped to the range of $150-200 billion.[1] The immediate reasons were a combination of factors—a big leap in military spending, a cut in income taxes, and a failure to do more than slow the rise in civilian spending. While the overall tax level continued upward during the Reagan years, the rate of increase was greatly reduced. This was primarily the result of ending the rapid inflation of the previous two decades, which had regularly pushed taxpayers into higher brackets with steeply higher rates.[2]

America's fiscal predicament did not, however, arise overnight. The progressive failure to match outlays with income results from conditions developing since the early postwar years. America's world role and the heavy military spending that accompany it are undoubtedly a major element in any convincing explanation. Basically, three features in American fiscal practice stand out in sharp contrast to the pattern in most other advanced Western nation states. The first is the relatively high levels of military spending throughout the postwar period—high both as a percentage of gross national product (GNP) and very high as a percentage of government spending.[3] The second is America's relatively low level of civilian entitlements and civil spending in general, particularly by continental European standards. American entitlements seem particularly ungenerous toward the middle classes.[4] A third feature is more elusive but nevertheless palpable: the high level of inefficiency in federal spending programs. Inefficiency has always seemed particularly egregious in defense spending and, most recently, in the rapidly rising outlays for health care.[5] The reasons for this inefficiency seem both tactical—Congressional pork combined with inappropriate bureaucratic controls—and strategic—the lack of coherent general policies. These three features help to explain why a consensus on fiscal priorities is even harder to reach in the United States than in most other Western countries.

The conflict between guns and butter runs all through the postwar fiscal history of the United States, with competing bursts of military and civilian spending. The public has tolerated the United States' world role but has been increasingly reluctant to pay for it—in money or blood. Meanwhile the high level of military spending has limited civilian spending and entitlements—and hence, logically enough, public support for higher taxes. The public sector has remained much smaller in the United States than in continental European states, where the taxpaying middle classes receive a far more generous ration of public goods. Finally, the inefficiency of the American public sector not only wastes what resources there are, but also further discourages public provision of social goods. In some cases, notably health care, this results in further inefficiency. The combined public and private cost for health care in the United States is, for example, much higher proportionally than in France or Germany. Higher health costs squeeze private household budgets and further strengthen resistance to taxation.

To these three special features that help explain the fiscal crisis must be added a fourth: the ease with which the United States has always been able to finance its deficits, both fiscal and external. In the Reagan era, the bulk of the world's private savings went to finance U.S. federal deficits, despite the intense displeasure and discomfort of most European governments.[6] This capacity for manipulating the international economy to remedy the deficiencies of the American was, however, nothing new. It had become a regular part of American policymaking since the 1960s, when the United States was already running a troublesome external deficit. External balances continued to decline, and, by the early 1970s, America's long-standing trade surplus had turned into a deficit. By the 1980s, both trade and current-account deficits had reached levels previously difficult to imagine.[7]

No other country in the world could have continued to run such substantial and rising deficits over three decades. The United States was able to finance this deficit thanks to the dollar's international status. Here the superpower role provided a solution to the superpower's apparent "overstretch." But the endless manipulation of the dollar has proved to be an exercise of power that ultimately has undermined not only the world economy, but the superpower itself.

Broadly speaking, the United States has followed three distinctive formulas for manipulating the dollar to finance deficits. All three have worked for a time and then collapsed. Arguably, all three have left the real U.S. economy weaker than before.[8]

The first formula was developed under the Bretton Woods system of fixed exchange rates. The dollar's status as a formal reserve currency meant that foreign central banks were constrained to accept and hold surplus dollars as reserves in place of gold. The arrangement, the gold-exchange standard, presumed a prudent American monetary policy that would not create excessive international liquidity and thereby transmit inflation to other countries. The requirement to exchange dollars for gold, at the official price, was meant to limit excessive American monetary creation. In the end, it proved powerless to do so. Instead, the system came to rest, in effect, on forced loans to the Americans from their European and Japanese military protectorates. The superpower was asserting its hegemony. The linkage between military protection and supporting the dollar was made explicit.[9]

America's external deficits in this period could not be traced to any imbalance in the current account. The "basic" deficit arose when trade and current account surpluses were offset by heavy overseas military spending, corporate investment, and tourism—all of which gave America's external deficits an obvious imperial character.[10] As Charles de Gaulle put it in 1965, the Bretton Woods arrangement, by constraining European central banks to accept dollars in place of gold, was forcing Europeans to finance the takeover of their own industries by the Americans.[11] The Americans, of course, argued that they were merely providing "liquidity" to a world hungry for investment. The fact remained that the funds were tied to the priorities of American investors, who were, thereby, increasing their presence in allied economies. Americans could also claim that their deficits sprang from the high cost of defending Europe. Not surprisingly, the 1960s saw a sharpening of the "burden-sharing" debate within NATO.

In more purely economic terms, when America's domestic and foreign spending and investment were combined, the United States was "absorbing" more goods, services, and investments than its national economy was actually producing. The excess absorption was being financed by inflated credit in the form of dollars exported to other economies. Under the boom conditions of the 1960s, this naturally brought inflationary pressure on the foreign economies.[12] The situation grew progressively unstable as the Federal Reserve began accommodating the heavy military spending for Vietnam and the accelerating costs of Lyndon Johnson's "Great Society" by creating ever more, inflationary, credit.[13] But since American balance-of-payments deficits preceded severe domestic price inflation by several years, a good part of America's excessive credit was being dumped into the international economy, where it fed the offshore "Eurodollar" market.[14] This capital market, free from national regulation, was a magnet attracting still more capital from the United States. It permitted large sums to be mobilized not only for overseas investment, but also for speculation against the dollar. Ultimately, this greatly enhanced capacity for speculation was to prove the undoing of the Bretton Woods formula, as waves of private selling of dollars overwhelmed central-bank intervention.

By the time the Bretton Woods system finally broke down in 1971, the Americans themselves had grown tired of it. Its principal drawback was that it prevented devaluing the dollar. The dollar had grown "overvalued" as a result of the domestic price inflation that began to afflict the U.S. domestic economy during the Vietnam War. Being unable to devalue meant that American products were disadvantaged against foreign products. Hence the end of the long-standing American trade surplus in 1970. The United States tried vainly to persuade its competitors to revalue and finally abandoned its Bretton Woods obligations and let the dollar float.[15]

The transition to a system of floating exchange rates did not cure the American external deficit, which instead grew much worse.[16] Nor did floating dethrone the dollar from its international role, or prevent the United States from financing its imbalances by monetary manipulation. Under floating rates, there have been two distinct formulas for doing so. These might be called the Nixon formula and the Reagan-Volcker formula.[17] Like the Bretton Woods formula, both worked for a time but left the real economy weaker than before.

In its essentials, the Nixon formula consisted of an expansive fiscal policy, accommodated by an expansive monetary policy and accompanied by a "benign neglect" of the dollar's exchange rate. The formula was obviously inflationary—for the United States and for the world. It took frank advantage of what might be called America's comparative advantage in competitive inflation. Although foreign central banks resisted it, the dollar did depreciate sharply—almost 50 percent against the Deutschemark from 1971 to 1979, for example.[18] For most countries, such depreciation would have meant a sharp rise in domestic price inflation. Eventually, this is what happened in the United States. But the time frame was much longer than it would have been elsewhere. In the meantime, the dollar's depreciation seemed to work very much to America's advantage. It improved competitive prospects for American producers without hindering America's ability to spend abroad. America's advantage came from its huge and diverse economy that put it in a quite different situation from other European economies. Relative to the economy as a whole, the U.S. trade sector was only roughly one third of the size of most European trade sectors. The United States, moreover, was a net exporter of food and raw materials, and its major imports—oil for example—were themselves priced in dollars.[19]

Richard Nixon's formula was already being used in 1970, when he encouraged the Federal Reserve to expand the money supply. The ensuing dollar crisis of 1971 gave Nixon the occasion to jettison the Bretton Woods system and let the dollar fall substantially. This helped the beleaguered American trade sector, although not enough to prevent trade deficits in 1971 and 1972, and in most other years of the decade.[20] At the same time, Nixon imposed price and wage controls, which suppressed domestic price inflation until after his reelection in 1972. When controls came off at the beginning of 1973, explosive domestic price inflation followed immediately. There succeeded a series of further inflationary shocks, such as the explosion of grain prices and the four-fold increase of oil prices in 1974. In that year, the level of price inflation throughout the ten major noncommunist industrial countries had reached an astonishing 13 percent.[21] European governments, inclined to inflate away the ruinous wage settlements made after 1968, were doubtless partly to blame, but the Nixon Federal Reserve was the world's inflationary engine.[22]

The end of fixed exchange rates had also allowed Nixon to drop all capital controls. This left American corporations free to invest abroad as they wished and American banks free to participate fully in the burgeoning business of the Eurodollar market. After the oil shock, America's swelling liquidity, transferred through its enterprising banks, permitted the relatively easy "recycling" of loans to oil-importing countries. This mitigated the effects of the oil shock, but also delayed adjustment to it, and saddled banks with a dangerous level of insolvent debt for the next couple of decades.

By late 1973, exploding price inflation was finally prompting a monetary crackdown. A severe recession followed in 1974 and 1975, until the Nixon formula was resurrected by the Ford and Carter administrations throughout most of the latter half of the decade. The dollar continued its sharp fall against the yen and most European currencies.[23] By 1979, inflation had once more reached record levels, and a second oil shock followed the first. A general revolt in the oil, gold, and currency markets, together with a powerful political reaction against inflation in the United States itself, brought on a new period of monetary austerity, associated with the appointment of Paul Volcker to the Chairmanship of the Federal Reserve in 1979. A recession followed to usher in the Reagan era. In effect the United States ended the 1970s as it had ended the 1960s: heading into a deep recession exacerbated by stagflation. Meanwhile, a decade of monetary manipulation had helped neither the trade balance—which was in deeper deficit than ever—nor the real economy, whose rates of investment and productivity growth had fallen to new lows.[24]

The new decade soon brought a new formula. This Reagan-Volcker formula consisted of loose fiscal policy combined with tight monetary policy. The combination brought record interest rates and attracted a huge inflow of foreign capital. In effect, the United States borrowed back much of the credit it had created and exported under the Nixon formula. The capital inflows meant a very high exchange rate for the dollar, which kept down domestic price inflation. A moderate boom ultimately followed, financed by the inflow of foreign capital.[25]

In due course, the formula's longer-term costs forced its abandonment. These sprang from the unnaturally high dollar, which fell heavily on those parts of American industry subject to foreign competition. The result was a "rust belt" of bankrupt industries, principally in the Middle West. The costs were also catastrophic for dollar debtors of the previous decade, along with the financial institutions that held their debts. Hence the various domestic and foreign debt crises, most spectacularly the collapse of a good part of the American savings and loan industry, a financial disaster estimated at the time to cost the U.S. Treasury at least $325 billion in outlays.[26] As early as 1984, the Federal Reserve felt constrained to loosen its monetary policy.[27] As the decade continued, bursts of credit to avoid various financial disasters and lower the exchange rate alternated with returns to monetary austerity in the interest of preventing runaway speculation. By the end of the decade, the United States was falling into a deep and stubborn recession. Thus, the end of the 1980s, similar to the last years of the two previous decades, saw the United States caught in a period of recession and chronic stagflation—with oscillating monetary policy trying to avoid both inflation and a deeper recession.

Not surprisingly, the early 1990s saw a serious public malaise over the state of the economy. The 1980s had left the United States with radically increased fiscal deficits of a structural kind. The national debt, which had been roughly one trillion dollars in 1980, was over four trillion dollars in 1992, and had been growing since 1989 at the rate of $400 billion annually. Debt service had risen, as a percent of federal spending, from 8.89 percent in 1980 to 14.77 percent in 1990.[28] In effect, the United States had entered an era of "Ponzi finance."[29] An increasing part of the government's borrowing was being used to cover interest payments. The debt had grown self-propelled. With the collapse of the Soviet empire, the continuing American hunger for capital seemed likely to be more difficult for the rest of the world to accommodate. The opening of Eastern Europe and Russia to investment promised a greater demand for capital in the future. Germany's reunification and

Japan's own severe financial difficulties robbed world capital markets of two major savers. The Gulf War had similar effects on Middle Eastern savings.

Meanwhile, the growing share of U.S. budgetary resources eaten up by debt service grew harder and harder to square with growing demands for public-sector investments in infrastructure and education—needed, it was argued, to restore the economy to competitiveness.[30] At the same time, the lack of adequate public provision for health care in America, together with the rapidly escalating costs of the existing private system, began to be regarded as a major crisis for the federal system itself. Added to the clamor over health care was a broad public unease over increasing poverty and homelessness, rising crime, growing anger and despair in the urban underclass, and increasing racial and ethnic tension throughout the society.

Giving new force to these perennial arguments over the size and responsibility of the public sector was a growing public sense that the real economy was not performing well. While the United States had been notable for its capacity to produce new jobs, most were in the low-paying services. Despite the large increase in the number of wives at work, real incomes for American families had been stagnant for well over a decade.[31] The huge current-account deficit, despite the dollar's sharp depreciation, suggested a radical decline in American competitiveness in precisely those high value-added industries that could support higher wages. Decades of statistics showing relatively low U.S. investment and productivity growth gave substance to those fears of decline.[32] America's poor long-term investment and productivity performance began to be traced, not implausibly, to the bad fiscal and monetary habits I have been describing. All the formulas for manipulating the dollar had, after periods of minimal success, ended up in stagflation. Perpetual oscillation between austerity and inflation could be seen, in itself, as a great inducement to speculation rather than to serious investment in the real economy.

All of these issues began to form a giant cloud over the Bush administration, which had succeeded the Reagan administration in 1989. While George Bush had the good fortune to be in office for the Soviet collapse, it brought him surprisingly little political benefit. The public was proving much more concerned with stagnant living standards, declining competitiveness and financial fragility. It had grown commonplace to blame the outsized fiscal deficit for the domestic malaise. Durable economic improvement was thought to be unlikely without serious fiscal reform. Bush, who had once described Reaganite macroeconomic ideas as "voodoo economics," tried to bring the deficit under better control by agreeing to modest tax increases and cuts in military spending.[33] But he seemingly lacked the concentration and determination to push through major budgetary improvements. Saddled as he was with his own Reaganite party and a Democratic Congress, he probably also lacked the political means.

Instead of fiscal reform, Bush tried to capitalize on America's triumph in the Gulf War. He began to pin the fate of his administration to a commanding American global role in the "New World Order."[34] Some of his rhetoric seemed to have been borrowed from Henry Luce's "American Century" of the 1940s. In this, Bush misjudged both the international situation and the American political mood.

The Gulf War proved less the harbinger of a "unipolar" Pax Americana, as Bush claimed, than the "last hurrah" for unilateral American global interventionism. The conditions did provide a near perfect occasion to demonstrate American power. Iraq threatened the vital interests not only of its neighbors in the region, but also of all the Western powers and Japan. Thus the United States had willing military allies, eager to participate in order to exert influence over the outcome, and financial allies able to defray the costs. The Soviet collapse meant that the ample U.S. forces still in Europe could be withdrawn without fear. The military situation was ideal for demonstrating the prowess of American air, naval, and land forces developed in the long Carter-Reagan build-up. The terrain lent itself to effective use of sophisticated weapons and there was no need to take and hold hostile urban areas. Some analysts argued there was no need for a land war at all. Militarily and geopolitically, however, these were not conditions that could be generalized into a new American-dominated world order.

In fact, the United States would soon have difficulty hanging on to its hegemonic position in Western Europe. As the Yugoslav crisis demonstrated, Europe after the Cold War had new security problems, with new complex political and economic dimensions that the Americans were neither well-suited nor much disposed to take the lead in addressing. Nor did the major West European powers seem eager to legitimize a renewed American hegemony.

In any event, the New World Order had little durable appeal with Americans at home. The American public was not inclined to see the end of the Cold War as an historic opportunity to extend and consolidate American global hegemony. It was more inclined to see it as the long-delayed opportunity to rejuvenate America's national political economy.

Bill Clinton's campaign was adept at focussing on the long deterioration of America's economic competitiveness and social harmony. His solution was selective public investment in infrastructure and education, together with a radical reform of the health care system. It was not really Clinton, however, who set the campaign debate but Ross Perot, whose primary focus was on the budget deficit itself. Perot was able to convince a substantial part of the electorate that the deficit was at the bottom of many of the nation's long-term economic ills. He was not opposed to reforms along the lines that Clinton was suggesting, but argued that nothing would succeed without repairing the basic macroeconomic framework by sharply reversing the growing fiscal deficit.

As Perot proceeded with his campaign, his analysis grew more radical. Unlike Clinton, Perot was not shy about making obvious linkages between cutting the budget deficit, finding money for necessary public investment and welfare, making sharp cuts in the military budget and pursuing a less grandiose foreign policy. Controlling the deficit or having serious policies of any kind, Perot began to argue, was not imaginable without a reform of constitutional practices. Something would have to be done about the habitual "gridlock" between the executive branch and the Congress. And something would have to be done about the highly corrupt Congressional system, whose election campaigns required huge funds and left individual Congressmen free to tailor legislation to suit those who could buy influence.[35]

In effect, it was Perot who made explicit the links between economic decline, world role and constitutional practice. His basic message was that the American political system was growing increasingly unviable. The basic problems of the American political system raised by Perot are as old as the system itself. They involve the principal issue of the Federalist Papers—the balance between executive energy and Congressional resistance. While the executive's tenure does not depend on a legislative majority, without such a majority it is difficult to carry through any kind of coherent program. In current circumstances, a genuine working majority is difficult to imagine. At best, an administration can bargain and compromise and hope that some semblance of its original plans will emerge through a process over which it has little real control. It is not, of course, that a directing power is located elsewhere in the system. Rather, the legislation and policy that emerges is the serendipitous result of innumerable private bargains. The consequences of such a system for the government's ability to control its own bureaucracy are what might be expected. At the moment, the American political process is merely a market—where every legislator is a private entrepreneur working on his own account. His imperative need is to accumulate enough clients to meet the voracious demands for funds to finance his own election campaign. In the House of Representatives these elections take place every other year. Under such circumstances, party loyalty is minimal. The budget crisis thus emerges as a metaphor for the dysfunctionality of the system as a whole.

Obviously, all political systems have strong elements of bargaining and compromise. But, as the budget crisis suggests, the United States has lost its balance between the power to govern coherently and the power to obstruct. The result is large-scale waste and plunder of public resources. Under such circumstances, it is not surprising that budgets can never be balanced and that unresolved domestic problems continue to accumulate and fester.

In some respects, the present American situation resembles conditions at the beginning of the century, when the inadequacy of the constitutional system was much discussed and reform movements and third parties sprouted on all sides. The resolution came through a strengthening of presidential power—a process often associated with various domestic reform movements—Theodore Roosevelt's "Square Deal," Woodrow Wilson's "New Freedom," and later, Franklin Delano Roosevelt's "New Deal." But the more durable strengthening of presidential power came as the United States adopted a major global role. That evolution was prefigured in the roles played by Wilson and Roosevelt in two world wars and reached its peacetime fulfillment with what might be called the Cold War constitution in the early postwar era. An "imperial presidency" became the solution to the inadequacies of the traditional constitution.[36]

The problem with such a solution was that it remained inadequate for civilian policy. Except in war or quasi-war, the presidency lacked either the institutional base or the political prestige to develop and impose coherent domestic policies. While presidents became all-powerful figures abroad, they grew increasingly impotent at home. This was a situation that could only reinforce the already dangerous tendency to divert too many resources and too much attention to the global role, while neglecting domestic civilian needs and undermining the real economy. Hence the national "decline" that has been such a fruitful topic over the past few decades.[37] Hence, too, the use of external power to compensate for internal imbalance and weakness. Thanks in part to its own constitutional inadequacies, the United States became a "hegemon in decline," relying on its power in the world system to compensate for its growing weakness at home.[38]

The imperial solution began to break down seriously as early as the 1960s. This was the decade in which the American public revolted against the human cost of the imperial role, while the political system demanded a redirection of resources to civilian needs. This was also the decade when Europe began to mobilize itself to resist the exactions of its declining hegemony. The next two decades witnessed the playing out of the struggles that followed from these reactions. The Soviet collapse and the American fiscal crisis brought the constitutional game to a new present phase.

Clinton's election plus the Perot phenomenon registered wide public dissatisfaction with the status quo. But Clinton himself received considerably less than a majority of the votes cast.[39] Much of the public probably always doubted his ability to resolve the worsening "gridlock" that he and Perot brought into the open. The hopeful counted on a Democratic president to instill some return to party discipline within a nominally Democratic House and Senate. Nevertheless, so much compromise was required to put together a majority that the administration had great difficulty in pushing through major policy changes in any form. In early 1993, the protracted struggle over a "budget agreement" showed how tenuous Clinton's nominal Congressional majority actually was. And although the agreement did raise upper-middle class and corporate taxes, it promised no more deficit reduction than a similar agreement negotiated by the Bush administration two years earlier. At best, it seemed likely merely to stabilize the deficit at its already high level.[40] In the process of achieving the agreement, moreover, the new administration was forced to jettison a good part of its plan for targeted public investment, arguably its own best idea in the campaign.[41]

In its second year, the administration pushed through the North American Free Trade Agreement (NAFTA), but with massive defections among Democratic legislators and, therefore, only with substantial Republican support—not surprising since NAFTA was itself a Bush administration initiative. In that same year, the administration took on the formidable challenge it had set for itself: conceiving and carrying through Congress a basic reform of the health care system. The tenuousness of its majority soon forced it into a maze of contradictory compromises and no significant health-care reform was passed during the 103rd Congress. The president's approval ratings plummeted to new lows. Significantly, perhaps, he began to show a new interest in foreign policy—with an intervention in Haiti, and, rhetorically at least, a significant expansion of the North Atlantic Treaty Organization (NATO).

Meanwhile, the 1994 mid-term elections gave Republicans control of both houses of Congress for the first time since 1955. In the ensuing 104th Congress, House Republicans, demonstrating unprecedented discipline, proceeded to pass most of their election platform, the "Contract with

America," within a few months and with little alteration. In the process, the first steps were taken toward significant budget cuts. Under their dynamic new Speaker, Newt Gingrich, House Republicans seemed to be forging themselves into a disciplined European-style party, united behind a coherent program.

In mid-June 1995, as I write, no one can tell the fate of this bold Republican experiment. The future may not favor its continued political success. While fiscal balancing is widely supported in theory, the further it proceeds, the more opposition it is likely to generate. In any event, many people find the Republican budgetary priorities, which mainly favor cutting welfare and entitlement programs, inadequate as well as mean-spirited. American welfare is modest, by European standards at least, and Republicans also favor Reaganite tax cuts, increased defense spending, and expensive foreign policy commitments, such as NATO enlargement, any of which may derange plans for balancing the budget.

More generally, the whole Republican program seems too negative to provide effective answers to long-standing American problems. These arise as much from the inadequacy of the public sector as from its overextension. Whereas Clinton was elected in 1992 to provide an efficient civilian public sector, the Republicans captured the Congress in 1994 on a platform that promised to reduce that sector as far as possible. In effect, the Democrats came in with a program but proved unable to form a disciplined majority to enact it; the Republicans have a coherent majority but lack a serious program. To be fair, it is difficult to govern the country from the House of Representatives, and it is clearly premature to dismiss the most interesting constitutional development in several decades. In due course, the Republicans may evolve a more balanced approach to mastering the budget deficit and a more positive view toward government in general. Indeed a certain convergence between Republican goals and those of the Clinton administration is not unimaginable. If Republicans capture the White House in 1996, without losing their coherent Congressional majorities, they could be in a strong position to effect real changes in the habits and even the structure of the American political system.

If, instead, the Republicans fail to break through the frustrating constitutional pattern of recent years, what will follow? Clinton's political fortunes may revive, but even if reelected, he may never regain the initiative for major reforms. As long as the Democrats continue to appear an aggregate of special interests and cannot produce a coherent majority in Congress, Clinton (if reelected) would probably prove merely another of those caretaker presidents—one who presides over an increasingly inadequate and troubled federal system. In such circumstances, the American malaise may well move to a more radical stage.

Disaffection from normal political parties and, indeed, from normal political practices and structures still appears widespread. Without a revival of the imperial presidency, what other direction could reform take? Within the federal government itself, the root ailment seems to be the lack of an efficacious coordination between the executive and legislative branches. Woodrow Wilson, as a young professor, once suggested a parliamentary system, with a prime minister depending on a majority.[42] In recent times, France seems to have found a reasonable arrangement to combine presidential power with a strong government with a majority. In the French system, and indeed in most European systems, the legislature can throw out a government but not change the details of its budget or meddle with the details of its policies.[43] Such a change would be a revolution in American constitutional practice, but perhaps no greater than what the French experienced in 1958.

In all such fanciful discussions of reform, America's continental scale and diversity is the reality that distinguishes the American system from most other Western or Westernized democratic nation states. Rather than a comparison of the United States with a European nation state, perhaps a more appropriate parallel is between the United States and Europe's own nascent confederation built around the European Union. Put in this perspective, both the failings and the achievements of America's federal system can be better understood. To some, the parallel also suggests that the United States has grown too centralized to be governed properly.

The relative power of the states and the federal government is, of course, another ancient topic of American constitutional debate. Today, it is easy enough to argue that America's federal government is "overloaded." The problem with redistributing power is that the states lack the legitimacy or, in most cases, the scale to cope successfully with the major social and economic problems of a modern society. In this respect, the European Union's "Europe of States" possesses a more promising distribution of central and "regional" power for the kind of articulated governance that a large continental system requires. Obviously, the more centralized American system also has features and powers that Europe has not achieved, and perhaps does not want. In any event, no one can legislate that America's existing states become the cultural, political, economic, or moral equivalents of Europe's nation-states.

George Kennan, among others, has recently been advocating bold steps in a European direction. He suggests a regrouping of American states into thirteen regional entities—including three large urban agglomerations—New York, Chicago, and Los Angeles. These super-states would be more like German *Länder* than American states, and would therefore assume many current federal powers. This would not only permit solutions better adapted to what are often quite different regional conditions and propensities in America, but also allow greater experimentation with diverse solutions. Kennan imagines that the super-states on the Latin border (Florida/Puerto Rico, Texas, or the Southwest, including Southern California) might grow increasingly Hispanic in their population and culture. He leaves open the nature of their relationship with neighboring Latin American states, except to suggest that intimate relations would be natural and in everyone's best interest.[44]

Kennan's suggestive, if Delphic, comments about the Hispanic presence in the United States raise the familiar issues of "multiculturalism" and "historic revenge," issues that currently bedevil many American universities. They can be used either to support a relaxation of central control, which is Kennan's position, or a strengthening of it. Traditionally, the United States has always sought to impose English through "Americanization" in the schools. This part of the tradition will probably continue to prevail. Most Hispanic immigrant families are poor and lack formal education. Mastering English is likely to remain their obvious route to economic success and cultural advancement. But there seems no reason why Spanish language and Latin American culture cannot be taught in schools as well. If this means that regions of the United States ultimately become bilingual, it is hard to see this as a diminution of American culture.

Such a prospect will undoubtedly frighten many people. The reaction could at least indirectly reinforce the tendency to strengthen the federal government, perhaps also to retain or seek new hegemonic duties abroad. In justifying its actual or possible excursions in Africa and the Caribbean, the Clinton administration has been employing Wilsonian rhetoric easily adaptable to a much broader foreign-policy agenda. Recent enthusiasm for enlarging NATO in order to bring "stability" to Central and Eastern European states suggests just such an evolution. Among American political elites of the older generation, moreover, there remains a strong feeling that only attachment to the world role can keep America's motley population in some kind of civic discipline. And the American role in the world is not, after all, the product merely of American ambition to fulfill it. There remains the possibility of some major new geopolitical enemy sufficient to return American priorities to a Cold War pattern. Enlarging NATO may bring back the Cold War to Europe. In Asia, a nuclear-armed China grows ever more powerful. With Russia weak and Japan relatively disarmed, no indigenous military equilibrium is likely among Asia's major countries. Reluctance to see Japan become militarily independent—particularly as a nuclear power— could easily be used to justify a continuing American protectorate. China, too, may find an external enemy necessary for maintaining inner cohesion.

It may be doubted, of course, whether the American public feels a sufficient attachment to Asia to support the sort of existential commitment that was made to Europe in the Cold War. Nor are America's economic interests in Asia as promising as is often assumed. In many respects, Asia is the source of America's economic problems rather than the solution. Trade remains highly unfavorable to the United States, nor is it clear what will make the balance improve in the foreseeable future.[45] If American business needs a large area for lucrative investment and cheap labor, Latin America may seem a safer bet. This is not to suggest that Americans will lose interest in Asia, merely that they will not mobilize their society to remain the dominant power there.

In any event, there is no reason to accept the familiar dichotomy of the 1930s—between an America that is imperial and an America that is "isolationist." The present American mood might better be described as "measured internationalism." Students of American public opinion have long noted the decline of sentiments that can properly be called isolationist.[46] The great bulk of the public accept the need to play a major external role, less from a craving for grandeur than to protect the nation's own security and prosperity. But there is also the deep suspicion that America's allies have been "free-riding" too long for their own good, or for the health of the United States.

A policy of regional coalition-building and devolution fits well with such a mood of measured internationalism. Logically, it should mean support for European integration, including efforts to build a "European pillar" in the Alliance, preferably within NATO. These are long-standing American positions, but they may be advanced in the future with fewer second thoughts. Until now at least, America's role in the Yugoslav crisis has shown a strong American diffidence toward pulling Europe's chestnuts out of the fire. Yugoslavia has also illustrated a renewed American interest in using the United Nations. Engagement in the Security Council's machinery has a certain logical drift of its own—toward multilateralism and away from hegemony. It remains to be seen, of course, whether these trends will survive the bipartisan enthusiasm for NATO enlargement, or the Republican distaste for the UN and for multilateral arrangements in general. Most probably, so long as no enemy superpower threatens the United States, the drift toward regional self-help in Europe and multilateralism in the world will continue to suit the basic American mood. That this mood is both an opportunity and a challenge for European confederalism seems obvious. It should not, however, lend much encouragement to nationalist European policies that count on an American safety net.

Ideally, the end of the bipolar era will lead to a rejuvenation of state institutions on both sides of the Atlantic—perhaps even to a certain convergence of structures. Europe's nation-states need to strengthen their collective arrangements for ordering a continental market, maintaining regional security and taking an effective role in sustaining global order and balance. The United States, by contrast, needs to devolve power from its overloaded central system, while at the same time making the federal machinery more efficient, politically and administratively.

To return to the observation made at the outset, America's current economic, political, and social problems do not arise from no longer being a hegemonic superpower. Rather, they are the result of having been one for too long. The end of the Cold War gives the United States a splendid opportunity to recoup its inner strength and balance. It means more resources should be available for civilian needs. It should permit the gradual reform of what has become an excessively wasteful and overcentralized federal system. It should also help encourage America's elites to devote more of their attention to domestic rejuvenation and less to world management. Such a shift will doubtless be inconvenient. In the end, however, it may prove not to be a bad thing—either for the United States, or for its friends in the world.

Such a view may reflect an American inclination for more optimism than seems reasonable. But even if the United States is entering, as I see it, a certain crisis as a continental nation state, nothing ordains that its government and people cannot rise to the occasion. Given the history of the past century, the nature of America's current predicament is not difficult to grasp, nor is there any reason to be greatly surprised at it. The remedies require some imagination, courage, and luck—but not to a degree that makes success unimaginable. The United States was founded, two centuries ago, as an experiment "to decide the important question, whether societies of men are really capable of establishing good government from reflection and choice, or whether they forever destined to depend for their political constitution on accident and force."[47] The experiment is certainly not over.

◆ NOTES TO CHAPTER 2 ◆

1. *Economic Report of the President* (Washington DC: U.S. Government Printing Office, 1991), p. 375. The deficit figure is artificially lowered by including as income the surplus funds collected for social security, as well as the interest that the Treasury pays to itself for that accumulated surplus. See, for example, David P. Calleo, *The Bankrupting of America* (New York: Morrow, 1992), pp. 44-45; Joseph White and Aaron Wildavsky, *The Deficit and the Public Interest: The Search for Responsible Budgeting in the 1980s* (Berkeley: University of California Press, 1989), pp. 313-15; and Paul Blustein, "Alternate Social Security Plan Gaining: Hill Expected to Take Pension Plan Out of Budget Calculations," *The Washington Post*, February 16, 1990, p. A10.

2. For a discussion of the reasons for the rise in the deficit during the Reagan presidency, see David A. Stockman, *The Triumph of Politics: Why the Reagan Revolution Failed* (New York: Harper and Row, 1986), especially chapter 12. On unlegislated tax increases, see Joseph Pechman, *Federal Tax Policy* (Washington DC: Brookings Institution. 1987), pp. 114-16; and Douglas A. Hibbs, *The American Political Economy: Macroeconomics and Electoral Politics* (Cambridge, MA: Harvard University Press, 1987), p. 296.

3. For a comprehensive breakdown of federal outlays, including military spending, see *Economic Report of the President* (1991), pp. 376-77. For military expenditure as a proportion of GNP and government spending, see Calleo, *Bankrupting of America*, pp. 199, 210.

4. Complete data on levels of civilian spending is given in *Economic Report of the President* (1991), pp. 376-77. A comparative analysis is given in OECD, *Public Expenditure on Income Maintenance* (1976) and *Economies in Transition: Structural Adjustment in OECD Countries* (Paris: OECD, 1989). For an account of the relative decline of the American middle classes, see Frank Levy, "Incomes, Families and Living Standards" in Robert E. Litan et al., eds., *American Living Standards: Threats and Challenges* (Washington DC: Brookings Institution, 1988), p. 136.

5. For inefficiency in U.S. defense spending, see Edward N. Luttwak, *The Pentagon and the Art of War* (New York: Simon and Schuster, 1984); David P. Calleo, *Beyond American Hegemony* (New York: Basic Books, 1987), pp. 115-120 and 256, note 21, or *Bankrupting of America*, pp. 54-60; for an analysis of health care provision, see *Health Care Systems in Transition* (Paris: OECD, 1990); and *The Changing Health Care Market* (Washington DC: Employee Benefit Research Institute, 1987). In addition, a full description of the U.S. health care system and the need for reform is given in *Economic Report of the President* (1993), pp. 119-69.

6. See Harold van Buren Cleveland, "Europe in the Economic Crisis of Our Time: Macroeconomic Policies and Microeconomic Constraints," in David P. Calleo and Claudia Morgenstern, eds., *Recasting Europe's Economies: National Strategies in the 1980s* (Lanham, MD: University Press of America, 1990), pp. 160-63.

7. In 1970, the U.S. trade balance was $0.8 billion in surplus. By 1980, this had changed into a deficit of $31.4 billion and by 1989 the deficit had grown to $129.4 billion. The current account deficit grew from $5.87 billion to $99.01 billion between 1982 and 1984. *Economic Report of the President* (1991), pp. 402, 406.

8. For a fuller description of these formulas, see Calleo, *Bankrupting of America*, pp. 102-21.

9. In particular, this involved loans from Canada, Germany, and Japan; see Calleo, *Bankrupting of America*, pp. 107-08.

10. The "imperial" deficit is explained in Calleo, *Beyond American Hegemony*, pp. 85-87. Full statistical tables for 1962-1963 can be found in *IMF Balance of Payments Yearbook*, vol. 19 (1968) 1, and for 1964-1968 in vol. 21 (1970) 1.

11. Press conference, February 4, 1965, in *Major Addresses, Statements and Press Conferences of Charles de Gaulle* (New York: French Embassy, Press and Information Division, 1967).

12. De Gaulle speech, above; Jacques Rueff, "Le problème monétaire international" and "Le déficit des balance des paiements des Etats Unis," *Oeuvres complètes,* E. M. Claassen and G. Lane, eds., *Politique économique* 3:2 (Paris: Plon, 1980). See also, Calleo, *Beyond American Hegemony,* pp. 84-85; Harold van Buren Cleveland and W. H. Bruce Brittain, *The Great Inflation: A Monetarist View* (Washington DC: National Planning Association, 1976), pp.13-16, and, for international responses, pp. 31-48; and W. Max Corden, *Inflation, Exchange Rates and the World Economy* (Chicago: University of Chicago Press, 1986), pp. 85-94.

13. See Cleveland and Brittain, *Great Inflation,* pp. 31-35; for data on the growth of the U.S. money supply, see *International Financial Statistics Yearbook* (Washington DC: International Monetary Fund, 1980), pp. 54-55.

14. For an introduction to the workings of the Eurodollar market, see Susan Strange, "International Monetary Relations" in Andrew Shonfield, ed., *International Monetary Relations of the Western World, 1959-1971* vol. 2 (London: Oxford University Press, 1976), pp. 176-94. The estimated net size of the Eurodollar market in 1970 was $57 billion, compared with total U.S. gold reserves of just $11 billion. BIS, *Annual Report,* no. 41 (Basel, Bank for International Settlements, 1971), pp. 127, 157. This does not prove in itself that the Eurodollar market was inflationary. Cleveland and Brittain assert that around 75 percent of the $54 billion was already counted as part of national monetary aggregates. Its size, therefore, did not reflect a commensurate real growth in money stocks beyond that growth already sanctioned by monetary authorities. Cleveland and Brittain therefore argue that the unprecedented price rise of the inflation of 1968-1975 cannot be blamed on the Eurodollar market. Nevertheless, with so large a volume of newly liberated capital, it could create instability for exchange rates when mobilized; see Cleveland and Brittain, *Great Inflation,* pp. 22-23.

15. For a description of "benign neglect" and the demise of Bretton Woods, see Susan Strange, "International Monetary Relations"; Robert Solomon, *The International Monetary System, 1945-1976: An Insider's View* (New York: Harper and Row, 1977). A defense of "benign neglect" is offered by Gottfried Haberler and Thomas E. Willet, *A Strategy for U.S. Balance of Payments Policies* (Washington DC: American Enterprise Institute, 1971), and Lawrence B. Krause, "A Passive Balance of Payments Strategy," *Brookings Papers on Economic Activity* 3 (Washington DC: Brookings Institution, 1970).

16. For full data, see *Balance of Payments of OECD Countries, 1965-1985* (Paris: OECD, 1986), pp. 10-11.

17. For a full description of these two formulas, see Calleo, *Bankrupting of America,* pp. 109-21, or *Beyond American Hegemony,* pp. 90-108.

18. The dollar depreciated against the Deutschemark by 46.8 percent between 1971 and 1979. *Economic Report of the President* (1991), p. 410.

19. The relative size of the U.S. trade sector can be shown roughly by calculating the sum of imports and exports as a proportion of national product. The proportion for the U.S. in 1993 is 19 percent. For Germany, however, it is 51 percent; for the United Kingdom, 52 percent; and for France, 41 percent. OECD, *Economic Outlook,* 53 (June 1993), pp. 55, 67, 73, 83. After the oil price shock, petroleum and petroleum products, priced in dollars, consistently accounted for between a quarter and a third of all U.S. imports. *Economic Report of the President* (1991), p. 404.

20. U.S. net merchandise trade (in billions of dollars): 1970, 2.6; 1971, -2.26; 1972, -6.41; 1973, 0.91; 1974, -5.5; 1975, 8.9; 1976, -9.48; 1977, -31.09; 1978, -33.94; 1979, -27.56. *Economic Report of the President* (1991), p. 402.

21. Cleveland and Brittain, *Great Inflation,* p. 54.

22. For a discussion of the relative responsibility of the U.S. and European governments for spiraling inflation, see Cleveland and Brittain, *Great Inflation.* The authors conclude that the U.S. Federal Reserve Bank's decision in 1971-1972 to follow expansionary monetary policies was largely to blame for the subsequent general inflation, but that European finance ministries (with the exception of the fiscally austere Germans) exacerbated the situation by trying to inflate out of recession (pp. 48-51).

23. Between January 1974 and December 1979, the dollar depreciated from 298.6 Yen/$ to 240.6 Yen/$ and from 2.81 DM/$ to 1.73 DM/$, depreciations of 19.4 and 38.4 percent respectively. Paul Volcker and Toyoo Gyohten, *Changing Fortunes: The World's Money and the Threat to American Leadership* (New York: Times Books, 1992), pp. 370-71.

24. For the trade balance, see note 20. Output per hour rose by just 0.9 percent in 1978 then fell by 1.1 percent and 0.2 percent in 1979 and 1980. *Economic Report of the President* (1991) p. 339.

25. Private foreign investment in the United States rose sharply after 1982. Between 1982 and 1989, private holdings of government securities by non–U.S. citizens rose from $25.8 to $134.8 billion; of securities other than government bonds from $25.8 to $134.8 billion; of corporate bonds from $16.7 to $229.6 billion; and of corporate stocks from $76.3 to $260.2 billion. This capital inflow was supported by high real interest rates and the consequent appreciation of the dollar. When the dollar began to weaken in 1985, partly as a result of deliberate U.S. government policy, private holdings fell, but foreign official holdings of U.S. assets began to increase dramatically. Official investment grew from $202.5 billion to $337.2 billion between 1985 and 1989, reflecting attempts to support the dollar and protect dollar investments. *Economic Report of the President* (1991), p. 401.

26. The minimum cost of $325 billion over four decades was reckoned by the GAO. Some estimates went as high as $500 billion. This included the interest cost of the additional borrowing that would be needed. See David E. Rosenbaum, "A Financial Disaster with Many Culprits," *The New York Times* June 6, 1990, p. A1. R. Dan Brumbaugh Jr., and Andrew S. Carron, "The Thrift Industry Crisis: Causes and Solutions," *Brookings Papers on Economic Activity* 2 (Washington DC: Brookings Institution, 1987), p. 354. A later government estimate was $130-$176 billion, which did not include future interest payments. (*Economic Report of the President* (1991), p. 173). Others have questioned whether the capital involved in the bailout should be seen as a *cost,* rather than merely a transfer of funds that will be reinvested at the same level, thus having no net effect on the economy. This appears to assume that there are no opportunity costs for malinvestment; see Calleo, *Bankrupting of America,* pp. 46, 135-38 and 234.

27. In 1984, the federal funds rate, a general indicator of the Federal Reserve monetary policy, was 10.23 percent, up from 9.09 percent in 1983. By the beginning of 1985, it had fallen to 8.35 percent. *Economic Report of the President* (1991), p. 368. For a discussion of Federal Reserve policy in this period, see William Greider, *Secrets of the Temple: How the Fed Runs the Country* (New York: Simon and Schuster, 1987), p. 17; or Cleveland, "Europe in the Economic Crisis of Our Time," in Calleo and Morgenstern, eds., *Recasting Europe's Economies,* pp. 163-65.

28. *Budget of the U.S. GOVERNMENT, Fiscal Year 1992* (Washington DC: U.S. Government Printing Office, 1991), Tables 1.3 and 3.1, Part Seven, p. 17, 31-36. For comparative statistics, see OECD, *Economic Outlook* 53 (June 1993), p. 142. For the growth of the U.S. government debt, see *Economic Report of the President* (1991), p. 377.

29. For an explanation of Ponzi Finance, see Cleveland, "Europe in the Economic Crisis of Our Time," in *Recasting Europe's Economies,* pp. 164-65; see also Calleo, *Bankrupting of America,* p. 268.

30. See, for example, Robert Reich, *The Work of Nations* (New York: Alfred A. Knopf, 1991), chapter 21, "The Decline of Public Investment," pp. 253-61; or Edward N. Luttwak, *The Endangered American Dream* (New York: Simon and Schuster, 1993).

31. See, for example, Frank Levy, "Incomes, Families and Living Standards"; Joseph Minarik, "Family Income," in Isabel V. Sawhill, ed., *Challenge to Leadership* (Washington DC: The Urban Institute Press, 1988), pp. 33-67; and Louis Uchitelle, "U.S. Wages: Not Getting Ahead? Better Get Used To It," *The New York Times,* December 16, 1990, section 4, pp. 1, 6.

32. For example, real GDP per employed person did not grow at all between 1973 and 1979, and from 1979 to 1988 by just 1.1 percent per annum. In comparison, the OECD average growth rates (without the United States) for the same periods were 2.4 and 1.9 percent and those of Japan, 2.9 and 3.0 percent. The effect of the move to service sector employment and low investment is discussed in Calleo, *Bankrupting of America,* pp. 127-28, 171.

33. For details of the October 1990 budget agreement, see *Omnibus Budget Reconciliation Act of 1990* (Washington DC: U.S. Government Printing Office, 1990). The package agreed by Congress aimed at reducing the federal deficit by $492 billion over a five-year period. However, it optimistically assumed a real growth rate of 3.3 percent, falling interest rates, and did not take account of either the Resolution Trust Corporation or Gulf War expenditures. For further details, see Martin Feldstein, "Bush's Budget Deal Made the Deficit Bigger," *The Wall Street Journal,* November 29, 1990, p. A12.

34. On August 8, 1990, President Bush spoke of a "new era" when deploying troops for Operation Desert Shield. The concept of a New World Order was introduced in a speech to Congress on 11 September 1990. *U.S. Department of State Dispatch* 1, no. 3 (September 17, 1990), pp. 91-94; cited in Lawrence Freedman and Efraim Karsh, *The Gulf Conflict, 1990-1991: Diplomacy and War in the New World Order* (Princeton: Princeton University Press, 1993) p. 215. For a broader discussion, see Robert W. Tucker and David C. Hendrickson, *The Imperial Temptation: The New World Order and America's Purpose* (New York: Council on Foreign Relations, 1993), chapters 1-4.

35. For Perot's campaign platform, see H. Ross Perot, *United We Stand: How We Can Take Back Our Country* (New York: Hyperion, 1992).

36. For a broad, learned, and possibly more optimistic discussion of cycles in presidential activism, see Authur M. Schlesinger, *The Imperial Presidency* (Boston: Houghton Mifflin, 1973) and *The Cycles of American History* (Boston: Houghton Mifflin, 1986).

37. See, for example, Paul Kennedy, *Rise and Fall of the Great Powers* (New York: Random House, 1987), and *Preparing for the Twenty-First Century* (New York: Random House, 1993), chapter 13; Calleo, *Beyond American Hegemony*; Report of the Comparison of the Skills of the Average Work Force, *America's Choice: High Skills or Low Wages* (Rochester: 1990); Richard Rosecrantz, ed., *America as an Ordinary Power* (Ithaca: Cornell University Press, 1976); Mark Green and Mark Pinsky, *America's Transition: Blueprints for the 1990s* (Lanham, MD: University Press of America, 1990).

38. See Calleo, *Beyond American Hegemony,* p. 149. See also Charles Kindleberger, "Systems of International Organization," in David P. Calleo, ed., *Money and the Coming World Order* (New York: Lehman, 1976); Barry Buzan, *Peoples, States and Fear: The National Security Problem in International Relations* (Chapel Hill: University of North Carolina Press, 1983).

39. President Clinton was elected with just 43 percent of the popular vote, the lowest figure since Woodrow Wilson in 1912 (42 percent). A survey showed that 57 percent of the population were concerned or scared by the prospect of a Clinton presidency. On the eve of inauguration, a *Time*/CNN survey showed that only 41 percent of the public thought that Clinton was completely trustworthy, 50 percent said they still had reservations. For an analysis of the 1992 election results, see Everett Carll Ladd, "The

1992 Vote for President Clinton: Another Brittle Mandate?" *Political Science Quarterly*, 108:1 (Spring 1993), pp. 1-28.

40. The Senate finally approved Clinton's budget plan on June 25, 1993 after a 50-49 vote with Vice President Al Gore casting the deciding vote. The package of spending cuts and tax increases will reduce the deficit by an estimated $500 billion through fiscal year 1998. The plan has been criticized, like the Bush plan of 1990, because it relies on optimistic assumptions about U.S. economic performance. The OECD, assuming weaker growth, low inflation rates and higher interest rates than those used by the Clinton administration, estimates that the 1998 fiscal deficit will be 15 percent higher than official U.S. forecasts suggest. See *World Economic Outlook* (Washington DC: International Monetary Fund, October 1993), p. 54. By the autumn of 1994, however, the results were somewhat better than expected—thanks to a strong recovery from the recession and much slower expenditure of the military funds Congress had authorized. See J. Lisco, "Squirreling Away," *Baron's*, September 12, 1994, p. 19. Many market analysis were predicting higher inflation and interest rates. Alan Abelson, "Mucho Macho," Ibid., pp. 5-6.

41. During his election campaign, Clinton, emphasizing that government should borrow only to invest, announced a plan to target investment of $219 billion on education, skills training and infrastructure development. See Robert Reich in *The American Prospect*, (Fall 1992), pp. 61-64. The plan in its original integrated form was, however, reduced in scale during Congressional budget negotiations, and finally represented an increase in Federal investment of just $7.1 billion for fiscal year 1994. *The Budget of the United States Government: Fiscal Year 1994* (Washington DC: U.S. Government Printing Office, 1993), p. 72. A supplementary plan announced early in the Clinton administration to boost growth and create jobs worth over $18 billion a year was killed by a Republican filibuster in April 1993.

42. Wilson's advocacy of a British-style Cabinet system stemmed from his perception that the power of the presidency had been seriously diminished by a succession of weak presidents following the assassination of Abraham Lincoln. A Cabinet drawn from the Congress itself would, Wilson believed, control the power of individual committees and ensure a strong, decisive, and accountable executive, regardless of the character of the president himself. His enthusiasm for reform along such lines, however, declined after the election of Grover Cleveland and then Theodore Roosevelt, two strong, charismatic presidents. See Woodrow Wilson, *Congressional Government: A Study in American Politics* (Baltimore: The Johns Hopkins University Press, 1981). For a brief introduction to Wilson's early views, see Aurthur S. Link, *Woodrow Wilson*. vol 1, *The Road to the White House* (Princeton: Princeton University Press, 1947), pp. 14-19.

43. For an explanation of French constitutional arrangements, see Raphael Hadas-Lebel, "The Governmental Structure of the Fifth Republic," *SAIS Review* (Special Issue, Fall 1993).

44. George Kennan, *Around the Cragged Peak: A Personal and Political Philosophy* (New York: W. W. Norton, 1993).

45. In 1992, the U.S. trade balance with Asia was $-84.05 billion compared with $-73.4 billion in the previous year. In contrast, trade with the two NAFTA countries, Canada and Mexico, had deficits of $-3.95 billion in 1991 and $-0.45 billion in 1992. Trade with Western Europe showed a positive balance of $16.13 billion for 1991 and $6.19 for 1992. *Survey of Current Business* (July 1993), pp. 16-17. The average annual trade balance between the United States and Latin America for the period 1989-1992 was $2.1 billion in surplus. OECD, *Economic Outlook*, 53 (June 1993), p. 186.

46. David Yankelovich, "Foreign Policy After the Election." *Foreign Affairs* 71:4 (Fall 1992), pp. 1-12.

47. Alexander Hamilton, *The Federalist Papers*, number 1, R. Fairfield, ed., (New York: Doubleday, 1966) p. 1.

·3·

Craving Normalcy:
The Japanese State after the Cold War

Michael J. Green

While economic integration and the end of bipolar confrontation are combining to weaken the integrity of the state in Europe and North America, the transformation of the international system has unleashed a new debate in Japan about the possibility of at last becoming a "normal state." At the core of the debate is the question of what is "normal."[1] Two visions prevail. One is presented by Ichiro Ozawa, a former Liberal Democratic Party (LDP) strongman and the chief architect of the 1993 anti-LDP coalition of then Prime Minister Morihiro Hosokawa. In his best-selling book, *Blueprint for a New Japan*,[2] Ozawa argues that Japan will become a normal state when the traditional layers of heavy bureaucratic regulation are reduced and prime ministers are able to respond directly to the peoples' will and international pressures for Japan to play a larger political role in global affairs. Ozawa's vision represents an injection of risk into the system—both in domestic and foreign policy. Risk means an end of the old order and possibly the displacement of uncompetitive members of the economy and society, but the rewards are higher economic growth, greater individual freedom, and enhanced international prestige.

The alternate vision of the future is offered by Masayoshi Takemura, also a former-LDP politician, who turned on his erstwhile allies Hosokawa and Ozawa in the spring of 1994 to engineer the implicitly anti-reform LDP-Socialist coalition of Prime Minister Tomiichi Murayama. Takemura argues in his bestseller, *Japan, A Small but Sparkling Country*,[3] that while some deregulation of the Japanese economy is essential, radical changes in the way Japan relates to the rest of the world are not necessary. Economically, Japan's exceptionalism and insulated market are sustainable. Politically, Japan has little to gain from seeking expanded missions in UN peacekeeping or international security. In short, the system has more than enough risk to suit the average Japanese citizen. Where Ozawa sees normalcy as the ability to define national interest (and take the risks necessary to achieve the goals therein), Takemura's version of normalcy means attending to the needs of an exhausted public that deserves a respite after four decades of strenuous economic catching-up.

In the West, Ozawa's prescription for change has suggested a bold new departure from the past, while Takemura's vision has struck observers as reactionary. In many ways, however, it is Ozawa who calls for a nostalgic return to an American-inspired model of deregulation at home and strongly articulated national interests abroad, and Takemura who reflects more closely the post–Cold War inward focus that American, Canadian, and European politicians are finding so effective at the polls. Both factors are at work in Japan. Opinion surveys show that the people want reform and a larger international profile for Japan, but they do not seem to want the attendant risk.

Ozawa's and Takemura's are not the only visions for Japan (their rival in the LDP, Ryutaro Hashimoto, advertises his book with the banner headline "I *also* have vision").[4] But the Ozawa and Takemura perspectives best capture the difficult choice Japan faces. The foundations of the old system have been shaken down by recession, the end of the Cold War, and the growing consequences of seeking insulation from the international economy. The first stage of the transformation of the state—destruction of the old political order—has begun. The emergence of the new order will be driven by recently passed electoral laws that will encourage the formation of competing parties and coalitions. These new parties and coalitions will likely do battle along the lines suggested by Ozawa and Takemura. Whether deregulation, international activism, or reconstituted protectionism prevail, the role of the state in Japan will come into sharp focus for the first time since 1945.

THE ELUSIVE STATE, AND THE SEARCH FOR AUTONOMY

The Japanese polity shares most of the institutional characteristics of the other states under examination in this book, but approaches the post–Cold War era with two unique characteristics: first is the elusive nature of the Japanese state—or put another way—the disconnect between institutional structures and actual policymaking; second is the pervasive (though frequently futile) search for autonomy from potentially destabilizing external forces that is evident in all facets of Japanese statecraft. Both may be seen as legacies of Japan's sudden explosion into the modern world coupled with continued geographic insularity and insecurity. Before we can explain the potential transformation of the Japanese state in the years ahead, we must consider these elements that have characterized the Japanese state to date.

The concept of Japan as an "elusive state" was introduced to Western political literature by Japan-critic and self-proclaimed revisionist Karl Van Wolferen in a series of articles and books in the late 1980s. Much of Van Wolferen's description of Japan struck scholars as off-the-mark, but his clever description of Japan as a headless state "where the buck did not stop anywhere" was difficult to deny.[5] Those who attacked Van Wolferen's "Japan bashing" rarely acknowledged that his concept of an "elusive state" echoed the observations of one of Japan's most prominent postwar political scientists, Junnichi Kyogoku. In *Japanese Politics,*[6] Kyogoku argues that Japan imported the political institutions and laws of the West, but superimposed them on what remained an essentially feudalistic and premodern model of the state. The organs of the state thus remained weak, its laws contextual. The Supreme Court, prime minister, political parties, and government were all relatively unimportant in defining Japan's postwar political identity. Instead, feudalistic organizations within the state framework became the real sources of policy decisions and political competition: factions rather than parties; ministries rather than government; divisions rather than bureaux; corporations rather than communities.

The precedents for the elusive state can be found in earlier periods of Japanese history. The Tokugawa Bakufu was itself a military government superimposed on the imperial system of the previous millennium. After the first generation of Tokugawa leadership, the institutions of the shogunate became hollow shells within which clan rivalries reemerged. The Meiji restoration of 1868 was the culmination of these clan rivalries as much as it was a drive for modernization. Unable to impose a new modern state on top of the Bakufu, which was in turn superimposed on the old imperial system, the Meiji oligarchy eliminated the shogunate and "restored" the emperor. The bureaucracies and conscript armies they built were dominated by the Yamagata clan. With time the clan ties were replaced by the new feudalism of government ministries and army-navy rivalry. Japan's slide into the Pacific War was not the result of "fascism" as allied propaganda asserted in an effort to tie the axis powers in a single ribbon. Instead, Japan's war in China and attack on Pearl Harbor were the consequences of the prime minister's inability to control the bureaucratic rivalry and expansionism of an increasingly independent military clique. On 7 December 1941 the buck stopped nowhere.

However, if the imported Western institutions of the state have been weak in Japan, the drive for autonomy has not. Japan has brought this impulse into the postwar era with a singularity of purpose not found elsewhere among the advanced industrial countries. The search for autonomy is based on historical experience; its roots are geographic. Japan emerged in the middle of the nineteenth century with a clear understanding of the fate that had befallen China at the hands of Western imperialism. Thus, two centuries of self-imposed isolation in the Tokugawa era and four decades of rapid opening and modernization under Meiji were continuations of the same strategic goal—insulation against the West. During the Meiji Restoration the reactionaries had for their rallying cry "*Sanno Joi*" (revere the emperor and expel the barbarian). For the Meiji reformers it was "*Wakon Yosai*" (Japanese spirit with Western learning). At their core, they were promising the same thing—Japan would not be dismembered like China had been. The Chinese fatal flaw had been insisting on maintenance of the illusion that the Ch'ing Court was the center of the universe. Meanwhile, Western learning and technology (and opium, of course) undermined the actual Chinese institutions of imperial control. Japan chose to import wholesale the Western model of the state, but to retain control and build new insulation against external threats by creating autonomous Japanese institutions. In the last decades of the nineteenth Century, the Meiji Government privatized industry in an effort to create competitive domestic corporations. After learning how to conscript, train, and maneuver modern mass armies, the Japanese sent their French (after 1871, Prussian) military advisors home and prepared to practice their new techniques on the Chinese. After learning shipbuilding from its British allies, the Japanese Imperial Navy gave its business to indigenous companies such as Kawasaki and Mitsui. Ultimately, this led to an army that did not answer to the government, a navy that was driven by rivalry with the army, and corporations that formed into competing *zaibatsu* (business conglomerates) and intervened in domestic politics. The prime minister became weaker as the feudalistic parts of the state became stronger and more autonomous, but ultimately this served to insulate Japan from the ravages of a chaotic and unpredictable world . . . until, that is, the relentless pursuit of autonomy brought Japan into war against the entire world.

Elusive yet autonomous: On first blush these characteristics of the modern Japanese state seem in contradiction. Yet upon closer examination it is clear that they are complementary. Autonomy is the source of insulation and protection for the domestic institutions that together form the state with no center. One might call this feudalism. Put in a more positive way, it is what economist Eisuke Sakakibara refers to as Japan's "anthropocentric" system.[7] In the anthropocentric system government's role (or precisely put, individual ministries' role) is to nurture and protect economic organizations from destruction while their competition drives the economy. The system has worked well, but pressures for convergence (pressures that are economic, political, demographic, and geostrategic)—the same pressures hitting other advanced industrial countries—are raising the opportunity costs of the old system. These pressures are already behind the destruction of the old political regime and are forcing the choices articulated broadly by Ozawa and Takemura. With this in mind, we turn to the specifics of Japan's postwar political system.

THE 1955 SYSTEM

As in the prewar period, postwar autonomy rested not on the state, but on the fiefdoms within it. These fiefdoms: business *keiretsu* (associations), political factions, and ministries, have often been called the "iron triangle." The actors in the iron triangle captured U.S. occupation policy, which wavered between reform and recovery, but ultimately depended on existing bureaucracies and economic organizations for implementation of policy (in contrast to Germany where the bureaucracy was destroyed during the war). The Internal Ministry, the military, and the *zaibatsu* were disbanded, but ministries of foreign affairs, finance, and industry manipulated occupation policy to protect their own future. The iron triangle was solidified in 1955 when more than a dozen conservative parties formed into the Liberal Democratic Party which would rule until 1993 (and sneak back into a coalition the next year). Japanese political observers therefore refer to this as "the 1955 system." It was sustained by the simple principles of steady economic growth and low risk: mutually assured non-destruction, one might say, with strong economic organizations, powerful autonomous government ministries—and a weak and elusive state.

The Political Leg of the Iron Triangle

The political leg of the 1955 system was held up by the LDP, which established an electoral juggernaut that crowded out competing parties for almost four decades. The LDP's success could be attributed to three factors: flexibility, the electoral structure, and legitimacy. All three were functions of the Cold War environment and had the effect of continuing the feudalistic aspects of Japanese government.[8]

First, the LDP's flexibility was critical to its success. The LDP's platform was simple: opposition to communism, rapid and equitable economic growth, and strong support for the U.S.-Japan alliance. Within the party's ranks there were widely different views on issues of constitutional reform, the pace of remilitarization, and accommodation with the opposition. However, these more extreme ideas only saw the light of day when politicians associated with them rose to cabinet posts. Eventually, compromise with other faction leaders and cabinet ministers moved these views into the mainstream. Meanwhile, where the LDP was flexible and centrist, the opposition parties in Japan were often inflexible and off-center. The Socialist Party, in particular, was frozen along its Maginot line—prevention of a two thirds LDP majority in the diet that would allow constitutional reform (and abolition of Article 9, the "peace" clause). Since most Japanese voters felt uncomfortable giving the LDP more than two thirds of the vote, this guaranteed the Socialists' steady support from a minority of the voters. However, the Socialists' static defensive line and strong Marxist support within public sector labor unions created a disincentive for reaching out to a broader swath of the electorate. When new moderate-left parties emerged in the 1960s and 1970s appealing to a new class of suburban voters, the Socialists retreated further into their ideological bastion. The LDP, meanwhile commandeered many of the issues these new moderate-left parties had introduced, such as environmental protection.

The LDP's flexibility was not entirely a result of careful strategic planning. It had at least as much to do with a second factor behind the party's success: the electoral system in Japan. Each of the multi-seat districts of the powerful lower house of the diet was characterized by fierce competition between LDP candidates from different factions. In their effort to lock in the broad conservative vote, these LDP rivals established powerful support groups (*koenkai*) whose members' loyalty was nurtured by the rich patronage available to a long-term ruling party. Meanwhile, at the national level, factional rivalry meant that when one LDP prime minister stumbled, a reshuffling of factional balance of power would bring in a new face—creating the essence of change without the unpredictability and risk that comes with an actual change of ruling parties. Factional infighting in the party, rather than weakening the conservatives' base, made for a more dynamic vote-gathering machine. In effect, the elusiveness of the state—and of the LDP's center—was critical to the party's success at the polls.

The electoral system gave an additional benefit to the conservative LDP as well: gerrymandering. In spite of steady urbanization after the war, Japan's rural districts continued to hold close to the same number of seats throughout the postwar period. A Supreme Court decision determined that a discrepancy of more than three-to-one in the weight of rural versus urban votes would be unconstitutional, but even that ruling left conservative pro-LDP supporters in the countryside with a huge advantage over their urban and suburban compatriots.

Finally, the LDP's almost four decades of success hinged on the party's seeming legitimacy. First, this resulted from a demonstrated ability to manage the economy—or at least stay out of the way and let the bureaucrats manage the economy. Decades of high growth bought the party years of trust from the people. Legitimacy also derived from the geopolitical environment. The linchpin of conservative mainstream rule in postwar Japan was alliance with the United States, and thus the bipolar Cold War structure itself. The U.S. role in creating an atmosphere for long-term LDP rule involved much more than the depurging of conservative politicians during the occupation or the alleged funding of senior politicians by the CIA. Alliance with the United States formed the only point of consensus around which conservative politicians could converge in the late 1940s and early 1950s. Absent alliance, Japan's conservatives would have had to come to terms with fundamental questions of national security, where views diverged widely from advocates of unilateral disarmament to remilitarizing hawks. As the historian John Dower writes: "the reconsolidation and centralization of conservative authority during the Yoshida era was inseparable from the strategic settlement reached between the United States and Japan."[9]

Thus the 1955 system and the political leg of the Iron Triangle were Cold War constructs. Strategic settlement with the United States allowed Japan to defer the touchier questions of national interest and focus instead on economic recovery and political stability. LDP politicians were elected not to bring change or new directions, but to lobby the bureaucracies on behalf of constituents. National elections did not lead to new departures in policy, but to readjustment when economic inequities led to protest votes against the LDP at the polls (the LDP did well in times of economic slow-down but was punished when inequities in economic growth appeared). The Japanese people did not vote to define their state, they voted to choose their protectors and benefactors in a modern version of feudal democracy.

The Business and Bureaucratic Legs

The real business of the Japanese state was business, of course. Under LDP protection Japan's economy grew at a 10 percent real annual per capita rate from 1955 to 1970. Although economic growth slowed to 3 percent from 1970 to 1990, the fundamental pillars of the "anthropocentric" model of capitalism remained more or less intact. An almost risk-free haven was created for Japanese manufacturing firms by the *keiretsu* members cross-share holdings and a heavily regulated stock market. In the 1980s the average return on equity for Japan's top 350 industrial companies was only 8.5 percent, compared with 13.9 percent for the top U.S. industrial corporations for the same years.[10] In such an environment of "mutually assured non-destruction," large Japanese companies could afford to maintain lifetime employment; de-emphasize price; invest more in plant and equipment, and research and development; and satisfy investors by building market share through incremental technological improvements in products that rivals in all the other *keiretsu* were already selling—rather than through risky new ventures that might provide the higher yields required by intrusive stock holders in the West.

During this period, the exceptionalism of Japan's economic development defined Japan's overall relationship with the rest of the world. Economic growth created new insulation against global shocks. Japan's level of foreign asset valuation holdings in the domestic economy in the early 1990s was one twentieth the level of the United States (as a level of total assets). In fact, Japan's per capita ratio of foreign direct investment into the country has remained almost unchanged for four decades (and well below the average for the Organization for Economic Cooperation and Development), meaning that whether by strict currency controls (in the 1950s) or a high yen (in the 1980s and 1990s), Japan has kept intrusive foreign investment that might disrupt the "anthropocentric" system at a minimum. To say that Japan has had *no* external shocks would be misleading, of course, for the oil shocks of 1973 and 1979 (not to mention the less-known soy bean embargo shock of President Nixon) had a major impact on the

Japanese economy and psyche. The point worth remembering, however, is that those shocks—while they stunted economic growth—did not destroy any significant Japanese economic organizations or lead to new dependencies on foreign sources of technology or natural resources. In fact, Japan reduced its dependence on Middle East oil more effectively than either Europe or the United States following the oil shocks through a combination of conservation, diversification, and nuclear power development.

The government's role in this economic system was to back up mutual insurance by helping large uncompetitive firms to survive. The Japanese Ministry for International Trade and Industry (MITI) equalized competitiveness among companies by indigenizing, nurturing, and diffusing technology (weakening intellectual property protection of individual firms in favor of broadening the gains of new technologies across the economy). On the whole, as Richard Samuels has pointed out, MITI and industry reached industrial policy decisions based on "reciprocal consent" rather than government directive.[11] Where MITI's leverage was greatest was in creating anti-recession cartels to help endangered firms survive. High-technology industrial policy had fewer success stories (as evidenced by the fact that many of Japan's most competitive companies in the 1990s grew by defying the advice of MITI: companies such as Sharp, Sony, Honda, and Kyocera). The Ministry of Finance (MOF) played at least as important a role by guaranteeing that capital remained cheap, that banks did not fail, and that companies would not be vulnerable to the capriciousness of stock markets.

Was this a strong state? Certainly there was far greater government intervention in the economy than in the United States (though probably less than France), and MITI, the Ministry of Finance and the other economic ministries shared a common view of national economic interest. However, these bureaucracies policies were at the same time highly dysfunctional. MITI's policies on telecommunications, for example, have been driven as much by the goal of weakening the Ministry of Posts and Telecommunications as by rational economic planning.[12] Bureaucratic turf has mattered much more in Japan than in other OECD countries, for lifetime employment applies to bureaucrats as well as to mainstream corporate Japan. And Japanese officials have had a strong incentive to protect their economic constituencies and future nest eggs (the term *amakudari,* or "descent from heaven" describes the usual fate of Japanese officials, who almost all begin second careers in the private or semi-private sectors they regulated). Moreover, the system has had no accountability. Bureaucratic directives to industry generally have come in the form of subtle and untraceable "administrative guidance" rather than clearly delineated laws—further contributing to the elusiveness of the state.

Interagency feuding (in the most feudalistic sense) was often mediated by powerful LDP politicians who led policy *zoku* (caucuses). However, these political interventions often were efforts to create new campaign financing opportunities as much as they were well-informed policy making. Business also kept the bureaucracy in check by funding the LDP through Keidanren (the Federation of Economic Organizations). For decades Keidanren formed a near shadow government—preparing policy proposals, settling LDP leadership disputes, and even writing defense plans and strategy.[13] Since the state's national security goals were unclear, industry inserted its own goals instead. These dysfunctional elements of Japan's feudalistic system did not matter for much of the postwar period, however, because the economy continued to grow, income, assets, and technology were distributed more or less equally, and large uncompetitive players were insulated from foreign competition inside Japan. The problem came when the Cold War system ended and the costs of "anthropocentrism" escalated.

THE COLLAPSE OF THE 1955 SYSTEM

The 1955 system first began to show signs of "structural fatigue" in the late 1980s.[14] Rapid yen appreciation after the 1985 Plaza Accord and upward spiraling land speculation led to the "bubble economy" of the second half of the decade, and perverse disparities in income between land holders and the rest of Japan's struggling salarymen and farmers. Political scandals, which had always been a problem for the LDP, suddenly accelerated, revealing that politicians were engaging in stock speculation and bribery for personal aggrandizement rather than for political advancement and constituent services. Economic success and increased offshore production meant that industry was diversifying its political objectives and was less able to impose discipline on the LDP. When the bubble burst in 1991 and Japan entered its worst recession since the oil shocks of the 1970s, the LDP lost its credibility as an efficient manager of the economy. The end of the Cold War had already eliminated the ideological pillar of conservative rule and the Japanese people now had the freedom to consider non-LDP alternatives. With the birth of Prime Minister Morihiro Hosokawa's Japan New Party, and defections from the LDP that led to the creation of the Renewal Party (Shinseito) of Tsutomu Hata and Ichiro Ozawa and the Harbinger

Party (Sakigake) of Masayoshi Takemura, the stage was set for Japan's first non-LDP cabinet in almost four decades.[15]

When Hosokawa took power from the LDP, many revisionists claimed that the heralded "Hesei Revolution" (after the name of the Emperor's reign) was just a hoax.[16] After all, Hosokawa himself was once a member of the LDP—in fact, he belonged to its most corrupt and bloated faction, the Tanaka Faction. Hosokawa's backers, Hata and Ozawa, were members of Tanaka's retinue as well, before leaving the faction and the party in what cynics considered pure opportunism rather than crusading reform. Indeed, the successful reentry of the LDP into power in 1994, in an odd-couple alliance with their old enemies the Socialists, gives further fuel to the skeptics. Similarly, those who deny change point to the bursting of the bubble as nothing more than a cyclical recession that will do no structural harm to Japan's anthropocentric economic system.

The Japanese are a conservative people and disdain revolution, to be sure. But those expecting a return of the old system will be disappointed for two reasons. First, Japan's economic woes are linked to much more significant changes in global capital and technology flows and domestic demographics than the government's rosy economic figures suggest on the surface. Second, the Japanese diet has created a new electoral system of single seat districts that is almost certain to send all of the government and opposition party candidates cascading towards two or three competing parties that will undermine the autonomy of the ministries and force a sharper delineation of the economic choices Japan faces.

The Economic Transformation

Officially, Japan's post-bubble, post–Cold War recession began in May of 1991 and bottomed-out in October of 1993. Beneath this rather positive interpretation offered by the government, however, is a tsunami of devastating proportions. Put in its starkest terms, between 1989 and 1992, Japan lost asset values of 337 trillion yen, an amount comparable to 70 percent of the nation's GNP. 143 trillion of this amount was in land, the rest in hidden value assets ("*fukumi-shisan*") held in the form of stocks and overseas investments. This sudden disappearance of asset value caused a credit crisis for Japanese banks. Officially the top commercial and credit banks have bad loans totaling 13.7 trillion yen. Private research organizations put the amount at 60 trillion yen (close to $600 billion).[17]

Taken together, these figures all suggest that the underpinnings of Japan's anthropocentric capitalist system may no longer be sustainable.

Cross-share holdings of non-performing stocks become extremely costly for companies that are only maintaining cash flow by selling hidden assets. Similarly, the lifetime employment system of large companies has become too expensive to maintain. Officially, Japanese unemployment ranges between 2.5 percent and 3.0 percent, but in-company unemployment brings the real figure up to 7 percent (in a highly cynical move, Toyota recently established a special "elite" project team of 70 middle managers to study the reasons for in-company unemployment among middle managers). The high appreciation of the yen only exacerbates these difficulties. Thus giants such as Nippon Telegraph and Telephone (NTT) reduced their number of employees by 10 percent between 1990 and 1993.

To some extent it might be argued that this kind of restructuring will make Japanese companies leaner and meaner in the future. That certainly would be the case in the United States. However, for Japanese companies to down-size and focus on "core competencies" means abandoning traditional management practices such as lifetime employment, cross-share holdings of stock, and maintenance of stock earnings through the liquidation of hidden assets. In short, it means introducing more risk into the system. It will be extremely difficult for corporate Japan to emerge from the current recession "leaner and meaner," with its traditional management practices intact.[18]

Indeed, Japanese news media is replete with anecdotal evidence that Japanese companies are already taking dramatic measures in this direction: reducing redundant workers, selling off the non-performing stock of strategic allies and opening-up new alliances with foreign firms. The difficult choices have not been made, however, and it may still be that Japan crawls out of its three year recession *without* addressing the real structural problems that economists and far-sighted business managers are demanding. The current crop of executives in Japan, after all, are men who rose through the ranks by not making mistakes (that is, by avoiding risk). The newer companies that have been built from the bottom up by their current chief executive officers (CEO's) are the ones that are calling for a radical new management practices and an end to paternalistic bureaucratic interference.[19] But these are also companies that have reduced their Japanese image and have moved significant proportions of not only their manufacturing, but also their management and research and development, offshore. The silent majority of companies remain cautious, conservative, and domestic-oriented in their management philosophy.

The business community thus sees the need for change but is schizophrenic in pressing the government to bring it about. One classic example of this confusion stemmed from Keidanren, as it made the much trumpeted demand that the Hosokawa administration implement deregulation and simultaneously called on the government to create new regulations that would prevent the price of land from falling and jeopardizing corporations' hidden assets. Another example is Japan's effort to create a national information superhighway. Electronics companies are lobbying for the Ministry of Posts and Telecommunications to allow greater freedom to companies creating online services and software, while at the same time calling on the government to create a massive national information superhighway public works project.

While corporate Japan's love/hate view of deregulation and risk may be understandable in the short term, however, a number of trends are combining that will force the difficult decisions into sharper focus through the rest of the decade. One is the reduction of opportunities for middle managers. The lifetime employment system stresses seniority with guaranteed rewards for those who wait, but the average age of presidents of big companies is rising, while the number of potential posts for future senior managers is dwindling. Meanwhile, the real growth in employment opportunities for college graduates (who faced terrible prospects in the early 1990s) is in the service sector where there is greater labor mobility. In 1992 manufacturing output dropped by 1.3 percent in Japan while the service sector grew by 3.4 percent, bucking a trend in which the two sectors of the economy had been growing in tandem.[20] As the opportunity costs of participating in lifetime employment increase for elite university graduates, they will move into new areas, creating greater labor mobility and weakening the consensus behind anthropocentrism. Technology and capital flows also conspire against the old system. The massive debt of Japanese banks is discouraging lending, meaning that a rapidly growing portion of venture capital in Japan must come from abroad. Japan's traditional technology strategy of one way indigenization is also becoming untenable as massive, high-risk aerospace and computer projects require new levels of international collaboration in which Japanese companies will be expected by foreign partners to give as much technology as they get.

In short, the opportunity costs of maintaining the old system are likely to create greater cleavages within the Japanese polity: between those whose technological advancement is hindered by government regulation and those who depend on government to insulate them against the destabilizing impact of volatile financial markets, international competition or the high yen. The political framework within which these issues will be debated is already taking shape.

The Political Transformation

The rollcall of Japan's post-LDP reformist politicians could easily lead to skepticism. The leaders of the first anti-LDP coalition included Prime Minister Morihiro Hosokawa (formerly of the LDP Tanaka faction), Deputy Prime Minister Tsutomu Hata (also formerly of the Tanaka faction) and of course, the coalition's architect, Ichiro Ozawa (again, of the Tanaka faction). When the Socialist partners in the coalition withdrew their support from the cabinet and eventually through their lot in with the LDP and the smaller Sakigake Party to form a coalition government in the spring of 1994, the key figure behind the new government was former prime minister Noboru Takeshita. Takeshita was, not surprisingly, of the Tanaka faction, and continued his war on the rebellious Ozawa and Hata while pulling the strings of Socialist Prime Minister Tomiichi Murayama. Japan's process of political reform could be explained as little more than a succession battle that spilled over from the Tanaka Faction. In fact, the Socialists' complete repudiation of their own party platform (a condition for receiving the prime ministerial post in the coalition with the LDP) suggests that the process of political reform may have only resulted in the collapse of the left and strengthening of the traditional forces of corruption and conservatism.

Such a conclusion would be too facile, however, for in their enthusiastic rush to assure the voters of their commitment to reform, the current crop of politicians have introduced a new electoral system that virtually guarantees new political alignments in the future. Under Japan's old system, aspirants to the powerful lower house of the diet ran for one of 511 seats divided into 126 districts across the country. With an average of four seats per district and the probability that LDP politicians would be running against fellow party members (but fierce rivals), there was a strong disincentive to run a campaign based on policy issues and an equally strong incentive to join one of the LDP factions. To win in an election, politicians had to lock in a large enough segment of the district to be one the group of diet members elected. That meant continuous care and feeding of constituencies such as agriculture, small business, or even religious organizations. Politicians had to tap into organizations and promise to provide for them (locking into the anthropocentric system at the grass roots, local level). The voters, in turn, elected people who would effectively lobby on their behalf to the powerful bureaucracies in Tokyo.

Under the new system, passed into law in January of 1994 and effective since December of the same year, politicians will run either for one of 300 single-seat districts or for one of 200 slots that are distributed to parties in a list system divided into eleven regional blocs. This simple structural change will have an immense impact. First, single seat districts will weaken, if not destroy, the faction system. Moreover, single seat districts will create strong pressures against a single dominant party such as the LDP. Minority parties based on a strong constituency (such as the Komeito with its connection to the Sokkagakai religion) could survive in the list system, but to win in single-seat races politicians will have to build broader coalitions that are unified by strong thematic glue. One politician's theme will lead inevitably to counter themes from his rivals. Played out on a national stage, this will accelerate the formation of two or three parties that have the resources and issues to compete effectively in all 300 single seat districts across the country. Japanese voters may begin voting, not for a lobbyist in Tokyo, but for a party and politicians that represent a direction they wish the country to go. The difficult economic choices already outlined will provide the ingredients for each party's prescription for the future.

The end of dominance for a single party will mean a new role in the economy for Japan's bureaucracy. In the 1920s a two-party system led to politicization of the bureaucracy, with powerful *zaibatsu* lined up on opposite sides. The diet was much weaker in the 1920s than it is today, however, and the emergence of new party politics in the 1990s will likely have an even more divisive effect on the integrity of the ministries. Already, MITI has been racked with internal division as proxy wars between the rebels and loyalists of the former Tanaka faction have filtered down through the ministry's personnel decisions, terminating the career of at least one candidate for vice minister (the highest bureaucratic post). The prospect of continued changes in ruling parties or coalitions will make the elite bureaucracy a much less secure place to work. As expertise flows to other sectors of the political economy, the bureaucracy's efforts to control information and markets will dissipate. As lifetime employment in the bureaucracy weakens, so too will the ministries' concern with preserving the anthropocentric system in industry.

In the mid-1990s the evolution of political realignment has been characterized more by fits and starts than bold leadership, but the process will accelerate rapidly when elections are held under the new system. The two camps in 1995 have moved closer to forming institutionalized competing parties, but legacies of the old party allegiances remain. The current opposition parties: the Japan New Party, Renewal Party, Democratic Socialists, Komeito and smaller allies, have attempted to form a single party—the New Progressive Party (*Shinshinto*)—that may survive internal strife (particularly between Komeito and its secular rivals in the JNP). The ruling coalition partners, the LDP, Socialists, and Sakigake, have found cooperation at the polls much more difficult given their radically different grass-roots structures. The Socialists could easily split or be eliminated in voting under the new system, which would make their inability to cooperate with the LDP a moot point. But then, the LDP also has the potential to split as younger politicians are frustrated in their efforts to run in the single seat districts by their more powerful elders. In short, the process of political realignment, while it is showing signs of moving towards a two or three party system, could just as easily see further splintering into small parties in the short term before clear competitors emerge in the medium to long term.

It must also be pointed out, that in spite of broad visions for Japan's future presented by political leaders such as Ozawa and Takemura, these ideas have not yet animated politicians to form together, nor have they attracted constituencies in business to back one view or another in a systematic way. In the mid-1990s, Japanese politicians are more concerned with surviving the transition to a radically different election system than with creating parties or policies. They realize, however, that the first elections under the single seat/block system will wreck havoc upon even the best laid plans. Within a number of years, incumbents wanting reelection will band together in parties that have national reach and the battle lines will be drawn along the issues already introduced. Several outcomes are possible.

SOME SCENARIOS FOR THE FUTURE

For four decades the LDP led based on a national mandate for economic growth and anthropocentrism. Until the late 1980s, the two were not mutually exclusive. Now they are. Implicitly, the contradictory visions of Ozawa and Takemura suggest as much. If translated into concrete policy measures, each would transform the role of the state—bringing it into clearer focus—but in different ways.

Japan as a "Normal" Nation

There is widespread doubt in Japan that Ichiro Ozawa will ever be prime minister, but his formula for rebuilding Japan is not unique (many of the ideas were Yasuhiro Nakasone's in the early 1980s) and any number of new political leaders could make his plans their own. Under such leadership, the Japanese state would acquire the instruments necessary to calculate and articulate national interest. The prime minister's office would be equipped with independent sources of intelligence (independent from both the United States and the bureaucracies in Japan). Japan would turn membership on the United Nations Security Council into a platform for advancing a regional political agenda in Asia, including the dispatch of UN peacekeeping forces when sanctioned by the Security Council. The Japanese Government would utilize technological assets more to achieve national security goals, including strengthening of export controls and more explicit use of foreign aid to influence international political developments. At home, however, deregulation would be emphasized to allow new enterprises in software and information technology to move ahead rapidly. Deregulation of the financial markets would attract international players back from Hong Kong,[21] injecting much need venture capital into the system, but traditional *keiretsu* cross-share holdings would prove less rational. In order to compete internationally, more Japanese companies would be driven to joint ventures with Western firms comparable to the close Mazda-Ford relationship. The government would be less likely to prop up uncompetitive players. The aging of society and the prospect of hidden internal unemployment moving outside companies (so that the nominal and real unemployment rates converged) would require the establishment of a more effective welfare state (that is, the burden of the safety net would shift from companies to the government). Decentralization and the expansion of political appointments in the central bureaucracies would leave more of the initiative for creating welfare at the local level. Eventually, the decline or transformation of inefficient players might reduce excess capacity, loosen export pressures and depreciate the yen against other currencies. Japanese companies that emerged from this transition would be highly competitive internationally.

Japan as a "Small but Sparkling Country"

The alternate vision for Japan's future is that of Mr. Takemura. Again, there is a possibility that Takemura may never be prime minister of Japan, but his vision has as many antecedents and quiet supporters as Ozawa's. A small but sparkling Japan would attempt to sustain most of the management practices and government intervention of the traditional anthropocentric model of capitalism. However, the initiative in policymaking would gradually concentrate on the prime minister's party at the expense of the bureaucratic and business legs of the iron triangle. The Government would prop up uncompetitive players with large national projects, forcing a diffusion of technology internally and a sharing of the domestic market that would lead to overcapacity. This in turn would drive the yen up further against foreign currencies, raising the costs to consumers and competitive high tech players in the system. Japan might attempt to continue recycling its surpluses in foreign aid projects—particularly in Asia—but an aggressive push for membership in the UN Security Council or a role in international politics would be unlikely. Japan's initiative in foreign relations would be hampered by continuing surpluses that would keep nagging trade issues at the top of Tokyo's agenda with other states. Deregulation of financial markets would proceed at a slow pace, given the potential for a sudden unraveling of the *keiretsu* system. Japanese banks' bad loans would lead to higher interest rates that would combine with the erosion of corporations' hidden assets to choke investment over the mid-term. In the short term, the bureaucracies would be extremely powerful, but over time would weaken as political appointees and political intervention spread. As politicians assert a new grip on the organs of government, the spoils would be used to cement political alliances rather than to advance deregulation. Taken as a whole, the effort to retain old management practices could cost Japan significantly in terms of economic growth, but would be far less disruptive in the short term than the Ozawa model.

CONCLUSION

The wild card in both scenarios is the United States. Under the 1955 system, the U.S. government played the role of opposition party (by increasingly pressing for greater emphasis on consumers in the economy) and provided for Japan's security in the international system. Under either scenario described above, this role for the United States is likely to decrease— indeed, it already has. As a result, more responsibility for defining national interest will fall upon politicians. Given the new possibility of elections leading to actual changes in government, those politicians will be more accountable for their definitions of national interest than ever before.

The "normal state" vision of Ozawa takes a bolder definition of national interest, but it is one that injects risk in the system and would likely lead to displacement in Japanese society. The "small but sparkling country" vision of Takemura involves less risk in the short term, but probably carries greater risk in the long term. As the electorate is driven from one vision to the next by crises, there is a danger that external factors—particularly economic relations with the United States—could become the focus of resentment for the losers in the domestic transformation. The challenge for policymakers in Washington will be to manage the bilateral relationship in a way that discourages demagoguery.

The irony of Japan's dilemma is that the elusive state is being dismantled and a more accountable state created precisely because of Japan's increasing interdependence with the rest of the world. Japan, with some 15 percent of global GNP, can no longer justify its program of economic exceptionalism. Foreign pressure for change conspires with domestic economic and demographic pressures—and regional competition—to force on Japan a choice between embracing change, convergence, and risk, or struggling to maintain a high degree of autonomous control over its economic destiny.

Japan has faced this dilemma once before—in the 1920s. At that time the nation had just lost the last of its Meiji oligarchic leaders; new electoral laws were leading to an unstable but democratic two party system; Japan's bilateral security treaty with Britain was replaced by a series of ill-defined multilateral treaties in the region; and the Ministry of Finance was preparing to liberalize financial markets and move onto the gold standard—in effect converging with a Western economic system on the verge of turning projectionist. The pressure for convergence could not have been greater, nor the timing worse.[22] The displacement and loss of control that resulted led directly to Japan's autarkic policies of the 1930s.

Autarky is not possible in the 1990s, but marginalization is. Japan faces dynamic economic competitors and loosening ties to the United States that will give new significance to the direction of political leadership and the definition of national interest in the future. The elusive state can run, but it cannot hide.

◆ NOTES TO CHAPTER 3 ◆

1. Several of the themes in this essay were developed originally by the author with Richard J. Samuels, *Recalculating Autonomy: Japan's Choices in the New World Order* (Seattle: National Bureau of Asian Research, 1994).
2. Ichiro Ozawa, *Nihon Kaizo Keikaku* (Tokyo: Kodansha, 1993).
3. Masayoshi Takemura, *Chisakutomo Kirari to Hikaru Kuni, Nippon* (Tokyo: Kobunsha, 1994).
4. Ryutaro Hashimoto, *Bision obu Japan* (Tokyo: K. K. Besto Serrazu, 1994).
5. Karl van Wolferen, *The Enigma of Japanese Power* (New York: Alfred A. Knopf, 1989). The "elusive state" is introduced on pp. 25-50.
6. Junnichi Kyogoku, *Nihon no Seiji* (Tokyo: Tokyo Daigaku Shuppankai, 1984).
7. Eisuke Sakakibara, *Beyond Capitalism: The Japanese Model of Market Economics* (New York: Economic Strategy Institute, 1993).
8. Nathaniel Thayer, *How the Conservatives Rule Japan* (Princeton: Princeton University Press, 1969).

9. John Dower, *Empire and Aftermath: Yoshida Shigeru and the Japanese Experience, 1878-1954* (Cambridge: Harvard East Asian Monographs, 1979), p. 269.
10. Sources: Nomura Research Institute and Standard & Poors. Cited in Ide Masayuki, "The Japanese Financial System and the Competitiveness of Large Japanese Companies," paper for the Conference on Japanese Corporate Organizations and Finance, Australia National University, 1992, p. 14.
11. See Richard J. Samuels, *The Business of the Japanese State: Energy Markets in Comparative and Historical Perspective* (Ithaca: Cornell University Press, 1987).
12. See, for example, Chalmers Johnson, "MITI, MPT and the Telecom Wars," in Laura Tyson, et. al., *Politics and Productivity: How Japan's Development Strategy Works* (New York: HarperCollins, 1989).
13. Keidanren Boeiseisaniinkai, *Boeiseisaniinkai Junenshi* (Tokyo: Keidanren, 1964).
14. A phrase coined by Reizo Utagawa in *A Brave New World: Can Domestic Japanese Politics Change* (Tokyo: International Institute for Policy Studies, 1992).
15. For a fuller account, see *The United States and Japan in 1994: Uncertain Prospects,* (Washington, DC: The Edwin O. Reischauer Center for East Asian Studies, SAIS, The Johns Hopkins University, 1994).
16. See Chalmers Johnson, "The Tremor," *The New Republic* 209:6 (August 9, 1993); and Karel van Wolferen, "Japan's Non-Revolution," *Foreign Affairs* 72:1 (September/October 1993).
17. Hiroyki Tezuka, "Restructuring of Japan Inc." Statement before the Joint Economic Committee of the United States Congress, July 26, 1994. Mr. Tezuka is a former Brookings Scholar and serves as the Senior Representative of the NKK Corporation in Washington, DC.
18. For elaboration on this theme see Arthur J. Alexander, "Japan as Number Three: Long-term Productivity Growth Problems in the Economy," *JEI Report* (April 24, 1994).
19. See, for example, Kazuo Inamori, "Battling a Venerable Bureaucratic Tradition," in *Japan Echo* 20 (1994). Mr. Inamori is Chairman of the Kyocera Corporation.
20. Douglas Ostrom, "Lessons from Japan's Recession," *JEI Report* (November 11, 1994).
21. The combination of excessive regulation and recession has led to an exodus of Western financial firms out of Tokyo, see James Paradise, "Foreign Companies Say 'Sayonara' to TSE," *Tokyo Business Today* 62:11 (November 1994).
22. David Asher, "Convergence and Its Costs: The International Politics of Japanese Macroeconomic Liberalization, 1918-1932," unpublished manuscript, Cornell University Scholars Program, 1991.

·4·

Italy:
The Crisis of an Oligarchical State

Sergio Fabbrini

The crisis of the postwar Italian state has stemmed not only from the transformations that have affected all the Western democratic states, but also from the Italian state's specifically oligarchical nature (where oligarchical is understood to mean that specific organized minorities are able to utilize state resources in order to perpetuate their own power). The Italian state acquired its oligarchical character through the combined effects of institutional centralization and a centralized party structure. The combination of the Italian state as a centralized institution and the pervasive control exerted by political parties was responsible for the Italian state's democratic consolidation since the war. Nevertheless, on the basis of the prolonged economic and cultural modernization of the country in the postwar decades, that combination also caused the Italian state's crisis. This crisis became evident only at the end of the 1980s when, with the demise of the Cold War international system, the last crucial justification for the oligarchical Italian state disappeared.

THE CENTRALIZED STATE

After brief debate, the Piedmontese political elites that led the political unification of Italy rapidly adopted the Napoleonic model for the state.[1] As is well known, this is a pyramidal administrative structure, in which local bodies are mere appendages (articulations) of national institutions. Given that Italian political unification came about on the basis of heterogeneous regional situations, this was a momentous choice, especially since the Napoleonic model developed in a national context (France) very different from that of Italy. In post-revolutionary France, in fact, the centralized model was justified by the need to transfer to the periphery what the revolution of 1789 had accomplished at the center; a center that already possessed a clear-cut political identity and that was therefore endowed with strong public institutions.

Italy's situation was very different at the time of the country's unification in 1861. There was no national center as such. Indeed, three different cities—first Turin, then Florence, and finally Rome—were selected to be the national capital, and once Rome had been definitively chosen, that city had to be both the capital of Italy and the capital of Roman Catholicism. Meanwhile, the periphery of "the hundred cities and thousand communes" possessed ancient and clear political identities sustained by varied but entrenched local institutional structures. Thus, while France was traditionally identified by its capital, Italy was traditionally identified by its peripheries. Furthermore, the unitary Italian state had engaged in fierce conflict with the Catholic Church from the birth of the nation. The national center—already weak in terms of identity—was therefore also weak in terms of legitimacy. Consequently, difficulties inevitably arose when the centralized institutional model, which instead presupposed a strong center and limited polycentrism, was applied to a polycentric country with a weak and poorly legitimated center. Nevertheless, for almost a century (until the republican constitution of 1948) the goal pursued by the political elites of the country, in emulation of the French model, was to consolidate political unity by building a uniform administrative structure that covered the entire national territory.

At this level, the republican constitution of 1948 was an important innovation: By formally recognizing local autonomies, the political unity of the country was no longer identified with the uniformity of its administrative system for the first time since 1861.[2] By envisaging a regional state as an expression of the country's historical polycentrism, the constitution of 1948 formally acknowledged that political unity could coexist with a state articulated into differentiated local autonomies. However, and this is the crucial point, such recognition remained only formal. The regional administrations were only created in 1970, and once inaugurated they had scant legislative autonomy, no fiscal self-sufficiency, and functioned as autonomous bodies solely at the administrative level. Moreover, they possessed few representative means with which to impose their point of view in national decision-making. Of course, legislation introduced on a national scale encountered substantial difficulties when attempts were made to implement it in Italy's polycentric context. The outcome, therefore, was that the law progressively became a matter of negotiation rather than an indisputable value.

Accordingly, one may argue that in spite of the regional structure envisaged by the constitution, the postwar Italian state preserved its centralized character, even if this has been somewhat attenuated at the administrative level. Indeed, the introduction of regional administrations in 1970 was motivated not by considerations of state functioning, but of democracy—that is, by the political, and not the institutional, necessity to integrate the largest opposition party on the Left (the Italian Communist party, or PCI) into local government.[3] The reason for this is straightforward. The PCI had achieved such massive electoral support—between one-quarter and one-third of the national electorate—that its continued exclusion from the government was no longer possible. Yet the party's anti-system ideological connotations and its international links with the geopolitical bloc hegemonized or controlled by the Soviet Union meant that inclusion of the PCI in the government was equally unacceptable. This was a major dilemma, for which the solution was sought at the level of local government. With the creation of the regional governments, the PCI could assume (local) governing responsibility without this upsetting the international geopolitical equilibria that constrained the action of the national government.

This solution generated local political elites that came to control the administrative machinery of the regions, as well as the communes and provinces.[4] However, since these elites were bereft of significant legislative capacity and an autonomous fiscal base, they had to yield constantly to the strategic dominance of the national political elites. Moreover, given the need to adapt national legislation to local realities, the role of these local party elites was restricted to intermediation between the central state and local constituencies.[5] Local electorates cast their votes for those local political elites who proved most adept in obtaining resources from the center; although their ability to do so increased when they belonged to parties—or internal factions of them—with clout at the national level because the parties controlled the national government's resources.

Hence regional administrative decentralization was the outcome of bargaining among national political elites, and not of the increased capacity of peripheral political elites to apply pressure. The formation of different government majorities at the local level complicated, rather than reduced, the centrality of negotiation among the national political elites. Complication increased to the point that, with the electoral decline of the PCI, these local majorities no longer served to integrate the principal opposition party into local government, and local government formation was influenced more by national agreements among the parties in the government coalition than by local agreements among the parties most electorally representative of the region in question. In short, despite the introduction of regional administrations, the Italian state continued to foster institutional centralism and not popular self-government. This was a process that also influenced the more general interaction between society and the state: Given the centralization of state institutions, societal interests aligned in an equally centralized manner.[6] Pressure groups organized nationally so that they could negotiate issues of concern to them directly with the center. The result was a centralized system both at the level of the public powers and at that of interest organization. However, since political parties controlled the institutional powers of the center, it was they, and not the institutions of state, that guaranteed the linkage between the center and the periphery on the one hand,[7] and between interests and national decision making on the other. One may therefore say that postwar Italy is a case of the superimposition of a party-centralized state on an institutionally centralized state.

The Partitocrazia

Devoid of an efficient central administration and lacking an instinctive spirit of independence, the Italian state has been the private spoil of the political parties throughout its history. The annexation of the state by the Italian parties is of distant origin. Fascism itself, which gained initial legitimacy from its assertion of the preeminence of the general interest over partisan interests, moved in swiftly to occupy the state through the principal tool of partisanship, the political party. The action of the fascist party, especially during the 1930s, had enduring consequences. The defeat of fascism by the allies and—in northern Italy—by the armed movement of national liberation bequeathed to the victors a state humiliated by its utter lack of autonomy.

Thus, in contrast to France, Italy's institutional continuity was once again entrusted to non-state forces, namely the political parties, instead of being assured by the state administration. At the end of the Second World War, in fact, the anti-fascist political parties were the only organizational actors present in the country, and the only ones endowed with sufficient legitimacy to provide the country with a leading elite, whether administrative or political.[8] With the popular rejection of the monarchy by the referendum of 1946, the last element of state continuity was dismantled. Now entirely unconstrained either by state or society (both of which had been enfeebled by single-party fascist authoritarianism), the political parties found that they had extremely broad room for systemic maneuver, although their margins of political action were much more narrow. In fact, although they had inherited a humiliated state and a weak civil society, the parties found themselves operating in a political context potentially—and, in some parts of the country, actually—in a state of civil war. In no other country had the waning conflict between the two great totalitarian ideologies of the twentieth century—fascism and communism—been so dramatic as in Italy; and in no other country (apart from Greece) did the nascent conflict between the two ideologies that had defeated nazi-fascism—democracy and communism (and therefore the two world powers, the United States and the Soviet Union, that symbolized them)—loom so large. And, since then, no other country in the postwar period has internally replicated this conflict so faithfully,[9] to the point that the confrontation between democracy and communism has provided the leading Italian parties with their legitimacy, as well as their political identity.

Consequently, a model of democracy (as the interaction between the electoral system and the governmental system, and between these and the state as defined above) was built in Italy that preserved the central role of national political parties in both representation and decision-making.[10] And this model developed precisely because the parties were the only political actors able to control the ideological conflict that they themselves, indeed, actively fomented. Hence, the political parties adopted (and thus preserved) an electoral system that was highly proportional and reflected the ideological cleavages that the country inherited with the collapse of fascism and the onset of the Cold War. It was an electoral system that fostered the growth of what some have described as "polarized pluralism";[11] that is, a system as fragmented as it is structured by the influence wielded over the minor and peripheral parties by the two biggest parties: Democrazia Cristiana (or DC) and the PCI. Corresponding to this "polarized pluralism" in the electoral system, therefore, was a "bargained pluralism"[12] in the governmental system. Consequently, at the electoral level, postwar Italian democracy has encouraged voting behavior oriented by choice of a party rather than by choice of a government majority. Inevitably, this stimulated the growth of political parties with rigid identities and therefore politically distant from each other;

political parties that have consequently based their action on criteria of closure toward the outside and of the absence of competition to their interior. Indeed, despite their diverse organizational models (for example, "democratic centralism" in the case of the PCI, "currents and factions" in the case of DC), the major Italian political parties have had the features of introverted parties (parties with a prevalent concern to their own internal identity) and of cooptative parties (parties with an inclination to change leaders and policies through choices made from above).

Thus the Italian system of government has been progressively structured around multiple centers of political decision-making: on the one hand, parliament has asserted its independence from the executive; on the other, the executive has done exactly the same with respect to its leader (the head of the government). In formal terms, postwar Italian democracy is a classic example of parliamentary democracy: with an executive elected by the legislature and accountable to it; with a legislature constituted by two chambers enjoying equal powers; with a head of state elected by these two chambers—in joint session with representatives from the regional councils—and functioning as a mere guarantor. In concrete terms, however, unlike that of other countries with similar systems of government (Great Britain or Germany, for example), Italian parliamentary democracy has never evolved toward the strengthening of either the executive with respect to the legislature, or of the head of the executive with respect to the government. The reason for this is simple. The Italian parliament provided a crucial arena for bargaining between the pro-system parties—particularly the DC—and the principal anti-system party, the PCI.[13]

Herein reside the distinguishing features of the Italian postwar model for democracy. To begin with, the deep ideological cleavage between the two main Italian parties—democracy versus communism—precluded their alternation in government. This brought Italian democracy close to the consociational model distinctive to countries with ethnic-cultural cleavages so profound as to rule out recourse to the majority principle in order to regulate accession to government among political parties. Examples of consociational countries are Belgium, Holland, Switzerland, Israel, or Austria before 1966. The appropriate contrast is found in the alternation of majorities as happens in competitive democracies—such as Germany, Sweden, Ireland, Norway, Spain, Greece—or even more so in Westminster-style majoritarian democracies—Great Britain, New Zealand, Canada, Australia, and with their specific institutional features, in semi-presidential France and the presidential United States.

A second distinguishing feature, in contrast to the consociational democracies listed above, is that the ideological nature of the cleavage between the two principal Italian political parties—and the geopolitical constraints that it implied—prevented the full consociational integration of the PCI into the executive as part of a broad coalition. This created the conditions for potential disequilibrium in the democratic system. The disequilibrium was neutralized, however, by strengthening the decision-making role of the parliament, which has powers comparable only to those enjoyed by the American Congress, whose institutional strength, however, unlike its Italian counterpart, lies in the separation of powers system. The strengthened role of parliament enabled the formation of parliamentary majorities that were different and broader (because they included the PCI) than formally governmental majorities (that necessarily excluded the PCI).

In short, although excluded from the central government, but not from the local government, the PCI was able to influence national decision-making through its massive presence in the two legislative chambers (not coincidentally endowed with the same prerogatives and legislative powers) and, especially, in the parliamentary committees equipped with lawmaking power (and within which the opposing parties negotiated their respective positions and respective votes, to the point that most legislation was approved unanimously or by overwhelming majority). The governments of so-called *Solidarietà Nazionale* (1976-1979)—which were necessitated by the dual threats of terrorism and inflation—represented the closest approximation to the consociational model of broad governmental coalitions, and yet nevertheless saw the PCI associated with the parliamentary majority, but not directly involved in the government. This explains why the Italian parliament has been able to increase its prerogatives and powers with respect to the executive, especially since the reforms introduced in 1971. These reforms assigned decision-making power over the organization of parliamentary work to a committee composed of representatives from all the parliamentary groups, and required that committee to operate (largely) on the basis of unanimity.[14] Meanwhile, most other democratic parliaments have watched their prerogatives and powers decline to the advantage of their respective executives.

Just as the Italian legislature has maintained its decision-making autonomy from the executive, so too has the government maintained its autonomy from its leader. The decision of the Italian constitution-makers to call the latter "president of the council of ministers" and not "prime minister" (as in Great Britain and France) or "chancellor" (as in Germany) is already indicative of the institutional aim pursued by the Italian party elites since the war: avoiding any centralization whatsoever of the government's decision-making. Thus, with a president of the council forced to act as a first among equals, Italian democracy has assumed the form of a practically "acephalous" democracy.[15] Because the executive's coalition has been pieced together by the secretaries of the parties involved in the coalition agreement, and because the public-policy directions pursued by this executive have been defined externally to it (at party headquarters), it follows that its directive organ—the presidency of the council—has never been able to achieve decision-making autonomy.[16] And as in every acephalous or leaderless democracy, the predominant tendency among Italian political actors has been to reward leaders who perform a brokering role among the members of the coalitional pact rather than who assume an activist posture. The few activist Italian leaders have been neutralized as soon as possible, with important exceptions, in periods of change or transformation: Consider, for example, the unusually long—for Italian standards—governmental leadership of Bettino Craxi, who was able to remain president of the council of ministers from 1983 to 1987, benefitting from the serious electoral decline of the DC in the 1980s.[17] This explains why most Italian presidents of the council have been adept at mediation but bereft of a political vision, adaptable to every circumstance, and with a scant sense of national public policy problems.

The extreme proportionalism of Italy's electoral system, and its multipolar party system that excludes the second largest party in the country (the PCI) from government, suggest why Italy's system of government has come to assume a polycentric character: in order to provide the political parties with multiple decision-making arenas in which to broker the positions of their contrasting systems.[18] Put another way, the Italian system of government had to assume a decentralized character precisely in order to provide opportunities for systemically irreconcilable political parties to reach agreement, thereby preserving their common interest in maintaining their role as gate keepers to the national political process.[19] While the non-centralization of the system of government has shielded the political parties—and, in turn, their national elites—from competition, enabling them to prosper, the centralized nature of a vulnerable state—vulnerable because of its scarce institutional autonomy—has equipped national party elites with formidable (material and symbolic) resources with which to strengthen their control over civil society and its ideological cleavages. Hence derives the phenomenon of the Italian *partitocrazia*,[20] here interpreted as the parties'—rather than government's—domination of the state.

THE FOUR CHALLENGES

Albeit with marked contradictions, postwar Italy has been traversed by pro-found processes of economic and social modernization and of cultural sec-ularization. At the end of the 1960s political movements arose that, with the radicalism of their anti-authoritarian protest, signaled the changes that had taken place in the country's social and cultural relations.[21] These changes undermined the two essential features of the Italian version of consocia-tional democracy: namely the stability of the ideological cleavage and the vertical control exerted by the party elites on the political behavior of citi-zens. They were changes, therefore, that in the 1970s brought to the sur-face—as a consequence of the dramatic challenge of terrorism—a national democratic political culture which was shared by the majority of Italian cit-izens. This was a phenomenon of major importance, bearing in mind that never in its post-unification history had Italy displayed consensus on democracy of such proportions. However, it was not until the 1980s, and in particular with the end of the Cold War and the fall of the Berlin Wall in November 1989, that Italy's postwar political cleavages dissolved, resulting in a radical de-structuring of the electoral market.[22] Thus, in the 1980s, the centralized party state was faced by four challenges generated by its own evolution. Let us examine them separately.

The first challenge was the crisis of public finance. Once the national par-liament had decided, in the 1970s, to separate fiscal power (preserved by the center) from spending power (transferred to the periphery), the basis was laid for irresponsible budgetary policy: When there is no correspondence between those who levy taxes and those who spend them, the conditions for a growing public deficit are inevitably created.[23] Moreover, if the periph-eral public administrators can only spend, then they will seek to spend more and more in order to ensure their reelection. This dissociation between state budgetary receipts and local fiscal outlays prevented the Italian elec-torate from monitoring the financial soundness of the decisions taken by local administrators. Consequently, there was fertile ground for local cor-ruption, given that no one was aware of the budgetary criteria adopted in taking these decisions.[24] Equally deleterious for Italy's financial health have been the effects of its consociational party system. The executive's respon-sibility for budgetary policy evaporated because of the existence of multiple decision-making arenas in parliament and in the government for bargaining and agreement among the parties.[25] In Italy, the financial law presented to parliament by the government has never had—and could never have had—the features of a closed proposal, in the sense that the government stakes its authority on it. On the contrary, the budgetary proposal has been necessarily open in character, given that not only parliamentary groups but even individual parliamentarians can submit amendments regarding both income and expenditure. The experience of other European countries provides a wealth of contrasting examples. In France, parliamentary amendments to the government's financial proposal are inadmissible, except those eliminating or reducing an expense or increasing a revenue; in Great Britain, it is even inadmissible to present parliamentary amendments in order to transfer resources from one item to another in the budget's proposal; in Germany and Spain, parliamentary amendments, which in any case are not authorized if they concern obligatory expenses, require prior consent from the government in order be introduced to the discussion. Naturally enough, a budgetary policy like Italy's that is open to negotiation between government and parliament—and, indeed to negotiation between the two different political majorities—robs responsibility from the executive and thus inevitably gives rise to burgeoning public deficits.

The second challenge has to do with territorial relations. Throughout the postwar period, the regions of the center-north and the south of Italy have followed different economic trajectories. Today, few would maintain that this has been due to the exploitation of the South by northern companies. In real terms, the income of the southern regions has increased more than threefold since the 1950s. But the gap between the North and the South in terms of per capita income is the same as it was in the 1950s. Per capita income in the regions of the South is still 60 percent of that in the regions of the North. Of course, to have kept pace with the growth of income in the northern regions—which ranks among the highest in the world—is an extraordinary achievement, and today southern Italy is no longer an area of poverty. The point is, however, that this growth of per capita income in the South has not derived from growth in the productive capacity of its regions: At the end of the 1980s, the South produced less than 18 percent of national industrial output with 36 percent of the population. The growth, therefore, has stemmed principally—if one excludes earnings from organized crime—from financial transfers from the central state, bearing in mind that the South, with its percentage of the population, yields just 18 percent of national fiscal revenue. The result has been a net flow of resources in favor of the South, according to a model that has been aptly called "development without autonomy."[26]

Why has financial aid by the central state produced the perverse effect of increasing income but not productive capacity in the South? The answer is to be looked for in the South, not in the North, and specifically in the choices of southern political elites. These southern elites historically enjoyed scant legitimacy. It should be kept in mind that the South entered the era of mass politics at the end of the last century, not on the basis of aggregating collective identities as in the North, but on the basis of a clientelistic and individualistic mobilization. Moreover, southern elites were further delegitimated after the Second World War by their conspicuous absence from the great popular upheaval that, in the northern regions, led to the defeat of fascism.[27] Thus, with scant legitimation and as the expression of a society without collective identities,[28] the southern political elites came to use the massive financial aid provided by the republican central state to satisfy the particularized interests of clientele and kin,[29] and not to pursue policies of collective interest aimed at the creation of services and infrastructures for economic development. The contrast is with the local political elites of the North who were obliged to pursue economic development as the expression of collective identities, Catholic, lay, or Socialist.

For this reason, the economic constraints on firms in the South derive not from the North but from the paralyzing inefficiency of the southern productive and institutional infrastructure. This explains why the South has produced numerous political entrepreneurs but few economic ones. The abuse of national public resources by local elites was possible because these elites benefited from the constant support of the national governing elite. National elites faced considerable problems in consensus-building because they were obliged to contend with a strong Communist party in the regions of the North. They were able to solve their problems by drawing on the reservoir of clientelistic votes in the South and by forging alliances with the southern political elites. Not coincidentally, therefore, almost all political leaders in national government have had broad and solid electoral bases in southern Italy.[30] The result has been a lacerating contrast between private wealth and public disorder in the South which has generated ever greater demand for resources by the southern regions addressed to the central state. Continued calls for resources, however, only increased first the diffidence and then the hostility of the northern regions towards the redistributive policy of the state. After all, the five regions (Lombardia, Emilia-Romagna, Piemonte, Veneto, and Toscana) that give much more to the center in financial terms than they receive from it are located in the North.[31] This accounts for the explosion of a territorial crisis that, for the first time since the Second World War, threatened the political unity of the country.

The third challenge derives from the crisis of the Italian version of state capitalism. After an initial phase in which it stimulated modernization,

intervention by the Italian state in the economy—among the most extensive in Western democracies—has increasingly restricted itself to stabilizing power relationships among the principal economic actors on the market,
rather than seeking to increase the level of market competitiveness. The vast
public sector of the economy—run since the 1960s by an iron-solid political oligopoly, or by a Christian Democrat and Socialist duopoly—soon
reached an understanding with the private sector, thereby creating oligopoly control over the market as well. Thus, public intervention, originally
intended to curb the old oligarchies of private capital, instead consolidated
them by merging them with the new elites of state entrepreneurs. The
merger of public elites and private capital soon grew into powerful oligarchies of public capital. Hence derives the capitalism of "everything in the
family"[32] and "everything in the state"[33] that distinguishes Italy from other
Western market democracies as an authentic oligarchical capitalism.
Because of extensive public intervention in the economy and in society —
undertaken in the absence of political competition — the prolific (party-
based) families of public-sector oligarchies and the traditional (family-
based) oligarchies of private capitalism have been urged to find some sort
of "functional agreement," whether direct or indirect. Inevitably, in the
1980s, oligarchical control of the market came into direct and dramatic conflict with the myriad of small and medium-sized firms, technologically
innovative and strongly competitive in international markets, which had
been able to overcome the economic depression of the early 1980s thanks
to their organizational flexibility. Driven by post-industrial change and
supported in the regions of the center-north by efficient public institutions
and local financiers, these small and medium-sized firms contested the control of the market by private and public oligarchies supported, in their turn,
by the centralized party state. This explains the formidable pressure for the
privatization of state-owned enterprises, for the deregulation of financial
institutions, for economic policy no longer tailored to suit the interests of
great industrial groups: in short, the conflict between small firms and public oligarchies explains the neo-*laissez-faire* surge that, in Italy too, has
called for the drastic curtailment of the state's economic role.

   The fourth challenge derives from the crisis in the Italian version of
consociational democracy, which, combined with wide-scale public intervention, has solidified the oligarchical control of the political parties,
whether in the majority or in the opposition. Majority parties gained
strength because the central elite control over the huge resources of public
intervention rendered them practically impervious to internal challenges.

Minority parties strengthened because exclusion from governmental power forced national elites to emphasize the crucial resource of the political party, organized, as we know, according to a criterion (democratic centralism) that favored the stability of the leading groups. Control over the centralized state by oligarchical parties—some of which were permanently in government—led to the identification of the public administration (and of its elites in particular) with the parties rather than with the state. We have already seen that the Italian public administration has been perceived traditionally as the spoil of the political parties. If under fascism it was plundered by a single party, under the republic it has been looted by a coalition of parties.[34] Thus, at all levels of the state, the civil service sought (and found) its power and legitimacy in the parties and not in the public institutions. Given the absence of alternation between parties in government, this linkage between civil servants and political parties enabled the elite of the civil service to entrench its power, thereby transforming itself into a bureaucratic oligarchy. This process, in turn, triggered similar mechanisms of entrenchment among interest-group elites, who also found legitimacy in the support that they received from the parties—parties from which they originated or were destined to return. Ultimately, a pervasive intermingling came about between the various oligarchies of private capital, public capital, civil service, interest groups, and political parties; an intermingling coordinated by the parties themselves but framed by a strategy of relations that enabled each of these oligarchies to preserve its control over resources in its sphere of operations.

However, just as the economic oligarchies (private and public) came into conflict with new, numerous, small and medium-sized economic actors, so the political oligarchies (of the parties, pressure groups, and the civil service) clashed with a society that had grown increasingly open and autonomous. By dissolving the old ideological cleavage, the end of the Cold War removed the last justification for oligarchical politics—namely that oligarchical control was the price to pay if civil war in the country was to be averted. And in fact, the 1990s have seen an unprecedented mobilization of groups of citizens, public institutions (the judiciary), and economic sectors against the most grievous price exacted from the country by the oligarchical alliance: corruption. Political corruption had become the established method to ease tensions among the various groups in the oligarchical alignment.[35] And corruption strengthened the movement to change the electoral system based on proportional representation that had privileged oligarchical stability at the expense of programmatic competitiveness. The mobilization of opposition to the oligarchical state culminated in the referenda of 1991 and 1993 in which the overwhelming majority of electors voted to abolish the proportional system.[36] It was corruption that spurred the investigative judiciary (backed by vast public support) into action, first timidly and then with growing ruthlessness, as it prosecuted the crimes against the public administration committed by the party, bureaucratic, and economic oligarchies. The outcome of all this has been the moral collapse of the entire ruling class of Italian democracy since the Second World War, a collapse without precedent—in such proportions and in peacetime—in any democratic country.[37]

THE ITALIAN TRANSITION

While the first two challenges examined previously shook the centralized structure of the state, the last two seriously undermined its party nature. In the 1990s, these four challenges have triggered a twofold process of transformation: on the one hand, the formidable pressure exerted by large sections of the electorate in the central-northern regions for the decentralization of the state; on the other hand, an unprecedented mobilization of public opinion against the *partitocrazia* and for the replacement of consociational democracy by competitive democracy. These two processes of transformation have inaugurated an unforeseeable period of democratic transition.[38] Let us examine them separately, beginning with decentralization.

Like other Western democracies, Italy has been marked by widespread fiscal revolt in the 1990s, especially in the regions of the center-north. This revolt has resulted in the rapid electoral success of the new political actors (the *Leghe*, or Leagues) that promoted it;[39] political actors, indeed, that in a few short years have grown into the largest parties in the center-north regions, as well as a political force of crucial importance for the formation of the national government.[40] Very rapidly, therefore, this fiscal revolt has merged with popular dissatisfaction with the long-standing democratic inefficiency of the national state and its inability to respond to the needs of citizens. Finally, when the public debt and administrative inefficiency were linked in the public mind with the widespread political corruption uncovered by the judicial investigations, the explosive mixture provided by the delegitimation of the national state was ignited. All the national parties responsible for management of that state—including those of the Left because they had been, albeit to a more limited extent, participants in that management—were engulfed by the anger of the electorate and swept from the political scene.

Although the electoral appeal of the *Leghe* seems, in 1995, in decline, the outcome of their action has been numerous proposals, advanced by parties with a national posture, for the decentralization of the state, either into a form of federalism or of strong regionalism. For the first time since the Second World War, such proposals have sparked debate on the national identity of the country, reviving attitudes that had accompanied the country's post-unification history until the fall of fascism.[41] The dividing line continues to be: on the one hand, that the idea of Italian national identity had formed before the unitary state, and therefore did not depend on it; and, on the other hand, that the idea of national identity coincided exactly with the unitary history of the country.[42] Evidently, this is a distinction with powerful operational implications. If the Italian nation has its roots in a collective conscience and deep-rooted traditions, independently of the specific statist forms assumed by unified Italy, and if there was a history of Italy prior to unification constituted by multiple and diverse small nations or sub-nationalities or regional nations, then the unitary and centralized Italian state has been only one of many possible institutional outcomes, and the national identity encapsulated by the unitary state will survive the decentralization of the state. If, conversely, there was no Italian nation prior to unification, and if Italy is an exemplary case of the close interdependence between nation and state, then the transformation of the state may shatter the idea of nation-hood itself. In any case, it is certain, as it has been aptly pointed out,[43] that Italian national identity displayed marked ambiguities throughout the country's post-unification history until fascism. Under the fascist regime, it was transformed into aggressive nationalism, and thereafter Italian national identity was obliterated from public conscience as a reaction to its abuse by fascism.[44]

Whatever the case may be, there is no doubt that since 1943 Italian culture—both elite and popular—has shunted the concept of nation to one side. The principal parties that arose after the war, the DC and the PCI, were proponents of cultures that, although antagonistic, were both supranational in character. The concept of nation was consequently replaced—to an extent unique among the countries of the old continent—by that of Europe, and it was a concept that, with the 1950s, became the guiding principle of Italian governmental culture, both lay and Catholic. The Europeanization of the Italian governmental parties further heightened diffidence toward the nation. Moreover, although the PCI was long hostile to Europe, this position was motivated by supranational considerations—workers' internationalism—and not by deference to national interests. And this too fueled suspicion of the concept of the nation. At the popular level, the traditional non-distinction between nation and nation-state meant that rejection of the nation-state, because of the state's evident inefficiencies and iniquities, entailed rejection also of the nation. In short, the values of workers' internationalism (embraced by the opposition) together with the values of Europeanism, of pacifism and of international solidarity (embraced by the lay and Catholic parties of the center) have weakened the Italians' consciousness of nation-hood, which has consequently never been a point of reference for civil society—except, perhaps, when the national football team is playing.

Seen against the background of this absence of a deep-rooted national identity, proposals for the devolution of the Italian state have generated both assent and apprehension. The reason for assent is obvious: such proposals offer an answer to the fiscal and territorial problems now beleaguering the country. At the level of public finance, decentralization helps to sensibilize local political elites to the need to balance the budget. The transfer of fiscal as well as spending power to the periphery will enable citizens to exert closer control over the results of government decision-making. On the territorial level, devolution will assign responsibility to local governments, especially those in the South. The "development without autonomy" of the South may be overcome if local governments are obliged to create the institutions, services and infrastructures required for the growth of modern economies, on pain of electoral defeat. This will require the stable local governments that the South has never had. Hence derives the pressure for reform of the regional electoral system broadly in coherence with the principles—those of the majority vote and the direct investiture of the head of the executive—underpinning the reform of the communal electoral system approved by the national parliament in March 1993 and which, since its inception, has noticeably stabilized municipal governments. Moreover, economic competition is today determined by the quality of territorial systems of the regions and the municipalities; that is, by their ability to maintain, enhance or attract economic, financial, and human resources. However, although the benefits of reform proposals are evident, the apprehension that they arouse among not a few sectors of public opinion is understandable. Such apprehension is due precisely to the weakness of that sentiment of common belonging that alone can defend the institutional experiment of devolution against the risk of its degeneration into regional or macro-regional disintegration.

Let us now look at the second process: that responsible for going beyond *partitocrazia*. Whereas in France of the Fourth Republic the stimulus for political change was external to the political system—the rebellion of the French generals in Algeria against the decision by Paris to grant independence to that country triggered a crisis in the French consociative structure and initiated a process of institutional transition toward competitive democracy that was accomplished partly in 1962 and definitively in 1965— the stimulus for change in Italy has been internal, the combination of electoral referenda and judicial investigation of corruption. The August 1993 approval by parliament of a new national electoral law—three-quarters majoritarian and one-quarter proportional—set in motion a complex institutional reform of Italian consociational democracy aimed at creating the conditions for alternation in government by competing poles or party coalitions.[45] It is, after all, the absence of competitive changeover of governing elites for almost fifty years that has enabled elite groups to turn into entrenched oligarchies. It should also be borne in mind that the reform of the electoral system was preceded by less visible, but equally significant, reforms of important components of the Italian system of government. Here I refer to the 1988 abolition of the secret ballot in parliament, and to the strengthening, again in 1988, of the powers of the president of the council. The abolition of secret balloting weakened the legislature as regards its veto power, and empowerment of the president of the council strengthened the executive in terms of its technical and policymaking capacities. Simultaneously, moreover, electoral reform has induced the majority of the political forces that emerged from the March 1994 election to advance proposals for the adjustment of the central institutions (parliament, executive, and judiciary) to reflect the new majoritarian thrust of the electoral law.

Here too, however, while the advantages of institutional reform are evident, the apprehension that it has aroused is understandable. The national elections of March 1994 provided an extraordinary opportunity for fueling such apprehension. The 1994 elections, in fact, were won by a spurious coalition of center-right parties bound together by a curious and novel political "glue"—the charisma of a political leader who is also the head of a private multi-media empire.[46] Thanks to his control over the media, this leader was able to organize an authentic national political party that swept to power in the elections in less than three months. It was a phenomenon without precedent in established Western democracies, and one that showed that—in a transition of this size and with a market (like the Italian one)[47] unregulated by an effective anti-trust legislation in the crucial sector of mass communications—the power of the old *partitocrazia* can be replaced by that of a new "videocracy" rather than by that of the electorate.[48]

Since to date the political and economic reformers have been scattered and disorganized, they have been forced into an unequal power relationship with their rivals the oligarchies. Herein resides the danger, but also the interest, of Italian transition. The danger stems from the fact that this transition has come about in Italy without political guidance, unlike in France from 1958 to 1962 with the leadership of Charles de Gaulle and the technical-political elite that had gathered around him. The interest arises because this transition is the first to have involved bottom-up change in the model of democracy, in a context of the continuity of the democratic regime. It is difficult to predict the eventual outcome of these two processes of change. What is certain, though, is that if the outcome is positive, Italy will be able to discard the First Republic, and the oligarchical state with it, and move towards a decentralized and competitive Second Republic.

♦ NOTES TO CHAPTER 4 ♦

1. Roberto Ruffilli, *La questione regionale dall'unificazione alla dittatura* (Milan: Giuffré, 1971).
2. Sabino Cassese, *Il sistema amministrativo italiano* (Bologna: Il Mulino, 1983).
3. Ettore Rotelli, *La non reforma* (Rome: Edizioni Lavoro, 1981).
4. Marcello Fedele, "Classe politica e modelli di organizzazione," in Marcello Fedele, ed., *Autonomia politica regionale e sistema dei partiti*, vol. 3 (Milan: Giuffré, 1989).
5. Alfio Mastropaolo, *Il ceto politico* (Rome: La Nuova Italia Scientifica, 1993).
6. Marco Cammelli, "Regioni e rappresentanza degli interessi: il caso italiano," *Stato e mercato* 29 (1990), pp. 151-199.
7. Franco Cazzola, *L'amministrazione e i partiti in Italia* (Milan: Giuffré, 1988).
8. Pietro Scoppola, *La repubblica dei partiti* (Bologna: Il Mulino, 1991).
9. Frederic Spotts and Theodor Wieser, *Italy: A Difficult Democracy* (Cambridge: Cambridge University Press, 1986).
10. Sergio Fabbrini, *Quale democrazia* (Rome-Bari: Laterza, 1994).
11. Giovanni Sartori, "Bipartitismo imperfetto o pluralismo polarizzato?" in Giovanni Sartori, ed., *Teoria dei partiti e caso italiano* (Milan: Sugarco, 1982), pp. 7-44.
12. David Hine, *Governing Italy* (Oxford: Clarendon Press, 1993).
13. Massimo Morisi, "Il parlamento tra partiti e interessi," in Leonardo Morlino, ed., *Costruire la democrazia* (Bologna: Il Mulino, 1991), pp. 367-446.
14. Andrea Manzella, *Il parlamento* (Bologna: Il Mulino, 1991).
15. Luciano Cavalli, *Governo del leader e regime dei partiti* (Bologna: Il Mulino, 1992).
16. Maurizio Cotta, "Italy: A Fragmented Government," in Jean Blondel and Ferdinand Muller-Rommel, eds., *Cabinets in Western Europe* (New York: St. Martin's Press, 1988), pp. 120-37.
17. Sergio Fabbrini, "Personalization as Americanization? The Rise and Fall of Leader-Dominated Governmental Strategies in Western Europe in the Eighties," *American Studies International* 32:2 (1994), pp. 51-65.
18. Giuseppe Di Palma, "Establishing Party Dominance: It Ain't Easy," in T. J. Pempel, ed., *Uncommon Democracies. The One-Party Dominant Regimes* (Ithaca: Cornell University Press, 1990), pp. 162-88.

19. Morlino, ed., *Costruire la democrazia.*
20. Mauro Calise, "The Italian Particracy: Beyond President and Parliament," *Political Science Quarterly* 33:109 (1994), pp. 441-60.
21. Sidney Tarrow, *Democrazia e disordine* (Rome-Bari: Laterza, 1990).
22. Renato Mannheimer and Giacomo Sani, *La rivoluzione elettorale* (Milan: Anabasi, 1994).
23. Yves Mény, *Government and Politics in Western Europe* (Oxford: Oxford University Press, 1990).
24. Donatella Della Porta, *Lo scambio occulto* (Bologna: Il Mulino, 1992).
25. Paolo De Ioanna, *Parlamento e spesa pubblica* (Bologna: Il Mulino, 1993).
26. Carlo Trigiglia, *Sviluppo senza autonomia* (Bologna: Il Mulino, 1992).
27. Here it should perhaps also be noted that the South was liberated earlier by the Allies than the North.
28. Robert D. Putnam, *Making Democracy Work* (Princeton: Princeton University Press, 1993).
29. Joseph La Palombara, *Democracy Italian Style* (New Haven: Yale University Press, 1992).
30. Mauro Calise and Renato Mannheimer, *Governanti in Italia* (Bologna: Il Mulino, 1982).
31. Stefano Benvenuti Casini, Stefania Lorenzin, and Giovanni Maltinti, *Stima dell'impatto regionale dell'intervento pubblico in Italia* (Torino: Fondazione Giovanni Agnelli, 1994).
32. Alain Friedman, *Tutto in famiglia* (Milan: Rizzoli, 1988).
33. Fabrizio Barca, *Imprese in cerca di padrone* (Rome-Bari: Laterza, 1994).
34. Luciano Cafagna, *La grande slavina* (Venezia: Marsilio, 1993).
35. Alessandro Pizzorno, "Le difficoltà del consociativismo," in Alessandro Pizzorno, ed., *Le radici della politica assoluta* (Milan: Feltrinelli, 1993), pp. 285-313.
36. Carol Mershon and Gianfranco Pasquino, eds., *Ending the First Republic* (Boulder: Westview, 1994).
37. Gianfranco Pasquino, "Introduction. A Case of Regime Crisis," in Gianfranco Pasquino and Patrick McCarthy, eds., *The End of Post-War Politics in Italy* (Boulder: Westview Press, 1993), pp. 1-11.
38. Patrick McCarthy, "Conclusion: Inching Towards a New Regime," in Pasquino and McCarthy, eds., *The End of Post-War Politics,* pp. 160-75.
39. Tom Gallagher, "Rome at Bay: The Challenge to the Northern League to the Italian State," *Government and Opposition* 27:4 (1992), pp. 470-85.
40. Giacomo Sani, "The Anatomy of Change," in Pasquino and McCarthy, eds., *The End of Post-War Politics,* pp. 108-20.
41. Marcello Pacini, *Scelta federale e unità nazionale* (Torino: Fondazione Giovanni Agnelli, 1994).
42. Silvio Lanaro, "Federalismo e tradizione nazionale," in M. Sabella and N. Urbinati, eds., *Quale federalismo?* (Firenze: Vallecchi, 1994), pp. 115-33.
43. Gian Enrico Rusconi, *Se cessiamo di essere una nazione* (Bologna: Il Mulino, 1993).
44. Norberto Bobbio, "Quale Italia," *Reset* 13 (1995), pp. 16-18.
45. Gianfranco Pasquino, "Italy: The Twilight of the Parties," *Democracy* 5:1 (1994), pp. 18-29.
46. Adrian Lyttleton, "Italy: The Triumph of TV," *The New York Review of Books* 41:14 (11 August 1994), pp. 25-29.
47. Michele Salvati, "La crisi politica 1992/1994: come uscirne?" *Stato e mercato* 42 (1994), pp. 365-89.
48. Giovanni Sartori, "Video-Power," *Government and Opposition* 24:1 (1989), pp. 39-53.

·5·

A Crisis of the State?
The French Case

Julius W. Friend

*La France vient du fond des ages. Elle vit. Les siècles l'appel-
lent. Mais elle demeure elle-même au long du Temps. . . . De
part de la géographie du pays qui est le sien, de part du
génie des races qui la composent, de part des voisinages qui
l'entourent, elle revêt un caractère constant qui fait dépendre
de leurs pères les Français de chaque époque et les engage pour
leurs descendants. A moins de se rompre, cet ensemble humain,
sur ce territoire, au sein de cet univers, comporte donc un
passé, un présent, un avenir indissolubles. L'Etat, qui répond
de la France, est-il en charge, à la fois, de son héritage d'hier,
de ses interêts d'aujourd'hui et de ses espoirs de demain.*

CHARLES DE GAULLE, MÉMOIRES DE L'ESPOIR

Is there a genuine crisis of the French state today? The New Shorter
Oxford English Dictionary gives this definition of crisis: Greek, *krisis*, a
decision, the turning point of a disease. If France, among other states
today, is in the midst of a crisis, is this in the literal sense a crisis of the
state? The last few years have seen three crises that caused states to dis-
appear: in the German Democratic Republic in 1990, the Soviet Union in

1991, and the Yugoslav Federation, which can be said to have disappeared by 1992. Clearly, we are not discussing a similar phenomenon in France, or even a crisis of the regime, as often in the French past; the present crisis concerns the functions of the state.

The French state *is* in difficulties, in common with other modern developed states. Some of these difficulties are of long standing while others have come into focus more recently. The key date for this focusing is the year 1990, in which France was faced with the unwelcome unification of Germany and a presumed reduction of the French role in Europe. French policy attempted a *fuite en avant* (forward escape) urging rapid conclusion of a treaty on European Union, in order to reinsure the French tie with Germany and gain more leverage in monetary questions through the institution of a unitary European currency. The resulting Maastricht treaty turned out to be more divisive than integrating, and its 1992 ratification in a French referendum showed that the electorate was almost evenly split, though divided on lines of class and education.

Late 1990 also saw a renewed downturn in an economy long in difficulties, but which had taken a brief upturn from 1988 to late 1990. Unemployment, ominously ascending since 1974, dropped in those years, then rose again. These two shocks caused the French to reflect on all of the disquiets of the contemporary French state and society, which in concatenation amount to a considerable malaise, if not a crisis in the most literal sense.

France is attempting to cope with the readjustments arising from the abandonment of a state-guided economy, concomitant with the rise of a global economy. The welfare state, guarantor of social stability, is struggling with steadily mounting social welfare expenses that threaten the national budget. Among these expenses are payments for an unemployment rate that remains, apparently incurably, above 10 and currently above 12 percent. In addition, problems stemming from past (and possibly future) North African immigration pose momentous questions concerning the French sense of identity and the nature of the republican synthesis.

Decentralization has broken the old Jacobin role of the centralized state, incidentally opening wider access to corruption. The decline of humanist culture in French secondary education is deplored and connected with the decline of French as a world language.

Finally, the controversy over the Maastricht Treaty has focused all of these factors in the public mind at a moment when nothing much is going right for France in any respect. Also, France's international role, the centerpiece of Gaullist policies, was called into question by the end of the Cold War and German unification. Thus the sense of crisis is easy to understand.

France has, however, seen many crises, and if commentators in recent years have made the end of a French exceptionalism an instant cliché, France was, until not long ago, still living the polarization inherited from 1793. In this polarization, who could forget the long series of regime crises that in the nineteenth century saw France live through two empires, two monarchies, and two republics, then in the twentieth century, after the 1940 defeat, the emergence of a semi-fascist state, followed by two more republics?

Since the beginning of the nineteenth century, six crises have led to regime changes in France. Street action followed by political collapse characterized the brief revolutions that ended the reigns of Charles X in 1830 and Louis Philippe in 1848. The overthrows of Napoleon I, Napoleon III, and the Third Republic were caused by military defeat—itself a failure by the state to fulfill its most basic and ancient responsibility, the defense of the realm.

On May 8, 1870, Napoleon III's plebiscite ratified Prime Minister Emile Ollivier's new liberal empire with 67.5 percent of the vote. Only 14 percent voted against it, though a larger number of voters abstained. Four months later, after the news of the Sédan disaster reached Paris, the Empire fell.

Daniel Lindenberg has recently argued that there was no real crisis of the Third Republic in 1939-1940, and indeed "une réprise du sentiment civique, qui aurait certainement profité à la République sur la long terme."[1] He terms the events of 1940 less a crisis of the republic (more or less coterminous with the state, as I argue next) but rather "a crisis of the French elites, after a military defeat." Aside from the implicit suggestion that a crisis that brings down the system is not a crisis of the republic, one might conclude from this remarkable parallelism that only military disasters destroy French regimes, while crises simply fester.

Certainly this was the case with the Third Republic during most of its troubled life. The crises of the Boulanger movement, the Panama scandal, and the Dreyfus case, shook but did not overturn the system, which withstood the terrible shock of World War I and was troubled again by the Stavisky scandal in 1934, but survived for another six years. Yet during all of this time the Third Republic was not really legitimate for a sizable and very articulate minority of Frenchmen—Marianne was for Charles Maurras and those who thought like him "la gueuse"—the slut.

The Fourth Republic was not unfamiliar with scandals, but its nemesis was colonial war. In 1958 the return of Charles de Gaulle seemed the only way to avoid civil war. Ultimately, the Fourth Republic collapsed because it had insufficient authority to recognize military defeat, something de Gaulle could do only at the cost of two attempted coups d'état begun in Algeria. The disturbances of May 1968, which again shook the republic to its foundations, seemed to mimic the revolutions of 1830 and 1848, but produced no regime change.

The revival of confidence under Georges Pompidou, the successful alternation of power in 1981 and its variations thereafter (and the withering of a Communist party given to extreme language) have confirmed the legitimacy of a Fifth Republic, which its twice-elected president once called "the permanent coup d'état." The historian René Rémond described France's former "exceptionalism" as "the conjunction of seven or eight traits which the genius of our people had in the course of its history carried to extremes. [These were] instability, superiority of the legislative power over the executive, the number of parties, the power of the Communist Party, a taste for controversies on principle, making everything into an ideological debate, a society cut into two blocs, with a debate on laicity."[2]

Many signs now trouble the French sky, but none augur the collapse of the regime in order to give way to some sort of Sixth Republic. The Fifth Republic continues to enjoy more legitimacy than any other regime in France since the early eighteenth century.

For French republicans, in both the nineteenth and twentieth centuries, the state must be a republic if it is to be the incarnation of the nation. And disagreement on this point is implicit in the official title of the Vichy regime: the phrase "État français" proclaims that it was *not* the republic. De Gaulle, however, when asked at the liberation of Paris if he intended to proclaim the restoration of the republic, replied "la République n'a jamais cessé d'exister" (the Republic has never ceased to exist); the "French State" of Vichy was "null and void."[3] The state was the republic, and the so-called Vichy State had not existed. The phrase with which de Gaulle ended all of his speeches "vive la République, vive la France!" meant that the republican regime and the state were co-existential (see the common if not invariable capitalization of *République*). The legitimacy and moral force of the republic, hence of the state, were not affected by changes in its numeration or of its constitution; it remained "une et indivisible." A Fourth Republic might be succeeded by a Fifth, but this produced no void in the state's moral significance.

The trends that diminish the sovereignty and prestige of the nation-state are, as the chapters of this book indicate, ubiquitous. Still, they may have less impact elsewhere than in France. The state is perhaps more important, and was formerly more prestigious in France than in any other country.

Originally completely identified with the king, the state came at the Revolution to be identified with the nation, so that the term nation-state has had deeper meaning in France than elsewhere. It is significant that, in a language not much given to capital letters, in French the State, like God, can always claim the *majuscule.*

This state was deemed to be the incarnation of the general interest, as its laws voted by the National Assembly incarnated the general will. But today, to quote Diana Pinto: "The idea that that which conforms to the law, voted democratically, escapes the presumption of tyranny is a decidedly obsolete element of the political belief which served as a base for the French political system."[4] An example is ecology—public opinion demands information from independent sources, state organizations being suspect. Here, as with civil rights, the state cannot claim without rebuttal to be the evident promoter of the common weal. Its claims are questioned by international organizations both public and private. The state is also, for the first time in France, checked by judicial control. "The Assembly wills it" has joined "*le Roy le veult*" as an obsolete statement of what is more than formal law.

THE TROUBLES OF THE JACOBIN STATE

In the words of a remarkable report by leading intellectuals on French identity near the advent of the twenty-first century, "the state as a guarantor of collective values and the incarnation of the general interest has lost a part of its legitimacy, and its moral weakening creates a void which has not yet been filled."[5] Some of this loss belongs to the realm of cultural values, which will be treated later. An important part, however, concerns the general interest.

The centralized French state that emerged from the labors of the Jacobins and Napoleon laid claim to omnicompetence in the political and administrative sphere. The state needed to be strong, so argued the creators and supporters of the system, just because it had so many enemies—in the forces of reaction, dispersion, and disloyalty, and later of royalism, bonapartism, and clericalism. In the Third and Fourth Republics, the executive could be weak and the legislative quarrelsome, precisely because the administrative state was strong.

The Dirigiste State

After World War II the state took on new responsibilities, assuming the task of repairing, indeed re-embarking on, the building of an economy that had performed badly throughout the 1930s. Dirigisme saw in state direction the only means of rapid repair. The efficient secret of French dirigiste indicative planning was state control of credit—a commodity exceedingly scarce in the early postwar years in particular. Later, state allocation of credit remained important, but the state's role ceased to be unique. By the 1970s, the role of the state in planning and directing the economy had exhausted its original purpose. When the recession years began in 1974 the state attempted to resuscitate the economy with some of the same techniques, but without much success.

When the Socialists entered government in 1981 they meant to take a dirigisme that they believed benefitted only the capitalist class and used it to reorient the economy. Two years sufficed to disabuse them: they discovered that the French economy was in far worse shape than they had known, and could not recover without more austerity exercised inside a European capitalist economy. The French Right, meanwhile, had disowned the dirigisme it had pursued since World War II. Ministers of economics and finance with names like Pierre Bérégovoy and Edouard Balladur rivalled in their adaptation of the French economy to the international market, dropping currency controls, and tying the French franc to the Deutschemark. Thus under both Socialists and conservatives, the enthusiasm for the dirigiste state has largely disappeared.

The Welfare State
The welfare state came late to France. By 1900, 40 percent of the German population was covered by social insurance including accident, sickness, pensions, and unemployment insurance; no other European country came close to this. The first French legislation on social welfare came with a law on accidents in the workplace in 1898, followed in 1910 by a very modest pension plan for workers and peasants that was so low that only 0.5 percent of a worker's salary was involved. Meanwhile French union leader Léon Jouhaux argued that in any case only five percent of workers could benefit by it, by living to age 65. (A not dissimilar argument for retirement at 60 was given the author 73 years later by a Socialist leader.)

Not until the 1930s does one begin to see any extensive social legislation in France, with social insurance laws covering sickness, maternity, and old age with a four percent share from the employee and an equal amount from the employer. This covered only industrial and commercial employees, and only 30 percent of the population was thoroughly covered by these laws. In 1932 France began the practice of family allowances—legislation designed to keep up the birthrate. These have consistently taken a larger percent of social expenditures than in any other European country—in 1975, which was not the high point, this one item represented four percent of GDP.

The real expansion of the welfare state, which in French is called *l'état-providence*, (originally a pejorative phrase coined in the 1860s) took place after World War II. From 37.5 percent of the population covered in 1940 by any form of social welfare, the figure rose to 54.5 percent in 1955, to 68 percent in 1960, and to 86.8 percent in 1975.

Whereas French social transfers had been only 11.3 percent of GDP in 1950, by 1975 they had reached 20 percent—higher than in West Germany, where the figure was only 16.7 percent, and much higher than in the United States where it had gone from 3.8 percent in 1955 to 11.5 percent in 1975. This was of course a much higher GDP than in 1950—until 1974, after which the rises are largely due to inflation.

The breakdown of social transfer differs from country to country. This is most conspicuous in France where family allowances (*allocations familiales*) have continued to be a very high percentage of all social expenditures—as high as 29 percent in 1962, down to 20 percent in 1990, but rising and expected to rise further (this does not include unemployment insurance).

Social expenses in France in 1990 were 28.0 percent of GDP. They were undoubtedly higher in 1993, for which full statistics are not yet available, because of the rise in unemployment. Nevertheless, the idea that the welfare state has become too expensive, together with doubts about its effectiveness, is not new; it set in by the end of the 1970s, as it became clear that the prosperity of the "*trente années glorieuses*" was over.

The government's appropriation of GDP rose with the 1970s—in 1976 it was 39.4 percent for France, rising until the mid-1980s, when the Socialist government felt obliged to slow it down. A government that had entered office believing that it had a mandate to perfect the welfare state recognized that expenses were limited by national income. Despite the fact that the victorious conservatives in 1986 made no attempt to roll back retirement at 60, the idea of an ever-developing welfare state had received a mortal blow.

Two factors have increased the problem: unemployment, raising costs and lowering national tax income simultaneously, and the influx of immigrants (or rather, the recognition that they are a problem) concomitant with unwillingness to pay for them. Here the very size of immigrant families is a problem. The *allocations familiales* provide 615 francs for the second child, 1400 for the third, 2189 for the fourth, et cetera. They were introduced to raise the French birthrate (and probably did so) and the birthrate among the French of non-immigrant background remains much higher than the rate in Germany or Italy. Nonetheless, the *allocations* also provide an argument for the anti-immigrant polemic.

To what degree is the French welfare state in crisis, then, even with all its multiple problems? Despite the argument of conservative economists that high social costs are dragging down the developed economies, it is very unlikely that the welfare state as we now know it will be dismantled. The welfare state is also unlikely to expand. Almost certainly the new Chirac government will have to make some reductions as the expenses of unemployment compensation continue, while the population ages and the worker base contracts. In 1990, French old-age pensions were 29.2 percent of social expenses, or 8.6 percent of GDP, and are expected to rise by 60 percent by the beginning of the next century. The almost certain psychological effect of all this will be to make the beneficiaries of the welfare state suspicious of change, anxious about the future, and more resentful than grateful for the advantages they still enjoy.

Unemployment

In 1981, when unemployment had risen from less than three percent in the years of prosperity to 1.7 million, François Mitterrand campaigned against Valéry Giscard d'Estaing by proclaiming unemployment intolerable and promising to correct it. In mid-1995, unemployment stood at 12.6 percent. All governments have admitted their helplessness to solve this problem, and it has become a plague that discredits a French state that had believed it had control over the economy. Today, governments merely hope that they can do at least something to alleviate unemployment—not remove it.

Unemployment is, however, a differentiated phenomenon. In percentage terms, it hits hardest at young people between the ages of 15 and 24, and within this group affects young women more severely than men (23.8 and 15.7 percent respectively). The problem drops back sharply for those between the ages of 25 and 49, though it is still higher for women than for men (7 percent for men in 1992, 11.6 for women), and rises again for those 50 and older.[6]

While worse in 1994 than from 1989 to 1990, when it diminished to slightly over 2.2 million, unemployment has become a permanent condition of life for the young, especially those who are poorly qualified or lack qualifications entirely, and for the slightly older workers whose jobs have disappeared in the ongoing process of restructuring. A young person, there-fore, has indifferent hopes of rapidly finding a job unless he or she has been to a *grande école* of some sort or another—and even there instant employ-ment has become less certain. Early school-leavers, and particularly Maghrébins, find special difficulty in locating work. (Statistics are hard to come by, since a large percentage of young Maghrébins are French citizens and are not counted separately). Even those who are unlikely to lose their jobs worry about it and fear for their children's future. Unemployment began as an economic problem; it has long since become a social one as well, as sterile suburban neighborhoods and housing projects (*les banlieux et les cités*) fester and produce crime and despair.

Decentralization

Decentralization, according to most authors, limits national sovereignty in practice by making towns, departments, and regions more autonomous, and especially in limiting the role of the prefect. Certainly the original Jacobins, as well as the modern advocates of centralization find this to be the case. Former prime minister Michel Debré declared during the decentralization debate in 1982: "It is this fundamental text [article 3 of the *Declaration des droits de l'homme et du citoyen*] which distinguishes between decentral-ization and dismemberment. Decentralization stops where the national exercise of sovereignty begins. Dismemberment begins when the exercise of sovereignty becomes impossible."

Debré was only echoing the Jacobin deputy Billaud-Varenne, 189 years earlier, who saw in the departments set up earlier in the Revolution a "fed-eralism which would make the departments so many principalities and their administrators so many potentates and a menace for the unity of France."[7] Under Napoleon, the Constitution de l'an VIII (1800) and its attendant laws created the prefects, sub-prefects, and mayors who consecrated the idea of "*unité territoriale*" that lasted for 150 years.

In one recent work, Catherine Grémion notes that prefects, who hold in their hands the representation of the services of the state, are in recent years in post usually only 24 months, sometimes less, and thus cannot have much understanding of the problems of their department. (This is, however, not a novelty introduced by the decentralization reforms, though it may have become more frequent and common; prefects were always shifted often to keep them from "going native"). Grémion continues: "The symbolic presence of the state itself suffers from the new arrangements initiated by decentralization: for the voter, the department is now the president of the general council, the region is the president of the region, the state is in Paris."[8]

Other authors speak of the diminution of the state's role introduced by the effects of an increasingly globalized economy.

> Our territorial administration remains in a pyramidal mode, with the tip in Paris. We still think of territorial agglomerations in the same way: the capital, the chief towns of regions, other important cities, smaller ones, and finally the smallest rural communes. This is the pyramid of sovereignty, which in France, more than elsewhere, has modelled everything. . . . But the reality is different. Paris rules more in function of the concentration of enterprises and banks than by its function as capital. . . . If Paris is no longer the center, can one then identify another center of power, which is in the process of substituting itself, at least partially? The answer is no.[9]

The author speaks of certain nuclei in a non-homogeneous system, which orients the ensemble—the U.S. Federal Reserve Bank and the central banks of Germany and Japan. The decisions taken by these organizations influence by ricochet all countries and enterprises, but these centers are not sovereign in the way that the state used to be. The shrinking of sovereignty is not accompanied by the creation of other identifiable centers that could play a sovereign role, with far-reaching consequences. "Strikes, riots, or elections have no meaning, for the simple reason that there is no longer any identifiable power on which they can put pressure, in non-agricultural economic questions. Voting for the Right or the Left will only change the situation at the margins. Our territory in this respect is no more than a province of a world empire, without an emperor and without frontiers."[10]

In appealing to the state against factory closings, or demanding the creation of new jobs, "one can send a delegation to the prefect, board a bus for a manifestation in front of the Ministry of Industry or the DATAR, strew heads of cauliflower on the road or loose pigs among the CRS." None of this does any good, although the state has done what it can, and often promised "that the inexorable would not take place." "From important though not unique constructor of economic development and its balance, throughout the country, the state has become the regulator of the internal social consequences of economic evolution, largely through a policy of steadily increasing social transfers by means of unemployment insurance. All governments since the mid-1970s have done this."[11]

Thus, although the state continues to build autoroutes, to extend the high-speed train (TGV) net, to underwrite research, and to give major funds for training, the national sovereignty incarnated by the state has been progressively limited, even though nothing has changed in the royal forms used by the king of France to proclaim himself sole master.

> On the contrary, even, for decades the action of the state has been amplified and diversified, been extended to more and more areas. The Bottin administratif needs more than 1200 tightly printed pages to describe the organization of the state and its multiple ramifications. . . . But behind the appearances, three basic phenomena limit if not constrain the action of this majestic and still powerful apparatus: 1) building Europe; 2) the worldwide victory of *"la logique marchande"*—all governments since 1981 have had to use the same macro-economic policies, and the 1981-1983 exception proves the rule; and 3) decentralization.[12]

The Matter of Europe

That the French state is engaged in trying to build Europe—a potential superstate that could render it obsolete—is to the minds of many Frenchmen an abomination. One particularly articulate polemic against the Maastricht Treaty, written by former Pompidou adviser Marie-France Garaud and the Gaullist deputy Philippe Séguin (since risen to the influential post of president of the National Assembly), refers to:

> its primary intent, partly hidden, partly disguised. A political intent, to constitute a federal state on the ruins of existing nations. . . . The future Union worked out in Maastricht will be federal, but the word is not spoken. We are getting ready to abandon essential attributes of our sovereignty, but indirectly, first by the currency, and by one-way mechanisms put in place to block any retreat. . . . Now we find ourselves again at the heart of a long battle. Let us recall the essentials. Charles de Gaulle, but also Pierre Mendès France had in common, each in his own way, the desire to see Europe reorganize itself, but not that it be based on the abandonment of that which they dared call France's vocation, where they dared see its greatness.[13]

The defense of the Maastricht Treaty in the National Assembly debate by then Justice Minister Michel Vauzelle could, at first blush, have been taken as an attack on it, in his tortured explanation that no French sovereignty was being alienated:

> I wish solemnly to underline that there is no derogation here from the fundamental principle of national sovereignty. . . . France's sovereignty is inalienable, never-ending, and indivisible. . . . There can be no transfers from it, that is a definitive transfer of the sovereignty of a state. There can also not be any ceding of a part of sovereignty, because sovereignty is indivisible. Sovereignty is a principle that is superior to the constitution. Just as the sovereign people has a constituent power that itself is superior to the constitution, which it can revise or abolish if it wishes, in the same way the sovereign people can in its sovereignty limit the space in which its sovereignty is exercised. The people can thus perfectly well consent to a self-limitation, but this is anything but an abandonment.[14]

But whether Maastricht proposed that sovereignty be abandoned or self-limited is a quibble; sovereignty was to be transferred in part to a higher, European level. Of course, an ongoing process had already transferred large parts of sovereignty much earlier. The great precedent came in 1964, when a plea by a shareholder of a nationalized Italian power company argued that the Italian law nationalizing the electrical industry was contrary to the Rome treaty. Despite the Italian government's claim that the European Court of Justice had no standing, the Court ruled that "by creating a Community of unlimited duration, having its own institutions, its own personality . . . and, more particularly, real powers stemming from a limitation of sovereignty or a transfer of powers from the States to the Community, the Member States have limited their sovereign rights . . . and have thus created a body of law which binds both their nationals and themselves."[15]

The European Court's supremacy doctrine was accepted by the judiciaries and administrations of both the then and future member states (including Great Britain). The areas affected are agriculture, transport, customs, the social security of migrant workers, as well as Community directives intended to "harmonize country laws on such matters as taxes, banking, equality of the sexes, protection of the environment, employment contracts, and organization of companies."

Another area affected is preemption; that is, the question of whether a whole policy area has been actually or potentially occupied by the central authority so as to influence the intervention of the states in that area. An example is fishing conservation, where the court has held that individual states no longer have the right to establish conservation laws—even where there is no Community legislation. Environmental protection in general became a Community responsibility with ratification of the Single Act.

At the beginning of 1990 the French government abolished the exchange controls that had been introduced many years earlier, which were designed to protect the franc. The measure was taken as part of the Europeanization pushed by then Economics Minister Bérégovoy, but it was not disputed by people like former Economics Minister and future Prime Minister Edouard Balladur. Bank of France official Philippe Lagayette wrote in 1992:

> It is hardly necessary to recall that the liberation of capital movements is indispensable for diversified industrial economies, where all the large enterprises are at the same time importers and exporters. . . . The progress of integration of economies, European at first, but global as well, has made monetary policy a competence which can only be exercised in close coordination with those countries with which we have the greatest number of ties.
>
> The exercise of sovereignty thus consists in the first instance in recognizing that international ties tightly frame our monetary autonomy. Sovereignty is limited, not by discretionary choices, reversible at any moment, but by the very nature of the economic world built by the industrialized countries, and which makes for their prosperity. One must speak clearly: refusal to recognize the limits of our sovereignty would signify in reality refusal of the economic world which is our own.[16]

The speculative "pounding" on the franc, which culminated in the European finance ministers' decision in early August 1993 to broaden the band of the European Monetary System's float from 4.5 to 30 percent, was countered by Balladur's determination not to let the franc move far from the Deutschemark. Although much criticized, it is another example of the way nominal monetary sovereignty shows its freedom only by yielding to necessity, which is to say that even when France seemed able to break free of the constraints of German interest rates, the prime minister and his colleagues concluded that France's freedom was illusory.

Enormous areas that have always belonged to national sovereignty have thus slipped away from the national state, usually with relatively little protest that the French state was at risk. The fever that set in with German unification in 1990 and a relapse into recession from the short recovery of 1988-1990 brought all problems into sudden focus. The National Front campaigned against the Maastricht Treaty in part because foreigners from other countries of the European Community, if domiciled in France, would be able to vote in local elections. The Front argued that the next step would be voting rights for resident Maghrébins.

The control of borders is another ancient regalian right, and the modern French state has, or is alleged to have, lost control of immigration because large numbers of foreigners originally invited in for temporary work have unexpectedly multiplied and because resident communities attract co-nationals who enter illegally. It does little good to point out that the foreign population in France is no larger, percentagewise, than it was in the 1930s. The problem is in the perception, and the perception, for many more French people than will ever vote for the National Front, is that France now has far too many North African Muslims, and is likely to receive too many more.

Dominique Schnapper, after noting this unaltered percentage, says "The integrity of the nation then appeared threatened by foreigners, but the principle of the nation-state was not under discussion; no one thought of raising the question of the confusion of nationality and citizenship which constituted the intangible principle of political legitimacy." She adds that national integration could be under threat, if what she refers to as the "specificities of the new immigrant populations are susceptible of being transcended by the political project."[17]

These are questions that trouble at least the one-third of the French population that has consistently told pollsters that it hears something it likes in the National Front's language—roughly twice as many as have ever voted for Jean-Marie LePen. But as Schnapper points out, surveys cite an estimate of about five percent of young Muslims in Marseilles as actively practicing their religion, and at Toulouse, although all the young Muslims declared a belief in God, 87 percent of the young men and 72 percent of the young women said that they did not pray, while 94 percent of the young men, and 45 percent of the young women did not observe Ramadan. Islam for them has a value of giving identity.

Schnapper speaks of the development of a French Islam—a personal religion. The Beurs, young Maghrébins, are in this reading acquiring most of the characteristics that could allow them to be French in most senses, while still existing as a parallel community. But French Jews and even French Protestants have, to a certain extent and in different degrees, existed as parallel communities, and it is now generally recognized as a myth that all French people of Catholic background have at all times (including the twentieth century) been uniformly integrated into the general community. Whether the Maghrébins will be allowed to continue gradual integration is another question—prejudice might rise, as fundamentalism in North Africa becomes more frightening to France, and perhaps attracts even secularized Muslims. As they watch fundamentalist terrorism growing in Algeria, the French fear that they are about to lose control of their borders to a new wave of hapless but unwelcome Westernized Algerians.

The Servants of the State

The network of *grandes écoles* set up by the Revolution and Napoleon to educate the future servants of the French state have in the past (and indeed still today) served that state well. Until very recently, it was a title of great honor for a man to style himself, as Pompidou's Foreign Minister Michel Jobert once did, *"un grand commis de l'État."* But although members of the upper classes have continued to compete for entry into the highly selective *grandes écoles,* members of the upper civil service lost up to 20 percent of their purchasing power in 1980-1988, and high civil servants compared their salaries and their status unfavorably with managers in the private sector, whose prestige had also risen with a new cult of the entrepreneur. Private sector salaries in scientific and technical fields were frequently 100 percent higher than those offered in universities or public scientific institutions.

While civil servants have long left public employ for the private sector as they get older (*pantouflage*) the phenomenon now takes place with much younger people. Fifty-nine percent of managers between 25 and 40 years old responded to a survey by saying that they plan to leave the civil service. It is now commonplace for big companies to recruit talented young people immediately after their graduation from a *grande école,* assuming the cost of reimbursing the government for their tuition. Luc Rouban's 1993 study of high civil servants showed that 70.4 percent of *grand corps* members came from the upper classes. Such people are acutely conscious of the prestige of their jobs, and the decreasing prestige of the state affects the status of its higher servants.

Corruption

The lengthening list of scandals in French government and big business also drags down the prestige of the state. One clamorous and long-running scandal is the 1985 affair in which the state blood bank negligently (or criminally) continued to sell untested blood, often contaminated with the AIDS virus, to hemophiliacs and others, although an American process of sterilizing blood plasma was already available. Two senior doctors—state employees—have gone to prison, and in mid-1995 proceedings continue against three ex-ministers, one of them former Prime Minister Laurent Fabius, who are allegedly responsible.

Financial scandals also tarred the last years of Socialist administration. The financing of political parties had always taken place in the shadows, either with large contributions from business on the Right, or on the Left by using dummy consultancies paid for non-work by contractors working for municipalities controlled by the Left.

As campaign expenses mounted in the 1980s, with television assuming a larger role and unpaid militancy slackening off, more money was needed. The practices of the Socialist Party were encouraged by a see-no-evil policy from the highest authority in the presidency and a feeling that no harm could come to the operators. When scandals arrived, they were particularly painful for a party that had told itself that it was more moral than the Right. Perhaps the most serious scandal was the insider trading affair connected with the purchase of American Can Company by Pechiney in 1988, in which advance information benefited a businessman, Patrice Pelat, who was a close friend of President Mitterrand, and a Socialist maecenas, Max Théret. The director of the cabinet of then Economics Minister Bérégovoy, Alain Boublil, was eventually sent to jail for passing along inside information. Bérégovoy himself was accused of unethical behavior in accepting a one-million franc interest-free loan from Pelat, a charge that apparently weighed on him heavily and was in part responsible for his suicide in 1993.

The Right, too, had its scandals, and continues to have them. Former Defense Minister, François Léotard, narrowly escaped prosecution on a charge of advantageous purchase of property. Alain Carignon, Balladur's minister of communication and mayor of Grenoble, resigned from the government while facing a charge of misuse of funds and has been sentenced to a prison term.

Several of the most important businessmen in France, often graduates of *grandes écoles,* have also been recently accused of doubtful dealings. The head of Schneider, Didier Pineau-Varenne, was jailed by the Belgian government and is now the subject of an international arrest warrant which he is defying. Pierre Suard, head of Alcatel Alsthom, faces charges of misuse of funds, and the head of Saint-Gobain, Jean-Louis Beffa, faces accusations in another affair, which also involves Parti Républicain chairman Gérard Longuet. While none of these men has been convicted of anything as of mid-1995, the impression of wholesale corruption in the political-business class is strong; a new poll states that two out of three French company chairmen suspect that illegal practices are common in many companies.[18]

Decentralization has been described as a cause of some of the increase in corruption in France, but according to Yves Mény, author of a book on corruption, decentralization did not create corruption, but merely gave it new opportunities. Mény speaks of a "very severe devaluation of the state over the last decade, of the value [represented by the] State, of the value represented by 'the general interest.' The central value has become money, not money earned thanks to a spirit of enterprise but money often acquired very rapidly by speculation."[19]

Cultural Decline

The French "believed they were the center and the resume of what went on on the planet" notes the 1990 Leroy Ladurie report on French identity, which cites Jean-François Revel as saying that the "international vocation of French culture is considered in our country as necessarily passing through the diffusion of our language." The report continues: "The idea of the role of France, in politics as in culture, is refuted by the realities of this fin de siècle." Revel argues that the only reason now for foreigners to learn French can be the desire to acquire an exceptional intellectual tool—but "how can this be if French is not well written or expressed, as shown by the insufficient mastery of French by many students?" Just as serious, the vitality of a culture which is preponderantly literary and humanist is threatened by the retreat from a "classical curriculum."[20]

The French are uneasily conscious that French is no longer a world language, despite their promotion of *Francophonie.* French is spoken as a first language by only about 68 million people in Europe and Canada, and though it is an important vehicle in Africa and some other areas, it has been eclipsed by English, the first language of more than 350 million people in Great Britain, North America, Australia, and New Zealand, and the vehicle of commerce, science, and technology all over the world. French scientists are reproached by linguistic nationalists for giving papers in English at international meetings, but they feel that it is necessary in order to be understood.

In a speech that would be hard to imagine in the mouth of an American president, François Mitterrand said in the mid-1980s: "I regularly have sent me the statistics for foreign schools and universities on the teachers and pupils, the length of time, and the place occupied by French—whether obligatory or optional." Speaking of international institutions and scientific congresses where French is one of the official languages, but is not always used, he stated: "I want France to stop its participation in the organizations that ignore this obligation." He went on to say that the fault lies with the French, but that "no one listens to a people which loses its language."[21]

A recent governmental attempt to reverse the watering-down of French by the use of English or pseudo-English *franglais* was the new loi Toubon, forbidding the use of foreign words on the radio, on television, on shop fronts, or in advertising. It was emasculated by a July 1994 decision of the constitutional court in the name of the liberty of the individual. Even a champion of French and enemy of *franglais* like *Le Monde* (August 1, 1994) considered that "good sense has triumphed." When the rights of man are at war with the defense and illustration of the French language, the old order of things has indeed been shaken.

Stanley Hoffmann argues that the notion of culture is more central to the definition of Frenchness than in other countries, and that this is explicitly high culture, which always came from the top down, not from the *Volk*, as in German thinking. It was heavily based on literature and art, not on philosophy. Connected with this was a certain conception of France's relation to the world and a faith in the universal relevance of France's values and culture. It followed that France, to be France, had a permanent concern to play a major role in world affairs.[22]

Foreign Policy—France, Germany, Europe, and the World

"France cannot be France without greatness," is the famous phrase from the first paragraph of Charles de Gaulle's *Mémoires de Guerre,* and the general played a major role in convincing a country still affected by World War II, dispirited by the defeat in Vietnam and the unsolvable Algerian War, that it was still almost a world power. De Gaulle's success demonstrates that many of his countrymen were predisposed to believe him. As Hoffmann remarks, de Gaulle's position was a sort of therapeutic lie.

In the mid-1970s, there was much negative comment when President Giscard d'Estaing described France as a middle-sized power. But by the beginning of the 1990s the French were disabused. The end of the Cold War had shown that in the new world order or disorder France's supposed autonomy in world affairs was a myth. Instead, France faced a new relationship with the German partner it had carefully cultivated since 1950, first thinking of French hegemony, then that France at least had a political edge on the Germans—a seat in the UN Security Council, an independent nuclear force, coresponsibility for Berlin, and for the ultimate settlement in Germany.

After unification, these "trumps" in the relationship with the Federal Republic disappeared, and the new Germany loomed as more populous, more independent, and potentially more powerful. The uses of France's independent nuclear force were unclear; it could no longer be targeted at

Soviet cities. Even the future of the Security Council seat is uncertain: it could, in the near future, be shared with other European Union countries, or see its value diluted as Germany, Japan, and major Latin American and African countries join the council.

France's reaction to the new dispensation has been an attempt to re-knot the ties binding Germany to itself and the European Union, primarily along monetary lines, while maintaining much national discretion in security and other foreign policy affairs. The troubles of the Maastricht Treaty have placed the timing and even the realization of European monetary unity in doubt. France's role in the new Europe has been recast. Any advance toward a more closely tied, even confederal Europe, especially one diluted in directive power by the advent of Austria, Finland, Sweden, and later the Central European states, will almost certainly mean abandoning many symbols and institutions evocative of French national identity. Must France subsume its identity into a European one?

While waiting to see what role the new Germany will play in security arrangements outside the old NATO scenario, France has attempted an activist role in ex-Yugoslavia and Rwanda. The limits of its power are evident here—one might say the limitations of the present arrangements of international cooperation as well. One country can only make demonstrative gestures—a relatively large force associated with the UN in Bosnia, an almost-unilateral force in Rwanda. But these are inevitably short-term commitments and expensive ones at that. The willingness of France's leaders to take the lead in these crises, as a formerly activist United States lags behind, may flatter the nation at large as long as the expenditures in blood and treasure are not too great. But they also demonstrate that France's unilateral resources are limited, and that more comprehensive and permanent arrangements—by the European Union or the UN—have not only not been negotiated, but need more careful and extensive reflection by leaders and body politic than has yet taken place in any country. Those arrangements would inevitably leave a circumscribed role to any given nation-state.

CONCLUSION

The functions of the state in France, traditional and more recently assumed, are in multiple difficulties, though nothing resembling degenerative dissolution. The Jacobin state has suffered the impact of decentralization and scandals involving corruption that have blackened the reputation of French politicians and civil servants. The dirigiste state has been profoundly altered. The welfare state remains, but is in genuine crisis. The immigration question affects both the welfare state and the French sense of their national identity; while unemployment saps both the spirits of the unemployed and the potentially unemployed, and depletes the funds of the national treasury. Finally, the most basic of the state's regalian rights—control over territory, and the decisions of defense, peace, and war—are all now moving away from the control of the state and into still ill-defined European control. The state still has these rights, but cannot entirely exercise them.

Above all, the psychology of a proud nation flattered by Gaullist aspirations to *grandeur* has suffered as it takes account of its diminished power and potential—repeated shocks, all concentrated within the span of a few years. France will survive; the French state will survive, but altered and in further process of painful alteration.

◆ NOTES TO CHAPTER 5 ◆

1. Daniel Lindenberg, "Les Crises de la république," *Philosophie politique* 4 (1993), p. 134.
2. René Remond, *La Politique n'est plus ce qu'elle était* (Paris: Calmann-Lévy, 1993), p. 204.
3. Jean Lacouture, *De Gaulle I, le rebelle 1890-1944* (Paris: Seuil, 1984), p. 834.
4. *Entrer dans le XXIè siècle. Essai sur l'avenir de l'identité française. Rapport du groupe Horizon 2000 présidé par Emmanuel Le Roy Ladurie* (Paris: Editions la Découverte, 1990), p. 160.
5. *Entrer dans le XXIè siècle*, (Paris: INSEE, 1993), p. 148.
6. INSEE, *Annuaire Statistique 1993*, p. 116.
7. Quoted in Roland Debbasch, "Décentralisation et unité territoriale," in Jacques Moreau and Michel Verpeaux, eds., *Révolution et decentralisation: Le systeme administratif français et les principes révolutionnaires de 1789* (Paris: Economica, 1992), p. 114.
8 Catherine Grémion, "Pour un État correcteur," in Jean-Claude Némery and Serge Wachter, eds., *Entre l'Europe et la décentralisation: Les institutions territoriales françaises* (Le Chateau: Editions de l'Aube, 1993).
9. Jean-Pierre Balligand and Daniel Maquart, *La Fin du territoire jacobin* (Paris: Albin Michel, 1990), pp. 84-85.
10. Balligand and Macquart, *Territoire*, pp. 86-87.
11. Balligand and Macquart, *Territoire*, pp. 109-10.
12. Balligand and Macquart, *Territoire*, p. 110.
13. Marie-France Garaud and Philippe Séguin, *De l'Europe en général et de la France en particulier* (Paris: Le Pré aux Clercs, 1992), pp. 12-15.
14. *Le Monde*, May 7, 1992.
15. G. Federico Mancini, "The Making of a Constitution for Europe," in Robert O. Keohane and Stanley Hoffmann, eds., *The New European Community. Decision-making and Institutional Change* (Boulder: Westview Press, 1991), p. 180.
16. Philippe Lagayette, "Le transfert de la souveraineté monétaire," *Revue des Deux Mondes* (May-June 1992), pp. 61-62.
17. Dominique Schnapper, *La France de l'intégration: Sociologie de la nation en 1990* (Paris: Gallimard, 1991), p. 138.

18. *Financial Times*, September 8, 1994, citing a poll in *Le Monde* of the same day.
19. Yves Mény, "Les formes discrètes de la corruption," *French Politics and Society* 11:4 (Fall 1993), pp. 6-7.
20. *Entrer dans le XXIè siècle*, pp. 151-54.
21. François Mitterrand, *Réflexions sur la politique étrangère de la France: Introduction à vingt-cinq discours (1981-1985)* (Paris: Fayard, 1986), pp. 17-18.
22. From a lecture by Stanley Hoffmann at a conference on French identity at the Harvard Center for European Studies, May, 1994.

·6·

The Crisis of German Power

Dana H. Allin

Germany is troubled, as any casual observer will confirm. Its troubles include neo-Nazi thuggery and terrorism on the Right, neo-communist revival on the Left, complete desolation of any political class in the eastern part of the country, high unemployment, confusion about national purpose and identity, new disparities of wealth, plus a general disillusion with politics and politicians. But to assess German difficulties in the context of a broader crisis of the Western industrial state is to confront a paradox: The German state, faced with the huge and continuing challenges of unification, has performed rather well.

If we examine Bonn's performance with any objectivity, we cannot fail to be impressed. In a bloodless triumph, German diplomats negotiated the withdrawal of Soviet troops, the demise of the German Democratic Republic, and the fusion of two states and two diametrically opposed systems. The German government has dismantled obsolete East German industry, creating massive levels of unemployment, without, however, provoking a revolt or even very widespread protest. And despite the alleged disdain of Westerners for their new Eastern compatriots, Bonn has engineered a transfer of resources from West to East amounting, as Karl Kaiser points out, to two Marshall Plans a year.[1] In this age of taxpayer revolts, there has been nary a peep of protest.

Against this success, there are two main criticisms of the Kohl government's handling of unification. The first concerns the early decision to redeem East German marks for Deutschemarks at a rate of one-to-one. This decision had the practical effect of pricing East German firms out of business, since their employees were far less productive than Western workers, yet now had to be paid nearly comparable wages in the same currency. The second indictment is that Helmut Kohl was dishonest, or at least negligently stupid, when he promised, Ronald Reagan-style, that unification would be financed without any sacrifice in the form of higher taxes. And this lie and/or stupidity put such a burden of high interest rates on Germany's European partners that it smashed the European Monetary System (EMS) and effectively stalled European integration.

For this performance, Kohl hardly deserves a new chapter in *Profiles of Courage*. But it is far from clear that greater courage and honesty on Kohl's part would have meant that German unity could have been accommodated without considerable disruption to the European Community. The deeper cause of the European Union's crisis may be the fact that Paris and Bonn were so spooked by the implications of German unity that they rushed forward with a plan for accelerated European integration without really explaining to their people, or perhaps even understanding themselves, what it meant.

As for the flaws of the German currency union, Bonn officials respond that they did not have time to worry about economics; there were more pressing political perils that weighed on the very existence of the German nation state. The German Democratic Republic was imploding due to the suction effect of mass migration to the West. Soviet intervention and even superpower war could not be ruled out. The political situation had to be stabilized, and German unity negotiated quickly, to forestall violence and to take advantage of a window of opportunity that had been left open by Mikhail Gorbachev and Eduard Schevarnadze but which might slam shut at any moment. The subsequent coup attempt against Gorbachev, followed two years later by Moscow street battles between President Boris Yeltsin's government and leaders of the Russian parliament, convinced Bonn officials that they had been right.

German voters seem convinced too. In the 1990 elections that followed unification, they reelected the Christian Democratic Union (CDU)/Christian Social Union (CSU)-Free Democratic Party (FDP) coalition government by a wide margin. Four years later in October 1994, despite the intervening souring of some fond post–Cold War hopes, they handed the coalition yet a fourth term (albeit with an extremely narrow parliamentary majority this time). Kohl himself, if he remains in office until October 1996, will have been Chancellor for 14 years, surpassing the tenure of Konrad Adenauer and, arguably, leaving a comparable personal stamp on the character of the Federal Republic of Germany.

There is another sense in which the notion of a systemic German "crisis" rings false. Most countries in the world, including, it is fair to say, most industrial democracies, would count themselves lucky to have Germany's problems. It is not just that the country is immensely rich. Comparing what American society has achieved over the past four or five decades to what German society has accomplished over the same period leaves hardly any room for argument: Germany has constructed a superior model of social equity and stability. To be sure, this author is one who prefers the vibrancy and anarchic creativity of American life, on most days at least. Many non-Germans—especially entrepreneurs, intellectuals, writers interested in public life and public debate—find German society stultifying in its obsession with rules and order. But a good society, as Eric Hobsbawm has argued, is not organized "for the benefit of privileged minorities," who "can look after [them]selves. . . . Any society worth living in" is organized, rather, for the benefit of people of ordinary and minimal means.[2] And by this standard—measured in such terms as disparity of wealth, minimal standards of living, the condition of public spaces, and public amenities—Germany wins. Developments of recent years have forced a rethinking of the German model, but have not jeopardized its basic achievement.

Given these various successes, how does one account for the malaise afflicting the German public mood in the mid-1990s? Are Germany's troubles serious, or merely annoying? Is this a crisis, or just a period of vague dissatisfaction?

Overuse of the word "crisis" has debased its meaning. To mean anything more than simple difficulty, crisis must, as Charles Maier has put it, "[signify] a precarious systemic state in which an organism or a society hovers between decomposition and a rallying of collective energy." Crises need not be terminal, but the word "does suggest that the society and states that emerge after an extended period of turbulence shall have been transformed, not merely restored."[3]

There are three ways in which Germany can be seen to be struggling through a real crisis that fits this definition. One is economic and combines the complete failure of centrally planned socialism, under which a third of the country lived for almost half a century, with the partial obsolescence of a welfare capitalism that proved spectacularly successful throughout the Cold War. Second is a "moral crisis," as identified by Maier. In Germany's case this moral dimension is paramount; the new nation's moral and psychological sores will continue to fester well after economic unity has been achieved. Finally, and closely tied to the moral crisis, there is a crisis of German power and identity: the requirement to cope with and use its own power for a state and a nation that was allowed for 45 years to forget, or pretend to forget, that national power matters.

THE CRISIS OF WELFARE AND JOBS

Germany's economic predicament is, in one sense, unique: No other nation has had to grapple simultaneously with the failure of Communism and the growing difficulties of welfare capitalism. The more dramatic part of this predicament is of course the Communist collapse. Here was no question of transformation; rather, a new system must be built on the ruins of the old. Logically, the chance to start over again suggests some advantages, and it is reasonable to speculate that in the long term East German industry, largely rebuilt, highly capitalized, enjoying twenty-first-century regional infrastructure, will rank among the most productive in the world.

But a completely fresh start has not been possible. The most obvious reason is that the habits instilled by two generations of life in a regimented, full-employment society are not easily broken. Those older than forty have had the hardest time adjusting; indeed, throughout formerly Communist Eastern Europe, many of the numerous imported Western managers follow the so-called "Marriott Rule," refusing to hire anyone over thirty.

The state and the society's confused manner of dealing with the past has compounded problems of human capital. The abrupt end of East German trade with former Comecon partners was in large measure the inevitable result of the contraction of those various economies, especially the near collapse of the Soviet anchor. But the problem was made worse by the fact that a host of East German experts on East Central Europe and the former Soviet Union were considered unemployable because of their links with the old regime.

Another difficult legacy involved the question of property rights. Huge swaths of the German Democratic Republic had been expropriated, often from owners who settled in the West. In September 1990, a few days before the official reunification, the Bundestag passed a law entitling all those who had suffered expropriation to restitution.[4] Legal scholar Frederick Fucci has described the confusion that followed. "Because practically every industrial enterprise in the GDR was affected by one or several property claims, the application of the principle of restitution before compensation cast doubt on the legal title of industrial enterprises, and buyers refused to move forward unless clear title could be passed to them."[5] The tangle of actual and potential restitution claims held up new investment by a critical seven months.[6] This was a perverse result, since those Germans who had lost property but resettled in the West were very much the winners of the post–World War II system, compared to those who remained in the East. But the Bundestag was determined to make a concrete statement about the sanctity of property in a *Rechtsstaat*, that is, a state governed by the rule of law. As a result, even after unification it was the hapless East Germans who were forced to pay for Germany's crimes—in this case, the crimes of GDR confiscations.

Finally, Bonn mustered the moral courage to recognize that the crimes of the Communist East could not be undone, and that priority should be given in most cases to the present inhabitants. The Bundestag passed another measure, which, in effect, overturned the "restitution principle," by insisting that "persons with confiscation claims present, within stringent time frames, an investment plan for the properties affected." If such plans matched those of other investors, they could get the property back, but since it was generally impossible for the original owners or their heirs to compete with outside investors, the way was finally cleared for new investment.[7]

The state saved itself a great deal of trouble with one other bold and sensible decision—the setting up of a single holding company, or *Treuhandanstalt*, for the privatization of the GDR's 8,500 state-owned enterprises, along with nearly half the country's real estate and various special assets of the Communist party. In effect, this single holding company inherited an entire country.

This decision, which was pushed by the Bonn chancellory but formally approved by the GDR parliament in its dying days, was not a self-evident one at the time. Many East Germans argued plausibly that the enterprises and assets should pass on to the new state governments, who would be politically accountable for their privatization decisions. And yet, as Treuhand president Birgit Breuel has asserted, the cleaning of these Aeolian stables required some insulation from political pressures.[8]

Treuhand decisions were painful and controversial. State-owned enterprises were transformed into corporate firms with management boards to carry out cost reductions and massive layoffs. At the beginning of the trauma, left-wing terrorists shot to death the Treuhand president, Detlev Rohwedder. The climate was not improved by the behavior of many West German investors, whose main interest turned out to be shutting down potential competitors.[9]

But there came an early turn to more realistic, and humane, strategies. The privatizers started to insist on strict and detailed contracts mandating a certain level of employment for a certain number of years. Together with trade unions, employers associations and state governments, the Treuhand set up the German Labor Protection Law to promote "work-creation companies" that offered jobs to some of those laid off. The Treuhand also started a rather successful marketing campaign to reestablish trade connections and joint ventures with Eastern European countries. Such measures have helped purchase some surprising social peace in Eastern Germany, despite an unofficial unemployment rate of roughly 25 percent.[10] This calm cannot be explained fully by Germany's generous unemployment benefits. Treuhand president Breuel herself speculates that the East Germans, hardened by life under a grim regime, are just "extremely realistic."[11]

A time will come, however, when the East Germans stop blaming the GDR and start blaming the Federal Republic for their troubles. The outlines of these longer-term troubles are already visible. Early union/employers-association agreements mandated a general increase of East German wages to West German levels by 1994. The date was later moved back to 1996, and many employers simply ignore the mandate anyway, knowing that unions are unlikely to insist on enforcement if it means putting large eastern enterprises out of business.[12] Even so, wages in the East have gone up quickly, pushing unit-labor costs to 160 percent of the Western level by late 1994.[13] This development has encouraged a degree of capital intensity that bodes well for productivity, but ill for employment.

Western economists cannot claim, with the same old confidence, that painful restructurings today prepare the way for prosperity and full employment tomorrow. In the long run, Eastern Germany faces the same potential for a structural unemployment crisis as the rest of Germany, perhaps writ somewhat larger. And Germany's employment fears are part of a larger syndrome, for the specter of technology-driven unemployment has returned to haunt the Western world. Can modern industrial (or post-industrial) societies provide an acceptable level of employment? Are these societies likely to become increasingly divided, with a group of high-paid "symbolic analysts" (to borrow from Robert Reich) at one end, and a mass of marginalized, unemployed workers or low-paid service providers at the other? Political economists have raised similar questions since the beginning of capitalism. Earlier crises were overcome, whether through war, government spending, or the creation of new markets. But the threat has returned in the form of gross income inequalities in the United States, traumatic industrial restructurings in Eastern Europe, and persistent high unemployment in Western Europe.

In the early 1990s, German economists and economic policy makers were gloomy about the capacity of the German economic model, extremely successful throughout the postwar era, to cope with this new threat. The more obvious problems—such as a rather bloated welfare state and a series of social charges on hiring amounting to more than 40 percent of normal wages—could be fixed in theory. But the essence of political-economic culture was its consensus-based industrial policy, featuring union "co-determination" of company policies. This culture had kept wages increases in line with productivity throughout the postwar era, and was generally considered a key to the country's export-based prosperity. Pessimists have argued that such a system is incapable of accommodating real wage cuts, such as have kept unemployment relatively low in the United States.

Such an "American option" is still considered anathema in Germany. Even so, there is no reason to suspect that the German labor movement has abandoned its celebrated realism. A grim realism was certainly encouraged throughout 1993 by the worst German recession since World War II. In 1994 the German unions, led by IG Metall, showed considerable moderation in their wage demands. Unit labor costs fell 1 percent for the year, after rising 12.5 percent between 1990 and 1993.[14] Informed estimates put unemployment for 1995 at a record 3.7 million, with an overall jobless rate of 10 percent.[15] Since Germany will never be in the position to compete on the basis of low wages, it must rely on other sources of comparative advantage. But the opening of the Iron Curtain means that employees have fewer options than employers, who see an exit in the former Communist Eastern Europe, and are using it.

THE MORAL CRISIS

The demise of the German Democratic Republic was an event of liberation and joy, but it has brought problems that go well beyond its economic dimensions. Some comfortable aspects of the Cold War, from the privileged position of Berlin to the moral challenge of ideological struggle, are gone, and they are missed. The Harvard historian Charles S. Maier has argued that the end of the Cold War has contributed to a pervasive "civic discontent" or, to put it more dramatically, a "moral crisis" throughout the democratic West, which he compares to the 1870s and 1880s in Europe and America, and the 1920s and 1930s in Central and Western Europe. In all of these ages he discerns "a profound shift of public attitude along three dimensions: a sudden sense of historical dislocation, a disaffection with the leadership of all political parties, and a recurring skepticism about doctrines of social progress."[16]

Maier's analysis is important not least because it helps explain an odd aspect of the Western world's current malaise, the fact that Western societies are, in general, much calmer than they were even 15 or 20 years ago. There is no wave of terrorism such as afflicted much of Western Europe in the 1970s and early 1980s. There are no crippling waves of strikes. Politics seem dreary, tired, and not very effective, but they function nonetheless without the sort of explosive impasse that the concept of "political crisis" would suggest. Nor, generally speaking, is there an "economic crisis" in the sense of a debilitating, inflation-stoking struggle over national income share, such as was set off in much of Western Europe and the United States following the oil shocks of the 1970s.

Yet there has occurred a marked decline—in some cases, collapse—of public confidence. This crisis of confidence is evident now to a greater or lesser extent throughout the Western democracies, including Germany. To take Maier's first dimension, the "sudden sense of historical disorientation," no one in the West is more affected by the disorientation after the end of the Cold War than the Germans, even if they were the main beneficiaries of that end.

The disorientation of West Germans has to do with the new uncertainties of capitalism, (discussed previously) and new questions about their national identity and world role (discussed next). Among East Germans, disorientation involves the complete overthrow of everything familiar, expected and hoped for. After the euphoria of revolution, there is considerable disappointment with the realities of daily life. The new insecurities of life in a market economy are many—not just jobs, but the end of a system of guaranteed child care, for example. For writers and artists, to take another example, the secure and highly valued place they had in GDR society—the idea of artists as belonging to a well-defined, privileged and regulated "profession"—has been abolished. This brings new freedom; indeed, it returns artists to what is probably their proper and "natural" status, but it is a difficult adjustment. The tyranny of the market is nothing, morally, like the tyranny of a Communist state. But it is still a tyranny.

More profoundly disappointing for many of the political active is the sense that East Germans have little control over their political future. There are very few outstanding Eastern political elites, and there is some justice to the complaint from some East Germans that they have been as much "colonized" as liberated. This situation is not necessarily the fault of the Western colonists; there was a gaping deficit of experience in the East; many administrators and politicians came from the West and proved indispensably competent and even, as in the case of Saxony prime minister Kurt Biedenkopf, immensely popular. Moreover, the revolutionaries of 1989 turned out to have a vision for East Germany's future, a "Third Way" between capitalism and communism, that the East German electorate rejected out of hand.[17] This is perhaps tragic for those revolutionaries, but understandable for a population that had enough of economic and social experiments. The citizens' movement barely survives, in political terms, as junior partners in the Green/Alliance 90 coalition.

The most insidious blight on East German leadership is the poison legacy of the East German state security service—the Stasi. The release of Stasi archives has revealed a whole country that was caught up in the web of informers and informed-upon. There was a whole vast network of "IMs," *Inoffizielle Mitarbeiter*, that is to say, "unofficial colleagues," of the security service. Friendships, professional relationships, and even marriages have been shattered by what the Stasi files reveal. But how accurate are individual files? What did it mean to have "contact" with the Stasi? In a totalitarian system, who could avoid such contact? The saga of Brandenburg minister president Manfred Stolpe has personified eastern Germany's post-GDR trauma. Stolpe had worked through the Protestant church to aid the victims of state persecution. In doing so, he had many contacts with the Stasi, the nature of which has been the subject of long and bitter debate. Other church leaders, like the Protestant minister and last GDR defense minister Rainer Eppelmann, vehemently reject Stolpe's defense that he only did what he had to do. Brandenburg voters, on the other hand, have been more forgiving, reelecting him September 1994 in a landslide victory. Other Eastern politicians have been less fortunate; CDU politician Lothar de Maiziere was forced to resign his position as federal vice chancellor following allegations about his own Stasi contacts.

The Stasi net caught up the GDR's intellectual, literary and artistic elites as well. In a recent book, the East Berlin geneticist Jens Reich has detailed how the state made a conscious effort to compromise artists and intellectuals at all levels.[18] Christa Wolf is perhaps the most famous case—an apparently independent if not explicitly defiant fiction writer who turns out to have been, earlier in her life, an informer.[19] There were in fact vast milieus of underground artistic and literary culture, members of which thought they were carving out a private, civil space and even, in some cases, laying the groundwork for a peaceful revolution. When that revolution in fact came, and these artists were able to read their own Stasi files, they were dismayed to find that they had to come to terms with entirely new versions of their own personal histories.

In their old, private history, there had been a steady enlargement of artistic freedom and defiance, even within the artistic tomb of East German communism. As was true throughout Eastern Europe, the culture of rock music lent considerable energy to a limited sense of freedom's possibilities.[20] This sense of possibility was diminished, but not wholly destroyed, by the tremendous disillusion after the Soviet invasion of Prague, and, especially important in the East German artistic and literary scene, tremendous anger after the expulsion of East German poet and pop singer Wolf Biermann.[21] After Biermann's expulsion, many of those artists who could leave the country did so, but many others came closer together in what they thought were private gatherings, revolutionary cells for a new *"Ich-Bewußtsein,"* or self-awareness, in the words of one East Berlin artist who fled in 1984 to the West. At the time they seemed to be important achievements. But she now finds it impossible to take any pride in that achievement: "Today we know that the most enthusiastic participants in the underground scene had been placed there by the Stasi. And we also know that we must say goodbye to the illusion that there were niches and corners in DDR society that one could fill with artistic dynamite. In fact, there was round-the-clock surveillance, from the inside out."[22]

Perhaps this judgment is too harsh. Perhaps, after all, the regime only *thought* it could control this underground scene that it helped create, but was in fact helping to dig its own grave. In a sense, however, the validity of the judgment is irrelevant; what matters is that the artists and intellectuals are bitterly convinced of its truth. And the judgment has grim consequences for present civic culture. There is no East German de Gaulle to help create a positive myth of resistance (positive even if not wholly accurate), a sense of past solidarity that would be useful in forging a present-day community.

The problem is similar to that which West Germany faced after World War II. But the imperatives of the Cold War put an early end to denazification, and allowed the West Germans to ignore the many ex-Nazis among them. The East German elites, having shared complicity in a regime that was far less savage, are having no such luck. The watchword is still *Vergangenheitsbewältigung,* roughly, "grappling with the past." In practical terms, that means continued witchhunts and continued handwringing. It leads to such absurdities as the trial and conviction of former Stasi chief

Markus Wolf for espionage against Bonn, the same sort of espionage that the West routinely conducted against the East.[23] The occasional call for a blanket amnesty, such as that from *Die Zeit* publisher Marion Dönhoff,[24] are rejected as a first step toward "a kind of national amnesia."[25] The communist regime is demonized at the same time as Mikhail Gorbachev and former Hungarian foreign minister (now prime minister) Gyula Horn are lionized for their roles in bringing German unity about.

Some thoughtful Germans acknowledge this anomaly, but insist that descendants of the Communist (SED) regime have to be treated differently, because the East German regime was, over its forty-one year life, more repressive than the Polish, Hungarian or even, at the very end, the Soviet versions. "The point is, these were very *German* Communists," said one Social Democratis (SPD) politician who had been an East Berlin journalist until she was fired for a vaguely satirical magazine cover.[26]

□   □   □

German Communism's political legacy cannot yet be relegated to history. Most of the former Communist nations in East Central Europe have experienced a powerful revival of "post-Communist" parties, and East Germany is no exception. October 1994 elections made abundantly clear that the phenomenon of the PDS—the successor party to the Communist SED—cannot be ignored or wished away. In the Eastern Länder, the PDS with 1.7 million votes became the third largest party, well ahead of the FDP and the Greens, both of whom were routed in what used to be East Germany. In Berlin the PDS won four Bundestag districts outright, thus entitling the party to a Bundestag representation equal to its national vote share of 4.4 percent.

There is considerable disagreement about whether the PDS will fade before the next national elections or remain an enduring political force. The mid-term future of German politics depends very much on the answer.

Just under half of German voters in the October 16, 1994 national elections opted for a comfortable stability—a choice that translated into a thin government majority in the Bundestag. But the stability may prove illusory. The razor-thin margin of the coalition's Bundestag majority, the dramatic decline of the FDP, the SPD's strengthened control of the upper house of parliament (the Bundesrat), and the strong showing in the East of the post-Communist PDS all suggest a diminished capacity of the government to govern. To be sure, as Chancellor Kohl argued the night of the election, his new Bundestag majority of 10 seats is only two seats smaller than was Willy

Brandt's in 1969—and Brandt went on to conduct a bold, controversial, and ultimately successful *Ostpolitik*. Even so, it seems likely that this weakened government will now find it even more difficult to lead what is a still deeply divided country.

In this respect, Kohl's strategy against the PDS may have paid off in short-term election results, but seems problematic for the country's further political development. He was helped by the clumsy decision of Social Democrats in the eastern state of Sachsen-Anhalt to form a minority government with the Greens that depended for its survival on the abstention of the PDS. Thus it was possible for Kohl to charge the Social Democrats in general with insufficient vigilance against Communism. Given the historical circumstances, it was an incongruous appeal to anti-communism, as the old SPD strategist Egon Bahr reasonably complained: "Communism is dead, but anti-communism is still a powerful force."[27]

Kohl's campaign may have hurt the SPD, but it probably helped the PDS.[28] Even its harshest critics acknowledge that the PDS attracted voters from outside the old communist cadres. In particular, it scored well among young voters. Some observers see this as a reflection of resentment and wounded pride among eastern voters who are rebelling at the notion that 40 years of their history must be erased or, at most, remembered on West German terms. It is clear, at any rate, that genuine national unity is some ways away.

Throughout the early 1990s, however, it was the far Right rather than the post–Communist Left that captured the outside world's attention. The fabric of German civility seemed to unravel, as neo-Nazi gangs and skinhead thugs mounted full-scale pogroms against Turks and foreign refugees. During much of 1992 and into 1993, the morning radio news in Germany started off with what sounded like a ghastly weather report: a house of Vietnamese workers was attacked last night in Hoyerswerda; a Turkish family was burnt to death in Mölln. These outrages seemed even more alarming when considered in their international context—against the backdrop of far-right successes in France and Italy, not to mention Russia, where the party of nationalist demagogue Vladimir Zhirinovsky (himself having ties to the Munich rightist Gerhard Frey), received a share of the 1993 popular vote greater than Adolf Hitler's in 1930.[29] Was fascism proving to be the "last Internationale," in the words of one alarmed German historian?[30] Was this, to take up Maier's final dimension of "moral crisis," the ugly manifestation of a general loss of faith in doctrines of social progress?

German developments were in fact a great deal more ambiguous than such alarms would suggest. Immediately after the *Wende,* to be sure, the East Germans in particular expressed a natural and quite heavy dose of skepticism about any kind of social engineering along the lines of their disastrous experience with "real existing socialism." Nothing made it inevitable that East German youth would rebel only against the hypocrisies, economic failures, and police-state cruelties of the old regime; Communist ideology also included shibboleths and taboos for universal brotherhood and against racism. It is also true that the extreme German right has shared philosophically in the general program of modern, far-right populist movements in Western Europe, described by Hans-Georg Betz as blending a "rejection of individual and social equality and of political projects that seek to achieve it," an "opposition to the social integration of marginalized groups," and an "appeal to xenophobia, if not overt racism and anti-Semitism."[31] That certainly describes the official ideology of Germany's *Republikaner.* It also describes the practical ideology that Trier sociologist Roland Eckert identified in a study of 150 violent, right-wing criminals, who generally glorified war and violence, saw social inequality as inevitable and desirable, and viewed life as a conflict of ethnic and national groups.[32]

But in discussing German right-wing extremism, one needs to be careful. Leaving the volatile immigration issue aside for the moment, it is difficult to see where far-right ideology has had a significant impact on Germany's ideological center of gravity. There is certainly nothing in Germany like the erstwhile right-wing governing coalition of Berlusconi, Bossi and Fini in Italy. Nor have the *Republikaner,* or any other far rightist party, had the same core of enduring support enjoyed by France's National Front or Austria's Freedom Party (FPÖ). Indeed, the recent election successes of antiestablishment parties have been all on the political Left, as already noted. The *Republikaner,* with 2 percent of the national vote, failed again to reach the 5 percent threshold. This was roughly the same result as in the first all German election of 1990; it suggested that, after a high of 7.1 percent in the 1989 European elections and 12 percent in 1992 Baden-Württemburg state elections, the *Republikaner* constituted a spent force.[33]

This important point has been obscured largely in the international alarm that neo-Nazi terrorism and violence has inspired. The political threat posed by far-right parties is insignificant, especially compared to Italy and France. Unified Germany is not Weimar II; there is no present danger to the democratic order. In the wake of the murders of Turks, *millions* of Germans took to the streets of most major German cities for candlelight marches (*Lichterketten*) of solidarity with the victims.

This is not to say that the disorders of the early 1990s are unimportant. On the central matter of immigration, the autonomy and sovereignty of the German state has been impaired because the protective barrier of the Iron Curtain is gone, because the jumbo jet and cheap air travel are ever more factors in international migration, and because Islamic and African populations are booming. Refugees and other foreigners will continue to come to Germany and will remain in large numbers; their treatment will continue to be an important measure of the "quality," if not the stability of German democracy.[34] While stability seems sure, the quality is threatened, and the German government has failed in various ways to take the threat seriously enough.

In general, a confused and uncertain state conceded too much of the early initiative to skinheads and neo-Nazis. Partly this was a result of the breakdown of authority in the East. The disturbances of 1992 followed a depressing pattern. First came the decision to locate large numbers of refugees in East German dormitories, which were often old People's Army barracks. The housing arrangements were made without regard for the worsening socio-economic climate, and without any serious plans for protecting the asylum seekers. For gangs of youths—unemployed, bitter about their prospects, their heads filled with racist slogans and vague ideologies of glorified violence—the refugee and foreign-workers' housing presented an obvious target. When the gangs attacked, to their delight they found that the police response was pathetic. This, as Eckardt notes, was a critical factor that made East Germany the site of some of the most frightening riots. Eastern police forces were discredited and demoralized; they often lacked the authority to write traffic tickets that would not be thrown away the next moment.[35]

In the East German towns of Hoyerswerda and Rostock, during the long pogroms that terrorized and eventually drove asylum-seekers away, television cameras captured an chilling parallel to the Third Reich: throngs of townspeople standing by, cheering and, in some cases, helping out with the odd stone and Molotov cocktail. "There were seldom any clear fronts in Rostock-Lichtenhagen," *Der Spiegel* reported. "The police at times fought not against a defined group of thugs, but against an entire neighborhood."[36] This sobering fact does have to be balanced against the later *Lichterketten*, and it provided a tremendous morale boost to the thugs. Not only were they being cheered as heroes; they were conquering heroes, since the inevitable response of the authorities to these horrors would be to relocate the refugees. And such successes inevitably inspired other attacks across Germany.

The extreme Rightists were able to score a victory nationally as well, due to both the government's and the SPD opposition's inept handling of the immigration issue. As a matter of principal, Germany accepts no immigration, but until 1993 it had one of the most liberal political asylum laws in the world.[37] Anyone claiming to be politically persecuted in his home country had to be admitted into Germany until his or her claim was investigated. It was generally assumed that 90 percent of the claims would prove groundless, but since the investigation of claims, plus the appeals process, generally took years, this law had the practical effect of completely opening German borders. Between 1990 and 1992, Germany took in nearly a million refugees, more than the rest of the EC combined.[38] Proposals to tighten the law were resisted fiercely by the SPD and parts of the FDP, junior partner in the governing coalition. The opponents of change argued that Germany's history of Nazi persecution meant it had a solemn duty to give the benefit of the doubt to anyone claiming similar persecution. It was a good example of postwar German idealism: too much moralism; too little moral calculation. In the end, the law did have to be tightened, but by putting off decision until too late, Bonn had to bestow it as a political victory on the rioters and murderers.[39]

The *Verfassungsschutz* (Office for the Protection of the Constitution, a kind of German FBI) now worries about a long-term terrorist threat from the Right. There are signs that some of the more sophisticated Right extremists are organizing themselves into terrorist cells modelled after the left-wing Red Army Faction (RAF). The first targets appear to be "anti-fascists," a category that starts with the anarchic "*Autonom*" Left, but rapidly expands to include anyone too vocally opposed to the xenophobic outrages. In December 1993, a series of letterbombs went out to prominent Austrian socialists and minority advocates; among the victims was Vienna mayor Helmut Zilk, who had several fingers blown off. At about the same time, a list of two hundred "enemies" circulated in rightist computer mailbox networks in Germany.[40]

How, overall, should we assess the German state's performance in the face of xenophobic violence and extremism? The state did show itself able to shake off a kind of moralistic paralysis and deal with the crisis. Changing the asylum law cut applications for refugee status in half.[41] At the same time, following public outrage at some of the lenient sentences handed down to right-wing thugs, the punishments were significantly tightened.

Serious acts of right-wing violence declined in 1993.[42] However belatedly, the state demonstrated that it could react pragmatically. What it has not been able to do is to summon the trappings and symbolism of moral leadership effectively. Consider the uninspiring manner in which it has dealt with the citizenship issue. Tightening of the asylum law was coupled with liberalized provisions for German-born children of foreign parents to apply for German citizenship. And yet the opportunity to turn this change into a compelling gesture of reassurance to Turks and other minorities was squandered; for in principle, citizenship is still determined by bloodlines, that is racial mythology.

A big part of the problem may be Helmut Kohl, who seems incapable of the kind of moral symbolism of Willy Brandt's electrifying fall to his knees at the site of the Warsaw ghetto. The chancellor has also suffered by constant comparison to former president Richard von Weizsäcker, whose public remarks speak eloquently to the German requirement for a new "civil courage."[43] Kohl, by contrast, has repeatedly refused to attend victims' funerals, and complains petulantly that German *left-wing* violence and terrorism does not get the attention it deserves.

But neither the chancellor nor, indeed, his center-right party are exclusively at fault. There is something in present-day German culture that stymies any very elevated moral discourse. In delivering the speech quoted above, von Weizsäcker was splattered with eggs hurled at him by screaming *Autonom* demonstrators. Kohl is himself the constant target of screaming and eggs; he shows less courage in facing them, perhaps, but part of the blame has to be shared by a Left culture so ready to demonize, to portray political opponents as Nazi apologists. It is not just the anarchists. German political culture is highly polarized even though, programmatically, there is not much distance between Left and Right. There seems little to argue about in terms of social benefits, but a tremendous willingness to do battle over historic symbols. In a nation with so much horrible history to argue over, this battle is, perhaps, the most debilitating shackle on the effectiveness of the state.

NATIONAL IDENTITY AND GERMAN POWER

"*Es kennzeichnet eben die Deutschen, daß die Frage, 'Was ist deutsch' niemals ausstirbt.*" After two cataclysmic world wars, the descent into Nazi bestiality, forty-five years of national division, and the disappointments of reunification, Friedrich Nietzsche's question—"What is German?"

—certainly lives on. Nowhere are questions of national identity more excruciatingly sensitive than in Germany. Nowhere are the answers less certain. And nowhere are they more important.

The problem, put simply, is to develop a vocabulary and ethos of national pride and community, without denying the national responsibility for the holocaust and other horrors of World War II. This is necessary for two reasons. First, symbols of national pride should not be surrendered to the far Right—not without a fight, anyway. Second, Germany has tremendous power that will be used, for better or for worse, in the European and international arena. It can only be used for the better if political leadership is able to develop and articulate an enlightened sense of national purpose.

The first reason should not be discounted merely because right-wing extremism appears, for the moment, to be contained. Numerous thoughtful Germans see the perceived illegitimacy of German patriotism to be a national liability. Retired German diplomat Klaus Blech emphasized this point with an aphorism: "There is nothing more dangerous than a stupid conservative, and nothing more necessary than an intelligent one."[44] The German historian Arnulf Baring (an intelligent conservative) argues that German democracy may indeed be more fragile than, for example, the British version.[45] German democracy has never been tested by hard times; economic difficulties seem manageable for now, but success cannot be taken for granted. Willy Brandt's controversial widow, Brigitte Seebacher-Brandt, identified the same dilemma when she observed that: "In Germany today, a Skinhead is considered a right-wing radical because he raises a sign that says, 'I'm proud to be German. . . .' When it is left to Skinheads and other questionable elements to be proud of Germany, we cannot be very cheerful about the future."[46]

The task of developing a sense of German national community will be difficult, of course. Lingering bitterness from the 1980s *Historikerstreit* gives some indication of just how difficult. Since this "Historians Debate" in many ways foreshadowed united Germany's self-analysis, it must be worrying that it could not be conducted in a more constructive spirit. The fury of charge, countercharge and character assassination, plus the rather silly obsession with the question of Nazi evil's "uniqueness," obscured the fact that protagonists on both sides of the debate were making some reasoned arguments. The left sociologist Jürgen Habermas was probably right to argue that not much in history can offer the Germans as much consolation as a future-oriented "constitutional patriotism."[47] But both *Frankfurt Allgemeine Zeitung* editor Joachim Fest and Erlangen historian Michael

Stürmer were also right to argue that the writing and rewriting of history cannot be abandoned simply because postwar German national consciousness is grounded in historical taboos.[48] And even though the Berlin historian Ernst Nolte's suggestion that the "'gulag archipelago' [was] more *original* [*ursprünglicher*] than Auschwitz"[49] smacks of moral mystification, he was nonetheless justified to complain that "[he] who criticizes the Third Reich in order to strike at the Federal Republic or the capitalist system must appear as the fool that he is."[50]

Taboos about the past are matched by shibboleths regarding the future. The German political class's near-unanimous commitment to European unity is, in itself, constructive and reassuring. But that commitment should not be allowed to turn into an alibi for not facing up to these pressing questions of national identity. Indeed, the older and better-defined nation states, for example France, and even Britain, may be in a better position to hand over much sovereignty to a European Union, because they can have a more reasoned public debate about what they are giving up and what they are to retain.

Germans, on the other hand, tend to throw the "nationalist" epitaph at anyone who, like Bavarian minister president Edmund Stoiber, challenges the Europeanists' conventional wisdom. To be sure, Stoiber has at times appealed in a disturbing fashion to some of the more retrograde elements of German nationalism. (He did so, moreover, without the political skill and evident good humor of his predecessor, Franz Josef Strauss.) But he was only stating the obvious with his reminder, somehow controversial, that the nation-state is not about to whither away.[51] National politics—whether French, Italian, British, or German—cannot and should not be abolished.

The most immediate institutional intrusion on German national sovereignty is the Maastricht Treaty's plan for transforming the European Monetary System (EMS) into a genuine monetary union with a European central bank managing a European currency. By abolishing the Deutschemark, Germany would be surrendering not only the instrument of its monetary hegemony in Europe, but also an important national symbol of postwar prosperity and stability.

There are sound economic arguments for the monetary union. But there are two outstanding dangers as well. The first is very simple: By abolishing the Deutschemark, while giving the German population the idea that the purpose is mainly to deprive them of excessive power, Europe's leaders risk undermining German confidence in European cooperation. That would be a perverse result if, as *Financial Times* editor Martin Wolf has argued, the main purpose of European Union is to retain German confidence in such cooperation.

The second danger is more subtle. It derives from the observation that nations tend to pursue some version of national interest, even if they pretend otherwise. Pretending otherwise, or pursuing such interests unconsciously, can be more dangerous than explicit *Realpolitik,* because it is more likely to cause confusion and misunderstanding. George Soros has argued convincingly that such confusion contributed to the unravelling of the EMS, which in turn has undermined general confidence in European integration. Confidence, or lack of it, is self-reinforcing; it drives what Soros called "the 'boom/bust sequence,' which can be observed from time to time in financial markets; and [which] is also applicable to the integration and disintegration of the European Community."[52]

For more than a decade after its inauguration in 1979, the EMS was a well-tuned mechanism for encouraging the economic convergence of EC member states. There were, to be sure, crises along the way, such as was provoked by the reflationary policies of the French socialist government from 1981 to 1983. But such crises tended to confirm the fundamental convergence of policy, as the French Socialists, for example, made a clear choice in favor of its economic partnership with Germany, even at the cost of high unemployment at home. It was, in Soros's terms, a condition of "near-equilibrium" in which the "divergence between the participants' thinking and the actual state of affairs . . . [was] relatively small and self-correcting. . . . "[53] Participants thought that overall European economic policy was increasingly determined by a strong and economically virtuous Germany—and they were, for the most part, correct. Expectations of Europe-wide, high-growth, low-inflation policies tended to support and ease the execution of those policies.

The change came with German reunification, which, because of East Germany's economic ruin, turned out to be far more expensive than the Bonn government originally wanted to admit. Germany's role in the European economy then fundamentally shifted. The Bundesbank, which had anchored the EMS from its 1978 beginnings, now started to pull the system loose from its moorings. Raising interest rates to fight the inflationary effects of Bonn's deficit financing of reunification, the bank also forced up the general rate of interest among its EMS partners—this at a time when Europe was entering its deepest recession since World War II.

The crisis was worsened by the actions of European leaders, who behaved as though nothing had changed. The system was based on the assumption that German anti-inflationary zeal would be accompanied by fiscal rectitude. But now, even though the fiscal side had gone awry and German price inflation was higher than, for example, French inflation, financial markets still required a premium of higher French interest rates to allow the franc to stay pegged to the Deutschemark. Rather than devaluing the franc, Paris dutifully paid the premium, with painful results in terms of unemployment.

The divergence between reality and expectations—at least as represented by the statements of EC leaders—became very large; what Soros has called "far-from-equilibrium" conditions. Around September of 1992, financial markets finally noticed the divergence and began their relentless assault on the EMS. British sterling and the Italian lira fell out of the exchange-rate mechanism. The franc, thanks to massive support from the Bundesbank, was held to its Deutschemark parity for another year. But finally, the franc had to be released from its strict EMS obligation; a radical enlargement of currency bands meant that the exchange-rate mechanism was, for the time being, suspended.

For Germany, three lessons can be drawn from this experience. First, German economic and monetary power is formidable and pervasive. Second, it follows that Germany's problems are Europe's problems: Germany, like America, has demonstrated than an economic hegemon is most dangerous when it is weakening.[54] Finally, an honest reckoning of German national interests is not an obstacle but rather a prerequisite for getting monetary union back on track. Specifically, Germany needs a full and open debate about the circumstances in which it could be in its national interest to trade away the Deutschemark.

There is nothing inherently unsolvable about Europe's current monetary crisis. The history of the EMS up to 1989 demonstrated a successful formula for member states to trade some monetary sovereignty for a greater overall mastery of their own national economies. It must be possible to find a new currency formula for reconciling the interests of the member states, especially since the alternative—permanent dissolution of the EMS—would mean the effective end of a European economic community.[55]

□   □   □

German confusion about national power is most evident in debates about military force. These debates started to gather momentum soon after Germany achieved unity and recovered something like full sovereignty. The Gulf War—and Germany's much-noted absence from the military coalition against Iraq—sparked a national controversy about whether and under what circumstances German military force might be used for purposes other than the direct defense of Germany's (or a NATO ally's) territorial integrity. This was couched as a constitutional question until July 1994, when Germany's highest court ruled that nothing in the German constitution precluded a responsible use of military force abroad, if exercised in the context of alliance obligations.[56] The deeper objection to the "out-of-area" use of military force was grounded, of course, in a moral argument; the German left in particular had adopted an increasingly pacifist worldview.[57] It was argued that the not-so-distant Nazi past gave the Germans an extra responsibility to seek peaceful solutions to conflicts and, above all, never to send the *Bundeswehr* anywhere the *Wehrmacht* had once marched.

This moral argument is illogical on at least two levels. First, it assumes that the Federal Republic of Germany is a kind of moral successor to the Hitler regime, which it is not. Second, although peaceful solutions are usually preferable, they are not always available. For segments of the German Left to insist that it should always be possible to find "political" rather than military solutions to conflicts shows little understanding of the lessons of German history; it ignores that fact that something like "total war" was required to stop Hitler.

It is important to bring some historical perspective to this criticism: Although a pacifist moralism can be annoying to Germany's allies, it is indeed a vast improvement on what came before it. The deeper question is whether German military culture—as it exists today and as it seems to be developing—serves or hinders European peace and stability.

To answer that question one should begin by distinguishing between two related but not-quite-identical sources of German foreign policy. One is the anti-military sentiment, which is an understandable, if not entirely logical, reaction to a traditional German militarism and to the horrors of the Third Reich. The second source was a postwar tradition of hard-headed, albeit enlightened, pursuit of German national interests. The phrase "national interest" is something of a taboo in German discourse, but certainly Konrad Adenauer was pursuing nothing else when he consciously set about tying the Federal Republic down in a web of Western institutions. Never again, Adenauer knew, could Germany afford to find itself isolated in its immense power, inspiring fear and rivalry among its neighbors. This *Westbindung* or "*Einbindungspolitik*"—a policy of intentionally restricting German freedom of action in order to earn the trust that would allow Germans to pursue their truly vital interests—was continued by Brandt and perfected by Hans-Dietrich Genscher.[58] Maastricht was part of the same logic: another step toward a European Union which, while theoretically restricting German power, was consciously tied to the fulfillment of an overriding German interest in reunification.

In a broad historical context, restraints on German power are welcome. If one takes World War I as the model for how European order can break down, then the inhibitions of the major powers and, especially, the neutralization of Germany as a great military power, must be considered positive. While the major outside powers have not done much to stop the carnage in former Yugoslavia, at least they have not been drawn in on opposing sides of the conflict.

If, on the other hand, one looks to Hitler-style aggression as the greater danger, then failure to take strong action against that aggression is far more disquieting than the threat of unstable coalitions spiraling out of control into general warfare. This is not to say that Serbia poses a general threat comparable to that posed by Nazi Germany. But the Western democracies' "corrosive feeling of inadequacy" about confronting Serbia is another element (as Maier argues) of general "moral crisis." It recalls the democracies' similar passivity in the 1930s and makes the post-1989 hopes for Europe "seem hollow," just as they seemed "after Ethiopia, the Spanish Republic, Austria, and Czechoslovakia were wiped out" in the years leading up to World War II.[59]

None of this is meant to imply that the world would be a better place if Germany suddenly reacquired a taste for unilateral military adventures. But that prospect looks extremely unlikely. More realistic, and therefore more disturbing, is the prospect of Germany constituting the European Union's pacifist core, preventing Europe from consolidating itself as an effective and responsible world power.

CONCLUSION

The post–1990 Federal Republic of Germany is successor to one of the most successful state formulas of the Cold War era. But that success was partly based on the artificial and, as it turned out, very convenient suspension of certain elements of state sovereignty and responsibility. It does not appear possible to continue this suspension. The Germans confront the paradox that at the very moment when the nation-state in general is in the midst of an historic crisis, they must finally come to re-embrace it as the organizing principle of national life.

Germany requires a *national* response, conceived and implemented by an effective state, to each of its three crises. That does not mean an egoistically *nationalist* response. The jobs crisis, for example, is obviously international in its causes and consequences. In a Europe of open borders, not to mention a world of open trade, an exclusively national solution would be nonsensical. But to win popular acceptance of various austerity measures—whether cuts in middle-class entitlements, stagnating and even falling real wages, or a continued burden of high unemployment—some measure of national solidarity will be required. The same holds true for the country's moral crisis, centered on the stubborn psychological divide between East and West.

Finally, the state must find some deeper reservoir of national feeling to tap into for fulfilling the country's international responsibilities, including military ones. That does not mean militarist nationalism, but rather a conception of higher values, tied to national values, for which it would be plausible to sacrifice one's life. This conception will be difficult to find, but is probably located somewhere between "Europe," "Germany" and simple humanity.

◆ NOTES TO CHAPTER 6 ◆

1. The total cost by the year 2000 has been estimated to amount to between DM 1.034 trillion and DM 2.3 trillion. See Heinz Suhr, *Was kostet uns die ehemalige DDR?* (Frankfurt am Main: Eichborn, 1990). Net transfers in 1991 and 1992 were DM 139 billion and DM 180 billion respectively. *Monatsberichte der deutschen Bundesbank,* March 1992.
2. Eric Hobsbawm, "The New Threat to History," *The New York Review of Books* 49:21 (December 16, 1993), p. 64.
3. Charles S. Maier, "Democracy and Its Discontents," *Foreign Affairs* 73:4 (July/August 1994), p. 51.
4. *Gesetz zur Regelung offener Vermögensfragen vom 23. September 1990,* text, as amended in Dr. Helmut Grieger, ed., *Codex Iuris, Wiedervereinigungsrecht II—Eigentum, Investition, Vermögen,* Second Edition, (August 1992).
5. Frederick R. Fucci, "Whither the Treuhandanstalt?" in Gale Mattox, Marian Gibbon and A. Bradley Shingleton, eds., *Dimensions of German Unification: Economic, Social, and Legal Analyses* (Boulder, Colorado: Westview Press, 1994), p. 22.
6. Ibid, p. 22.
7. Ibid, p. 22.
8. Birgit Breuel, in roundtable discussion with members of the Aspen/Draeger Study Group on Structural Unemployment, Berlin, May 18, 1994.
9. This is of course, a hard charge to prove, since it concerns the inner motivations of West German investors. But a number of East and West Germans involved in the privatization process are convinced of its truth, including Berlin banking figures who have said so in confidential interviews with this author, and including Breuel herself, who has said so publicly. Ibid.

10. The official rate of unemployment in the eastern Länder in 1994 was 14.6 percent, but some estimates, which include part-time and make-work schemes, place the correct figure at closer to 25 percent.
11. Breuel, Aspen/Draeger Study Group.
12. "Germany Survey," *The Economist*, May 21, 1994, p. 10.
13. Ibid, p. 28.
14. Deutsche Bank Research, "First Positive signals on the German labour market, but still no grounds for relief," *Focus: Germany* 138 (Aug. 30, 1994), p. 3.
15. Ibid, p. 7.
16. Maier, "Democracy and Its Discontents," p. 54.
17. The political programs of *Neues Forum* and *Bündnis 90* have their origins in the writings of the East German dissidents Robert Havemann and Rudolf Bahro. See especially Bahro, *Die Alternative* (Köln/Frankfurt am Main: Europäische Verlagsanstalt, 1977); and Havemann, *Rückantwort auf die Hauptverwaltung "Ewige Wahrheiten"* (Munich: Piper, 1971). Ironically, with the marginalization of the Bürgerbewegung, it is the SED successor party, the PDS, that has taken up the "Third Way" slogans. See the PDS manifesto, Gregor Gysi, ed., *Wir brauchen einen dritten Weg* (Berlin: Konkret Literatur, 1990).
18. Jens Reich, *Abschied von den Lebenslügen* (Berlin: Rowohlt, 1992).
19. See *Der Spiegel*, June 25, 1990, pp. 162-168; *Die Zeit*, July 27, 1990, p. 1.
20. Many East German artists cite the phenomenon of the Beatles as an important *political* event in their lives.
21. See the interview with Jurek Becker, *Der Spiegel*, July 18, 1977.
22. Inge Schmidt, speaking at an Aspen Berlin conference on "Art and Politics," April 4, 1994.
23. *The New York Times*, July 12, 1993, p. A13.
24. Marion Gräfin Dönhoff, "Die Nürnberger Prozesse: ein abschreckendes Beispiel," in Dönhoff et. al., *Weil das Land Versöhnung Braucht* (Hamburg: Rowohlt, 1993), pp. 78-79. Former president Richard von Weizsäcker has also come out in favor of an amnestie, albeit a restricted one. See his interview, "Das Strafen muß ein Ende Finden," *Der Spiegel*, January 1995, pp. 22-25.
25. Joachim Gauck, "Wut und Schmerz der Opfer," *Die Zeit*, January 20, 1995, p. 5. Gauck, a theologian, was placed in charge of the Stasi files after the end of the GDR.
26. Conversation with Berlin parliamentarian Anke Reuther, September 7, 1994 in Berlin.
27. Egon Bahr, conversation with author, September 21, 1994 in Berlin.
28. This, at any rate, was the assessment of many observers including former German president von Weizsäcker in "Das Strafen muß ein Ende finden," p. 23.
29. In Russia's December 1993 parliamentary elections, Zhirinovsky's Liberal-Democratic party won 23 percent of the popular vote, along with a lesser share of seats in the new parliament—66 out of 450, or 14.7 percent. In Germany's 1930 Reichstag elections, the Nazis won a popular vote of 18.3 percent and a comparable share of seats, 107 of 595.
30. The comment was from Berlin's Free University professor Wolfgang Wippermann; see Nicolas Kumanoff, *Right-Wing Extremism and German Democracy*, Report of an Aspen Institute Berlin Conference, June 18-19, 1994 (Berlin: Aspen Institute, 1994), pp. 3-4.
31. Hans-Georg Betz, *Radical Right-Wing Populism in Western Europe* (New York: St. Martin's Press, 1994), p. 4.
32. Kumanoff, *Right-Wing Extremism and German Democracy*, p. 6.
33. Betz, *Radical Right-Wing Populism in Western Europe*, pp. 17-19.
34. This is a point borrowed from Adrian Lyttleton, who speaks persuasively of the threat to the quality of Italian democracy from Berlusconi's right-wing coalition government. See Kumanoff, *Right-Wing Extremism and Italian Democracy*, p. 6; and Lyttleton, "Italy: The Triumph of TV," *The New York Review of Books*, August 11, 1994, pp. 25-29.

35. Kumanoff, *Right-Wing Extremism and German Democracy*, pp. 8-9.
36. "Ernstes Zeichen an der Wand," *Der Spiegel*, August 31, 1992, p. 20.
37. *New York Times*, December 8, 1992, p. A1.
38. Registered asylum seekers numbered 193,063 in 1990; 256,112 in 1991; and 438,191 in 1992. *Statistisches Jahrbuch für die BRD, 1993*, p. 73.
39. For a summary of the changes, "Dokumentation der Ergebnisse der Verhandlungen zu Asyl und Zuwanderung; Auszüge aus der Parteienvereinbarung zur Änderung des Asylrechts," *Der Tagespiegel* (Berlin), December 12, 1992, p. 2.
40. On the letterbomb to Zilk, "So friedlich," *Der Spiegel*, December 13, 1993, pp. 140-142. On the development of German right-wing terrorism, see the interview with Ernst Uhrlau, director of the Hamburg Verfassungsschutz, in *Der Spiegel*, September 14, 1992; see also Uhrlau's presentation to an Aspen Institute Conference in Kumanoff, *Right-Wing Extremism and German Democracy*, pp. 10-13; and the presentation of German Federal Verfassungsschutz officer Joachim Fricke, in Felicitas von Aretin and Matthias Brunk, *Rechtsextremismus in Deutschland: Wie Groß ist die Kriminelle Energie?*, report of an Aspen Institute Berlin Conference of Feb. 23, 1994 (Berlin: Aspen Institute, 1994).
41. "Zahl der Asylanträge stark gesunken; Kanther sieht inneren Frieden gestärkt," *Süddeutsche Zeitung*, March 10, 1994, p. 1. By October 1994 the number was down to 10,000 per month, roughly a quarter of the average for 1992. *International Herald Tribune*, November 16, 1994, p. 6.
42. From 2,584 in 1992 to 1,699 through November 1993. *Der Spiegel*, December 27, 1993, p. 70.
43. See, for example, von Weizsäcker's November 8, 1992 speech before a Berlin demonstration against xenophobia, "Wir alle sind zum Handeln aufgerufen," *Der Tagespiegel* (Berlin), November 9, 1992, p. 6.
44. At an Aspen Institute Berlin conference on *"Germany: Four Years After the Wall Collapsed,"* May 27, 1994.
45. Cited in Kumanoff, *Right Wing Extremism and German Democracy*, p. 18.
46. See Brigitte Seebacher-Brandt in *Estarrende Gesellschaft in Bewegten Zeiten*, protocoll of the Alfred Herrhausen Gesellschaft für Internationalen Dialog, 1. Jahreskolloquium, June 11-12, 1993 (Stuttgart: Schäffer-Poeschel Verlag, 1993), p. 123.
47. Jürgen Habermas, "Eine Art Schadenabwicklung; Die apologetischen Tendenzen in der deutschen Zeitgeschictsschreibung," *Die Zeit*, July 11, 1986.
48. "The process of historicization will continue, for it has the most powerful imaginable ally on its side: time. That Habermas . . . not only calls for a static understanding of the Nazi regime, but also fights against passing time, makes him the advocate of a hopeless cause": Joachim Fest, postface to *Historikerstreit* (Munich: Serie Piper, 1987), p. 390. See also Michael Stürmer, "Geschichte in geschichtslosem Land," *Frankfurter Allgemeine Zeitung*, April 25, 1986.
49. Ernst Nolte, "Die Vergangenheit, die nicht vergehen will," *Frankfurter Allgemeine Zeitung*, June 6, 1986. Emphasis added.
50. Ernst Nolte, "Die negative Lebendigkeit des Dritten Reiches. Eine Frage aus dem Blickwinkel des Jahres 1980," *Frankfurter Allgemeine Zeitung*, July 24, 1980.
51. See the interview with Stoiber, "Es gab einmal eine europäische Bewegung in Deutschland . . . das ist vorbei," *Süddeutsche Zeitung*, November 2, 1993, p. 14. On the controversy unleashed by Stoiber's interview, see *Frankfurter Allgemeine Zeitung*, November 4, 1993, p. 1; November 8, 1993, p. 1; *Der Spiegel*, November 8, 1993.
52. George Soros, "Prospects for European Disintegration," delivered as the Aspen Institute Berlin's Wallenberg Lecture, September 29, 1993.
53. Ibid.
54. On the American case, see Dana H. Allin and David P. Calleo, "Geostrategic Trends and the World Economy," in Desmond Ball, ed., *Australia and the World: Prologue and Prospects* (Canberra: Australian National University, 1990).

55. "The important point about my boom/bust theory," argues Soros, "is that there is nothing inevitable about it. The typical boom/bust sequence is initially self-reinforcing and, eventually, self-defeating, but it can be aborted or diverted at any point." Speaking in the depth of the 1993 recession, Soros had his own prescription for restoring confidence: France should abandon its "franc fort" policy and allow its economy to grow and exports to rise at the expense of Germany's; an even deeper German recession would then bring down Frankfurt interest rates to a point where the economies were more compatible. At that point, monetary union should be imposed, not gradually but immediately. See Soros, "Prospects for European Disintegration."

56. "Das Urteil des Bundesverfassungsgerichts vom 12. Juli 1994" in *Europa Archiv*, 15 (October 8, 1994).

57. Although there are some realists in the Party leadership, the SPD as a whole remains adamant that German forces participate only in traditional UN peace-keeping missions. Recent Party resolutions promise that as long as the SPD maintains its veto power, "there will be no participation of the Bundeswehr in wars of the Gulf War model." Instead, conflict will be prevented by an international security system based on "the rule of justice" and "non-aggression." SPD, *Perspektiven einer neuen Außen- und Sicherheitspolitik,* Resolution passed by the SPD convention in Wiesbaden, November 16-19, 1993 (Bonn: Vorstand der SPD, Referat Öffentlichkeitsarbeit, 1993), pp. 13-15.

58. Gunther Hellmann, "Einbindungspolitik: German Foreign Policy and the Art of Declaring 'Total Peace,'" unpublished paper presented at the XVIth World Congress of the International Political Science Association, Aug. 20-25, 1994, in Berlin; and Timothy Garton Ash, "Germany's Choice," *Foreign Affairs* 73:4 (July/August, 1994), pp. 65-81.

59. Maier, "Democracy and Its Discontents," p. 55.

·7·

Fin de Siècle Canada:
The Federal Government in Retreat

Gregory P. Marchildon

The general public has never been more dissatisfied with the performance of the Canadian state. Anger and alienation seem to pervade
an environment in which politicians and public servants now try to
operate. The last federal election in October 1993 witnessed the decimation
of two of Canada's three national parties and the phoenix-like rise of two
new regional parties, one representing Western Canada's frustration with
Ottawa, the other urging Quebec's withdrawal from the federation. Many
of the new members of Parliament belonging to the Reform Party and the
Bloc Québécois are first-time politicians sent to Ottawa to redress historic
wrongs on behalf of their region with little regard for the national interest,
and in the case of the separatist Bloc from Quebec, quite hostile toward the
concept of a "Canadian national" interest.[1]

In a sense, the 1993 election was a product of the country's national referendum held one year earlier. At that time, a majority of Canadian citizens
voted *against* a constitutional accord designed to keep the country together
by attempting to accommodate the virtually irreconcilable demands of
Quebec and the Western provinces, as well as Aboriginal Canadians. The
tortuous two years that led to the Charlottetown Accord of August 1992 was
the most open, democratic, and expensive (almost $300 million was spent

by the federal government alone) constitutional process ever undertaken by a national polity. In a public referendum held in October 1992, Canadian voters nonetheless voted against the compromise, despite the fact that the agreement was supported by the governing party, the two largest federal opposition parties, aboriginal leaders, and ten provincial and two territorial governments of diverse political background.[2]

The purpose of this essay is to diagnose the most important domestic and international factors responsible for the country's current malaise. I argue that the Canadian state that emerged after World War II and the Canadian identity that it fostered has now become dysfunctional. The central government's vigorous attempts to construct a pan-Canadian nationality have been thwarted increasingly by the nation- and state-building efforts of Quebec since the 1950s, as well as the state-building efforts of certain provinces outside central Canada that have piggybacked upon Quebec's gains to improve their previously peripheral position relative to Ottawa. These competing efforts, particularly those that began in Quebec during the early 1960s, and pursued by the provinces of Alberta and Saskatchewan during the early 1970s, have rapidly devolved power to the provincial level of government. Meanwhile the formal institutions, constitutional laws, as well as Ottawa's general approach and assumptions, have remained highly centralized. As a consequence, provincial governments have taken on increasing responsibilities since the 1960s. At the same time, encouraged by its lopsided power over taxation and thus spending, the federal government remains immersed in areas of provincial jurisdiction. This has produced constitutional confusion, some duplication of programs and services, and much overlap in terms of responsibilities.

INTRODUCTION TO THE CANADIAN STATE

The "state" has a different connotation for federal and confederal entities such as the United States, Canada, Germany, and Switzerland than it does for unitary states such as France and the United Kingdom. The less centralized the federal or confederal state, the more decision-making authority is exercised by substate political units. In other words, the "state" is far from monolithic. As illustrated in Table 7.1, whether we use as a measure the autonomous fiscal capacity or the total expenditures of the two constitutionally recognized levels of government, Canada is the most decentralized country in the advanced industrial world.[3] With the weakest central government relative to the United States, Germany, and most surprising,

Switzerland—the country conventionally thought of as the most decentralized in the OECD—Canada also lays claim to the weakest government at the municipal or local levels.[4]

TABLE 7.1:

COMPARATIVE DECENTRALIZATION IN CANADA, SWITZERLAND, THE UNITED STATES, AND GERMANY.

Level of Government	Canada	Switzerland*	United States	Germany
Allocation of public sector revenues before transfers				
Federal/Central	49.0	53.3	59.4	64.1
Province/Canton/State	40.5	24.6	24.4	22.3
Municipal/Local	10.5	22.1	16.1	13.7
Allocation of public sector revenues (except debt loan repayments)				
Federal/Central	43.6	48.5	55.9	59.4
Province/Canton/State	40.6	29.3	23.5	24.6
Municipal/Local	15.7	22.2	20.6	17.1

*Swiss public sector revenues and expenditures for 1984, the most current data collected by the International Monetary Fund (IMF).

Source: IMF, *Government Finance Statistics* (Washington, DC: IMF, 1993).

Moreover, due to the enormous areas of responsibilities that have fallen to provincial governments over time, the federal government transfers a significant percentage of its relatively small share of public revenues to the Canadian provinces (and the provinces, in turn, transfer a large share of their total revenues to the municipalities for which they are constitutionally responsible). The result is evident. Canadian provinces exercise a degree of political power unmatched among substate units in the OECD.[5] Nevertheless, the provinces are hindered by the truncated nature of their taxation powers as delineated by the constitution and defined by the courts.[6]

This was not always the case. Before social program spending on health, welfare, and education began to grow exponentially in the 1960s, the federal government took a far greater share of revenues in order to fund what were then its relatively more expansive responsibilities.[7] By the 1970s, however, when such social spending had become the largest part of public expenditures, a gap emerged between the revenue-generating capacity of both levels of government and their respective expenditure responsibilities. The federal government used its financial muscle to set national standards in program and service delivery, creating in effect an intricate federal-provincial social safety net. Federal transfers came in the form of shared financing and conditional grants, later institutionalized in the Canada Assistance Plan (CAP) and Established Program Financing (EPF). Over time, however, the federal government's control over this complex intergovernmental fiscal arrangement began to weaken as federal tax revenues declined relative to the provinces, and as provinces, especially Quebec, began to opt out of national programs.[8]

In summary, Canada has become a country in which the provinces bear the burden of fiscal responsibilities yet must depend upon Ottawa for the revenue necessary to meet them. It is the most decentralized country in the advanced industrial world yet it remains burdened with a constitution that ranks among the most centralized. And it is a country in which one province, Quebec, is already exercising many of the powers of a full-fledged Westphalian state, including critical aspects of immigration and foreign policy.

Soon after the election of the Parti Québécois in the autumn of 1994, a draft bill now passed in Quebec's National Assembly declaring Quebec a sovereign country, and a referendum on the province of Quebec's separation from the federation slated for 1995, the continuing existence of the Canadian state once again has been called into question.[9] In reality, a sizeable number of the francophone Québécois elite has been working toward a decentralized option at least since the 1960s. They have achieved much in practice but little in constitutional terms, and this has prompted more radical sovereigntists to demand secession. Although a referendum on "sovereignty-association" failed in 1980, the collapse of the Meech Lake Accord ten years later gave new potency to the secessionist argument. Today even English-Canadians are beginning to prepare for what they had previously believed was unthinkable—the possible balkanization of what had been one of the most politically stable and wealthy countries in the world.[10]

This conflict over the appropriate balance between centralization and decentralization has long historical roots. Although originally referred to as a confederation,[11] Canada's first constitution, the British North America Act of 1867, was highly centralist. Drafted while the Civil War was raging, the English-Canadian Fathers of Confederation wanted a central government with the lion's share of powers in order to minimize arguments based on "states' rights." In an ideal world, they would have preferred a unitary state but the French-Canadian Fathers of Confederation insisted upon constitutionally empowered provinces in order to protect and enhance the jurisdiction of Quebec as the principal homeland of French-Canadians.[12]

By the mid-twentieth century, the relationship between the central government and the government of Quebec had become increasingly strained as the federal government used the emergency created by the Second World War to control taxation and construct a national social safety net that would act as a Keynesian-type stabilizer. While defensive at first, the Quebec government's position became more aggressive during the "Quiet Revolution" of the 1960s—the process of rapid social and political modernization that would eventually create a French-speaking Québécois business elite. At this time, Quebec began to opt out of various federal programs, receiving funding from the central government in order to administer its own programs. Although some grumbled about the precedent being set, opting-out did, at least temporarily, improve relations between Quebec and the central government.[13]

In the 1970s, however, constitutional politics became more adversarial as the question of the proper balance between central and provincial power was pushed to the foreground. Provincial governments dedicated to greater decentralization and even separation were elected. The Lougheed and Blakeney governments of Alberta and Saskatchewan demanded the right to use resource revenues for economic diversification in order to lessen what they considered Western Canada's debilitating dependence on Central Canada.[14] In Quebec, René Levesque's Parti Québécois government wanted to take the province out of the federation, albeit on terms that preserved the largest degree of economic integration possible.[15]

To some it seemed as if the Western provincial governments had joined forces with the separatist government of Quebec in a bid to decentralize the country. The Trudeau government in Ottawa attempted to turn the tide through centralizing measures, initiating an era of confrontation between the two orders of government. High-tax energy policies were designed to transfer western oil and gas royalties from provincial to central government coffers, and "national" energy pricing—controlled by a federal agency—subsidized "imports" to central Canada at the expense of Western-Canadian producers.[16] Then, fighting the Parti Québécois in the referendum campaign of 1980, Pierre Trudeau made vague promises of constitutional renewal if the people of Quebec voted against the sovereignty option.[17]

After winning the campaign, the central government unilaterally attempted to impose and repatriate[18] the constitution without the "renewal" —interpreted as decentralization in Quebec and some regions of Western Canada—originally promised. The provinces opposed the federal government's action both politically and legally, finally forcing a negotiated settlement with all provinces except Quebec, which continued its opposition to the constitution. While the Western provinces (now joined by Newfoundland) received constitutional recognition of their control over resources, Quebec could not have received what it was demanding without a wholesale dismantling of the central government. Quebec withdrew until new governments in both Ottawa and Quebec City were installed in 1984-1985, beginning a new round of constitutional talks aimed at bringing Quebec back into the constitutional fold.[19]

By this time, however, a new force had emerged making agreement more difficult even with a newly elected federal Conservative government more willing to accept a certain degree of decentralization together with a newly elected Liberal government in Quebec more committed to working out its future within the confines of the federation. Long ignored and forced to live on the periphery of Canadian society, the Aboriginal peoples of Canada began to push for constitutional recognition of their special status, particularly the "First Nations" of Canada, who soon began to argue for a third, constitutionally recognized, order of government. When Quebec's request for constitutional recognition as a "distinct society" was accepted by the provincial governments in the Meech Lake Accord negotiated in 1987, the leaders of the First Nations argued for a broad recognition of their right to self-government. Most believed, on both historical and legal grounds, that their right to self-determination was stronger than Quebec's, eventually pitting those First Nations with claims to territory within Quebec against the government of Quebec.[20]

The protracted debate between 1987 and 1990, while it involved the traditional argument over the division of powers, was more concerned with the constitutional entrenchment and protection of certain "national identities." In particular, discussion focused on the official status that should be accorded the province of Quebec as the homeland of the majority of Canada's francophones, and the Aboriginal peoples as Canada's First Nations. These differing identities ultimately came into conflict. The Meech Lake Accord, while recognizing the special status of Quebec, did not recognize the special status of Canada's First Nations, and Aboriginal anger at this exclusion did much to prevent the ultimate ratification of the Accord in 1990.[21]

The Meech Lake fiasco, however, was not simply the failure of an agreement because of the exclusion of one group. It was also the natural outcome of two nationalisms on increasingly different paths—English-Canadian and Québécois. By 1990, a majority of Quebecers primarily identified with Quebec instead of Canada. In his first public speech outside Quebec after the Parti Québécois's election victory in September, 1994, separatist premier Jacques Parizeau told an audience at the Canadian Club in Toronto that:

> In the sixties and early seventies . . . Pierre Trudeau and René Levesque each held one end of the identity cord and tugged hard. At first, Trudeau was far ahead. Seventy percent of French Quebecers said "Canadian," when asked about their identity. A quarter of a century later, the proportions are exactly reversed. This fall, 70 percent of French Quebecers state their identity as "Quebecers," not "Canadian." It is the result of a long, steady rise.[22]

The statement is misleading in the sense that it ignores the fact that in a federal state it is natural for people to hold dual loyalties, and that the majority of Quebecers still hold a second "Canadian" identity. The statement is nonetheless accurate in assuming that most Quebecers have shifted their primary identity from Canada to Quebec, now thinking of themselves as "Quebecers" rather than as "French-Canadians." Moreover, there can be little doubt that the strength of the Québécois identity, juxtaposed against the fragility of the English-Canadian identity, threatens the future of a country administered from Ottawa. Add to this the rising nationalism of the First Nations and Western discontent, and you have a country populated by diverging identities, rather than a nation-state bonded by common sociocultural assumptions. This situation is exacerbated by a host of internal difficulties and external threats—many of which are common to advanced industrial countries but which are particularly troubling in the light of the present fragility of the Canadian state.

INTERNAL DIFFICULTIES

It may be true, as one postwar-political historian suggests, that despite the Canadian governments very early commitment to Keynesian economics, this commitment was "neither unequivocal nor firm."[23] Nonetheless, the form in which Keynesianism, broadly defined, was translated into Canadian economic policy bears more similarities than differences with the advanced industrial countries examined in this volume. One shared characteristic was the use of social spending as an automatic stabilizer. From 1945 until the oil crisis of 1973, Canadians constructed the programs that would together constitute the social safety net.[24] Although more frail than the nets constructed by certain Western European states such as Great Britain and the

Scandinavian countries by 1973, Canada's social safety net compared well with most OECD countries, and was unquestionably deeper and stronger than the minimalist net constructed during the postwar period in the United States. Governments generally believed that programs delivering benefits to the old, the infirm, the sick, and, in particular, the unemployed stabilized aggregate consumption thereby smoothing the inevitable business cycle fluctuations in aggregate investment and national income growth.[25]

Another characteristic of the pre-1973 Keynesian consensus was the pursuit of full employment through the occasional use of counter-cyclical fiscal policy. Simply put, this meant governments spending more than current revenues to bolster consumption and investment, and thus employment, during recessions and doing the opposite during periods of very high growth. Of course, it was assumed that the budget deficits incurred during recessions would be offset by the surpluses enjoyed during the booms.

In a 1945 policy white paper, the Canadian government formally committed itself to using Keynesian policy to achieve "a high and stable level of employment and income," one of the first advanced industrial countries to do so.[26] Canada's use of counter-cyclical policy may have been sporadic, and perhaps even ineffective at times, but in reality there was no OECD country that consistently and effectively applied Keynesian policy.[27] And whatever lack of consistency in the application of the policy from 1945 until 1973, Canada and most OECD member states enjoyed a rate of economic growth unsurpassed in their history. Consumption, income, and investment all marched together keeping unemployment low.[28] The Keynesian consensus held strong in this environment of success, at least until serious problems began to emerge after the oil shocks of the early 1970s.[29]

The difficulties encountered by Canada after 1973 were faced by all of the countries covered in this volume. These problems included: considerably slower rates of economic growth as measured by gross domestic product (GDP) and GDP per capita; slower rates of productivity growth as measured by labor productivity and total factor productivity; higher rates of inflation; extremely high (nominal) interest rates; stagnation of household disposable income; and much higher rates of unemployment. Inevitably, the old equation between budget deficits and surpluses broke down as, year after year, governments attempted to increase consumption and investment in an ultimately futile attempt to lower unemployment. Instead, public debt began to climb along with inflation and interest rates even while employment growth sputtered. The end result was stagflation—low growth and high inflation—that marked the period from the oil shocks until the end of the 1980s.[30] The 1990s began with a recession that was more pronounced in Canada than virtually all other OECD countries. Since that time, the advanced industrial world has entered a slightly different phase, one still marked by low income, productivity, and employment growth, but now accompanied by low inflation—in Canada's case, even periods of deflation. On the other hand, years of piling up deficits have created another crisis—a chronic public debt problem in which the compounding pressure of interest costs on accumulated deficits have kept real interest rates high and forced governments to raise taxes even while shifting money from social programs to debt servicing.

As a consequence, the high growth, high employment policies and the social safety nets that typified the aristocracy of advanced industrial countries have been unraveling, in Canada's case since at least the mid-1980s.[31] In addition, the public has become increasingly dissatisfied with governments that take more in terms of taxes yet deliver increasingly less in terms of programs and benefits. In other words, countries that spent the majority of the postwar years building the social welfare state based upon the taxes of a broad middle class, are quickly losing their middle-class constituency. This should not have been as traumatic a process in the United States for the simple reason that a social welfare state on the Western European or Canadian model was never built. However, as David Calleo points out, although social spending and thus taxes have been lower in the United States, high military spending as well as the high cost of private health care, inner city poverty, and deteriorating infrastructure have produced the worst of both worlds: taxes that may be low by international OECD standards, but still far too high considering the paucity and poor quality of public programs and services that benefit the broad middle class. As a consequence the American middle class is even more zealously anti-tax than the middle classes in higher-tax OECD countries.[32]

The American experience contrasts sharply with that of the Canadian middle class that has traditionally benefited (perhaps disproportionately so relative to the poor) from the universal social programs created after the war. To some extent, the Canadian identity is bound to these programs. Since the United States provides the frame of reference for the Canadian identity, those features that distinguish the two societies take on great significance. Canadians have traditionally taken great pride in their version of the social welfare state, particularly their public health care system, assuming that it has created a "kinder and gentler society" than that of the United States. To the degree that popular strands of the social safety net are being weakened in order to service interest on public debts, both provincial and federal, Canadians are less able to distinguish themselves from Americans. Whatever the reality, almost all Canadians do "see their political society as more committed to collective provision" than American society, which is perceived as placing disproportionate emphasis on individual initiative, freedoms, and rights.[33]

A large portion of the national debt was accumulated through the persistence of Keynesian deficit spending after 1973—a policy error Canada shared with most OECD countries. Some of the Canadian debt, however, can be attributed to the ongoing jurisdictional competition between orders of government and the overlap or duplication of public services and thus tax expenditures this encouraged. Even in areas where federal and provincial actions were coordinated to some extent—health care, welfare, and education being the three most obvious examples—the funding transfer formulas themselves are so complex that they have created their own specialized bureaucracies in Ottawa and the provincial capitals. Even more insidious is the extent to which such federal-provincial "cooperation" has distorted spending patterns. The provincial desire for federal revenue is so powerful that spending decisions are often dictated by spending formulas more calculated to maximize "federal dollars" than to maximize the delivery of public services at minimum cost. The consequence is higher debt at both levels of government, and the well-earned distrust of a population that rarely distinguishes between federal and provincial dollars because it must pay for both in the form of income and consumption taxes.

Since the oil crisis, the vicious circle of growing deficits, growing debt, and growing debt service charges at both levels of government have today produced a combined debt to GDP ratio of almost 100 percent, one of the highest in the OECD. Nonetheless, in the face of high interest rates and downgrading by international bond agencies, both of which increased the cost of debt servicing, provincial governments have made tremendous progress in slowing their rates of spending and borrowing, and, accordingly, have recently reduced their net debt to GDP ratios. In sharp contrast, the federal government has been allowing its debt to GDP ratio to spin out of control since the early 1980s, despite the fact that its superior access to revenues should have enabled it to implement an even more stringent deficit-reduction program than the provinces. According to economist Ronald Kneebone, the "federal government was the most indebted" of Canadian jurisdictions yet made "the least impressive improvement in its debt position" in both the 1980s and in the early 1990s.[34]

Why has the federal government behaved so differently from the provinces? According to Kneebone, the fact that the federal government has the capacity to print money through the Bank of Canada, protected the federal government from downgrading by international bond rating services and therefore reduced the threat of a lending cutoff. The federal government's bond status was never changed despite the fact that it was doing less, often significantly less, than all of the provinces to get its financial house in order. But now it has reached the point where even the ability to monetize the debt is being discounted by the bond rating agencies, forcing the federal government to take its own debt problem seriously for the first time.[35]

Responding to this crisis, the federal government announced three initiatives in the 1994. The first is a federal program review in which the central government is analyzing all programs and services with a view to eliminating those that duplicate, or overlap with, existing provincial programs. Second is social security reform that is attempting to revamp the Canadian social safety net and, in the process, reduce expenditures. Third are the so-called "efficiency of the federation" agreements, bilateral agreements between the central and provincial governments aimed at eliminating the overlap and duplication of services, as well as reducing and simplifying administrative and regulatory procedures and laws in concurrent areas of jurisdiction.

All three initiatives signal a massive withdrawal, as the federal government extricates itself from areas of provincial or even concurrent jurisdiction.[36] The costs of such a shift are obvious. Since virtually every effort involves financial downloading to the provinces,[37] this will generate more federal-provincial conflict over which jurisdiction carries the historical and constitutional responsibility for the programs and services in question. There will also be an inevitable erosion of national harmonization and standards with consequent costs to a mobile citizenry. In the longer term, the erosion of nationally based programs and services and the reduction of equalization payments to poorer regions, is likely to increase the average person's regional or provincial identification at the expense of a national identity.

Although not as obvious, further decentralization does have a potentially beneficial side. To begin with, the provinces have already proven that they are more fiscally responsible than the central government, in large part because they operate in a more punishing financial environment. Second, substate governments such as the provinces are often more responsive to the democratic, educational, cultural, and linguistic needs of their population. Third, social policy experimentation in the areas of health care delivery,

welfare provision, and education, without federal payments, is more likely
to lead to innovative ways of reducing cost and improving service than single
programs directed from Ottawa. Competitive, decentralized federalism at its
very best limits unsuccessful experiments to one province while encouraging the rapid spread of successful programs to other provinces. Finally,
decentralization might actually promote national unity as Quebec and the
Western Provinces no longer find Ottawa an impediment to different trajectories of development within their own provinces and regions.

EXTERNAL THREATS OR INTERNAL IDENTITIES IN CRISIS?

I have already argued elsewhere that recent continental trade agreements
such as the Canada-United States Free Trade Agreement (FTA) and the North
American Free Trade Agreement (NAFTA) have neither caused, nor even
exacerbated, Canada's economic problems.[38] Indeed, according to the
OECD's economic estimates and forecasts for 1994 and 1995, Canada is the
fastest growing economy in the group of rich nations. The FTA and NAFTA
have, however, threatened a traditional pan-Canadian identity that unified
English-Canadians from coast to coast, even while strengthening a Québécois
identity. In the West, the notion of Cascadia, a natural economic region joining Alberta, British Columbia, Montana, Alaska, Washington, and Oregon
has taken hold since the signing of the FTA. And in the East, Quebecers feel
more secure about separation if they are assured that trade and investment
relations will be preserved through agreements such as NAFTA.[39]

The weaknesses of a pan-Canadian identity were exposed during the
1988 FTA election when English-Canadian nationalists opposed to the agreement with the United States found themselves struggling with Québécois
nationalists who supported the agreement.[40] The two identities were in clear
conflict both in terms of assumptions and objectives. From the English-
Canadian nationalist's perspective, the trade agreements not only have
encouraged further continental economic integration, but accelerated a
trend towards adopting American standards, institutions, and even social
and tax policies in place of Canadian standards, institutions, and policies.
From the Québécois sovereigntist's vantage point, the FTA and NAFTA
make Quebec less dependent on the rest of Canada economically, and
more capable of becoming a separate state within a North American free
trade space. Cultural assimilation with the United States is not feared; in
fact, Québécois nationalists feel more culturally protected from the
American influence than English-Canadian nationalists.

The two most bitterly fought elections in Canadian history, in 1911 and most recently in 1988, ostensibly involved the issue of freer trade with the United States, but were really concerned with the nature of the Canadian identity, and the threat that closer association with the United States posed to English-Canadian nationalism. During the so-called Reciprocity Election of 1911, the battle lines were clearly drawn outside French-Canada: on one side, Canadians who identified strongly with their status as British citizens with strong ties to the Empire; and on the other, Canadians who tended to view themselves as North Americans whose economic destiny lay in a north-south direction. The most vocal of the latter group were Western farmers—often immigrants from the United States or continental Europe with little or no familial or cultural connection to Great Britain. Both sides were powerful. The outcome was, however, decided by a third party little interested in the specifics of the free trade dispute. French-Canadian nationalists under the charismatic leadership of Henri Bourassa, founder and editor of *Le Devoir*, formed a temporary strategic alliance with pro-British and anti-American Conservatives against the Liberals and their supporters with continentalist leanings, and unlike almost eighty years later, the two opposing nationalisms worked together to defeat free trade.

Raising the specter of further political as well as economic integration with the United States, the free trade election of 1988 like the election of 1911 encouraged a wave of anti-Americanism.[41] This kind of nationalist sentiment was again most heavily concentrated in Ontario, but the nature of Canadian nationalism in that province had changed dramatically over the intervening years. The exclusive British-Canadian identity held by a largely British-immigrant population in 1911 has been replaced by a new Canadian identity based in part upon federal government initiatives from Ottawa including multiculturalism, bilinguilism, and a certain amount of cultural and economic protectionism vis-à-vis the United States.

Many English-Canadians in Western Canada have some difficulty identifying with a pan-Canadian nationalism constructed in Ottawa. Many, if not a majority, believe that certain federal initiatives and institutions such as bilinguilism and equalization payments have only served to keep the West down. Since the signing of the FTA and the NAFTA, some British Columbians and Albertans have even argued that the possible "deconfederation" of the country, sparked by Quebec's secession, would make them more prosperous.[42] Albertans in particular feel they have been the "milch cow of confederation," sending the equivalent of $160 billion (1993 Canadian dollars) more to Ottawa than they have received in benefits and services in return from the central government.[43] Long feeding upon such arguments, a Western separatist movement concentrated in Alberta and British Columbia with some support in Saskatchewan and Manitoba may yet become a serious political force if radical decentralization does not occur.[44]

In Quebec's case, closer economic integration with the United States poses little or no threat to national identity, now defined by a majority as a Québécois nation with a Québécois culture and the Québécois-French language. Quebec sovereigntists—those Québécois who support a separate nation-state—strategically supported the Free Trade Agreement (FTA) in the hope that this would make the Quebec economy less dependent on English-Canada, the real threat to their autonomy as they saw it.[45]

CONCLUSION

Although there are some obvious dangers associated with the further decentralization of the Canadian federation and the loosening of a pan-Canadian national identity, these do not imply a breakup of the of the country. Indeed, given the diverging trajectories of Québécois and First Nation nationalism as well as the Western Canadian desire for greater autonomy from Ottawa, any continued emphasis on centralism and a single Canadian identity may just serve to create greater disunity. At the same time, the current trend toward decentralization and multiple identities is not likely to push provinces into union with the United States. The decision-makers— the premiers and cabinet members of individual provinces—would never give up the extensive powers they enjoy under the current system in order to become little more than glorified municipal governments in the more highly centralized American system.

Nonetheless, if current trends continue—and the federal government's precarious fiscal situation almost ensures that they will—then the post-war–Canadian state is on the verge of great change. The first requirement for a smooth transition will be tax reform permitting the provincial, and likely Aboriginal, orders of government the necessary revenue-generating capacity in order to fulfil their extensive responsibilities. This will require more than incremental administrative change: the structure itself will have to be altered, including current constitutional authority.[46]

Rapid decentralization may in fact promote a greater degree of economic efficiency with provincial governments more responsive to the market disciplines of debt management, as long as such a devolution is accompanied by an economic union guaranteeing free movement of goods, services, capital, and labor. In cultural terms, the results are more ambiguous. The primary identity of most Québécois is already their province, and so little would be altered by decentralization. Only a minority of Western Canadians have ever identified with an Ottawa- (or Ontario-) based English-Canadian nationalism, but this number would shrink even more with further decentralization. While Canadians in Nova Scotia, New Brunswick, Newfoundland, and Prince Edward Island have perhaps the most comfortable sense of dual loyalties, the balance between national and provincial identities might be damaged by further decentralization. Certainly Atlantic Canada's economic future will be threatened by lower equalization payments. Ontario would be most affected by decentralization, in terms of national identity, although the province would be the most viable economic unit if the federation were ever to break apart. While previously the most supportive of the constitutional status quo, the Ontario government is now talking about a new confederation deal in which it would bear less of a burden in terms of supporting the poorer regions of the country.[47]

All of this is not to imply that the federal system as it developed from 1945 until about 1970 is undesirable. There were indeed many positive features associated with a more centralized federation. Nevertheless, too many obstacles now stand in the way of a return to the past. First, there is Quebec: Under no circumstances would it give up any of the powers and responsibilities that it has accumulated since the early 1960s. From the political and intellectual opinion leaders to the average person on the street, there is now a powerful consensus in Quebec that the province rather than the central government should fulfill most of the functions of the state.

The second obstacle lies in the West, where British Columbia, Alberta, Saskatchewan, and Manitoba will not agree to Ottawa having more say over their affairs for fear of a return to the days that their economic development was almost entirely dictated by Central Canada's requirements. Then there are the aboriginal First Nations who are demanding ever greater autonomy, and who are even now in the process of transforming their communities and land base into a third order of government. Fundamentally, this process involves a further devolution of power from Ottawa, which has had full jurisdictional authority over the First Nations and the reservations of land set aside for their habitation away from the rest of Canadian society. First Nation's land entitlement and self-government negotiations are forcing the federal government (often in conjunction with the provinces) to relinquish both land and jurisdictional control to the Aboriginal peoples.

Each of the above is a powerful obstacle preventing the federal government from pushing the country toward a more centralized state. But now the federal government itself has decided that its own debt situation requires that it retreat from its traditional areas of control and responsibility. Through social policy reform and the federal program review, Ottawa is attempting to jettison as much program and service baggage as possible, letting the provinces salvage what they can in the process. This process works against the basic instincts of the governing party and its federal bureaucracy, but the threat of disaster flowing from the enormous federal debt is shattering past certainties. As a result, all Canadians, irrespective of their views, are being pushed toward one of two destinations—an even more highly decentralized federation, or deconfederation itself.

• NOTES TO CHAPTER 7 •

1. Allan C. Cairns, "An Election to be Remembered: Canada 1993," *Canadian Public Policy* 20:3 (September 1994).
2. Leslie A. Pal and F. Leslie Seidle, "Constitutional Politics 1990-92: The Paradox of Participation," in Susan D. Phillips, ed., *How Ottawa Spends: A More Democratic Canada . . . ?* (Ottawa: Carleton University Press, 1993).
3. The impact on public sector management has been so great that the Fall 1994 (3:3) issue of *Canadian Public Administration* was devoted to the issue of decentralization.
4. See Stéphane Dion "Explaining Quebec Nationalism," in R. Kent Weaver and Keith G. Banking, eds., *The Collapse of Canada?* (Washington, DC: Brookings, 1992), p. 103.
5. On the concept of "province-building" see Alan C. Cairns, "The Governments and Societies of Canadian Federalism," *Canadian Journal of Political Science* 10:4 (1977). See also R. A. Young et al., "The Concept of Province-Building: A Critique," *Canadian Journal of Political Science* 17:4 (1984).
6. This is the infamous distinction between "direct" and "indirect" taxes, with provincial governments limited to the former, and the federal government permitted both forms of taxation. Peter Hogg, *Constitutional Law of Canada: Second Edition* (Toronto: Carswell, 1985).
7. Health, education, and welfare are areas of exclusive provincial jurisdiction under the Canadian constitution, and the federal government's use of its spending power through conditional grants and shared-cost programs to "Canadianize" social policy was vigorously resisted by Quebec throughout the postwar period.
8. Robin W. Boadway and Paul A. R. Hobson, *Intergovernmental Fiscal Relations in Canada* (Toronto: Canada Tax Foundation, 1993).
9. Province of Québec, "An Act Respecting the Sovereignty of Québec," first laid before the National Assembly, December 6, 1994.
10. An example of this mental preparation is the monograph series on "The Economics of the Breakup of Confederation" sponsored by the C. D. Howe think tank in Toronto. See: *Two Nations, One Money? Canada's Monetary System following a Quebec Secession* (October 1991); *Broken Links: Trade Relations after a Quebec Secession* (November 1991); *Parting as Friends: The Economic Consequences for Quebec* (November 1991); *Closing the Books: Dividing Federal Assets and Debt if Canada*

Breaks Up (January 1992); and *Tangled Web: Legal Aspects of Deconfederation* (June 1992). Another think tank, the Canada West Foundation of Calgary, also went through a similar exercise, albeit on a much more modest scale: see *The Economics of Quebec Separation: Consequences for Quebec and the Rest of Canada* (October 1992).

11. Unlike true confederal documents such as the first American constitution of 1781 in which *already-sovereign* states delegated limited legislative authorities to *newly-created* central institutions, the British North America Act was written by representatives of the existing colonies (in consultation with the Imperial government) in such a way to divide powers between the central and provincial authorities, with neither level of government permitted to modify the division of powers unilaterally—a federalist constitution in other words.

12. Gregory Marchildon and Edward Maxwell, "Quebec's Right of Secession under Canadian and International Law," *Virginia Journal of International Law* 32:3 (Spring 1992). For the most exhaustive historical view, see Arthur I. Silver, *The French-Canadian Idea of Confederation, 1864-1900* (Toronto: University of Toronto Press, 1982).

13. Kenneth McRoberts, *Quebec: Social Change and Political Crisis* (Toronto: McClelland and Stewart, 1988). Michael Behiels, *Prelude to Quebec's Quiet Revolution: Liberalism versus Neo-Nationalism, 1945-1960* (Montreal: McGill-Queens University Press, 1985). William D. Coleman, *The Independence Movement in Quebec, 1945-1980* (Toronto: University of Toronto Press, 1984).

14. John Richards and Larry Pratt, *Prairie Capitalism: Power and Influence in the New West* (Toronto: McClelland and Stewart, 1979).

15. Graham Fraser, *PQ: René Levesque and the Parti Québécois in Power* (Toronto: McClelland and Stewart, 1984).

16. Bruce Doern and Glen Toner, *The Politics of Energy: The Development and Implementation of the NEP* (Toronto: Methuen, 1985).

17. The tortured course of intergovernmental relations is superbly traced by Peter H. Russell in *Constitutional Odyssey: Can Canadians Become a Sovereign People?: Second Edition* (Toronto: University of Toronto Press, 1993). The official Quebec position is presented in a lengthy working paper entitled "Quebec's Traditional Constitutional Positions, 1936-1990," prepared by the Intergovernmental Secretariat, Quebec Government (November 1991).

18. The constitution was to be brought home (patriated) from Great Britain to Canada.

19. Roy Romanow et al., *Canada . . . Notwithstanding: The Making of the Constitution, 1976-1982* (Toronto: Methuen, 1984). Keith Banting and Richard Simeon, eds., *And No One Cheered: Federalism, Democracy, and the Constitution Act* (Toronto: Methuen, 1983).

20. Michael Behiels, ed., *The Meech Lake Primer: Conflicting Views of the 1987 Constitutional Accord* (Ottawa: University of Ottawa Press, 1989). For historical background on aboriginal demands, see Olive P. Dickason, *Canada's First Nations: A History of the Founding Peoples from Earliest Times* (Norman: University of Oklahoma Press, 1992), and J. R. Miller, *Skyscrapers Hide the Heavens: A History of Indian-White Relations in Canada, Second Edition* (Toronto: University of Toronto Press, 1991).

21. Andrew Cohen, *A Deal Undone: The Making and Breaking of the Meech Lake Accord* (Vancouver: Douglas and McIntyre, 1990).

22. Notes for Jacques Parizeau's speech at the Canadian Club, Toronto, November 22, 1994.

23. Robert M. Campbell, *Grand Illusions: The Politics of the Keynesian Experience in Canada* (Peterborough: Broadview Press, 1987), p. 2.

24. Although the federal government had passed the Unemployment Insurance Act (1940) and the Family Allowance Act (1944) before 1945, the funding for such programs was enriched in progressive stages after the war. Moreover, assistance to students through

low tuition fees and student loans, the Canada Assistance Plan in which the federal government shared the cost of postwar provincial welfare and social services programs, and a national public health delivery system, were all postwar initiatives. On the early evolution of Canadian policy towards the unemployed, see James Struthers, *No Fault of Their Own: Unemployment and the Canadian Welfare States, 1914-1941* (Toronto: University of Toronto Press, 1981).

25. Dennis Guest, *The Emergence of Social Security in Canada: Second Edition* (Vancouver: University of British Columbia Press, 1985), S. Ismael, ed., *The Canadian Welfare State: Evolution and Transition* (Edmonton: University of Nebraska Press, 1987), and Allan Moscovitch and Jim Albert, eds., *The Benevolent State: The Growth of Welfare in Canada* (Toronto: Garamond Press, 1987).

26. Government of Canada, Department of Reconstruction, *Employment and Income* (Ottawa: King's Printer, 1945).

27. See Campbell, *Grand Illusions.*

28. The average Canadian rate of five percent was low by 1930s and post-1973 standards, but was nonetheless higher than the average European Community rate of three percent or less before during this same period. Charles R. Bean, "European Unemployment: A Survey," *Journal of Economic Literature* 32 (June 1994), p. 573.

29. In some countries, such as Sweden, which had pioneered the social welfare net, the problems became evident a few years earlier. In "The Rise and Fall of the Swedish Model," *Journal of Economic Literature* 23:1 (March 1985), Erik Lundberg argues that "Sweden's ambitious application of the Welfare State ideology and the policy performance along the lines of the Swedish Model made the Swedish economy especially vulnerable to the external shocks of the Seventies and Eighties."

30. The international evidence and common trends can be found in Angus Maddison, *Dynamic Forces in Capitalist Development: A Long-Run Comparative View* (Oxford: Oxford University Press, 1992).

31. James J. Rice and Michael J. Prince, "Lowering the Safety Net and Weakening the Bonds of Nationhood: Social Policy during the Mulroney Years," in Phillips, ed., *How Ottawa Spends.*

32. David P. Calleo, *The Bankrupting of America: How the Federal Budget is Impoverishing the Nation* (New York: Morrow, 1992).

33. Charles Taylor, "Shared and Divergent Values," in Ronald L. Watts and Douglas M. Brown, eds., *Options for a New Canada* (Toronto: University of Toronto Press, 1991).

34. Richard D. Kneebone, "Deficits and Debt in Canada: Some Lessons from Recent History," *Canadian Public Policy* 20:2 (June 1994), p. 160.

35. Pre-budget consultation documents issued by the Department of Finance, Ottawa, October 1994: *A New Framework for Economic Policy* and *Creating a Healthy Fiscal Climate.*

36. This is not a sentiment that Lucien Bouchard, the leader of the Bloc Québécois shares but his view flies in the face of reality. See Jeffrey Simpson, "Ottawa is Loosening, not Tightening, its Centralizing Grip," Toronto *Globe and Mail,* November 29, 1994, p. A20.

37. The only exception would be in the case of "pure duplication," in which the province is already bearing the full cost of providing a service which the federal government exactly duplicates. The rule, however, is limited overlap rather than substantial duplication, and the provinces will be required to either expend the extra resources to cover the services no longer offered by the federal government or allow the elimination of the service.

38. Gregory P. Marchildon, "From Pax Britannica to Pax Americana and Beyond," *Annals of the American Academy of Social and Political Sciences* 538 (March 1995), pp. 151-68.

39. J. N. McDougall, "North American Integration and Canadian Disunity," *Canadian Public Policy* 17:4 (December 1991).

40. This clash between the two nationalities was aptly captured in: Philip Resnick with a reply by Daniel Latouche, *Letters to a Québécois Friend* (Montreal: McGill-Queen's University Press, 1991). See also Andrew Stark, "English Canadian Opposition to Quebec Nationalism," in Weaver, ed., *The Collapse of Canada.*

41. For a history of the 1998 FTA, see G. Bruce Doern and Brian W. Tomlin, *Faith and Fear: The Free Trade Story* (Toronto: University of Toronto Press, 1991).

42. The most notable examples include: David Bercuson and Barry Cooper, *Deconfederation* (Toronto: Key Porter, 1991); Patrick Grady, *The Economic Consequences of Quebec Sovereignty* (Vancouver: Fraser Institute, 1991); and Gordon Gibson, *Plan B: The Future of the Rest of Canada* (Vancouver: Fraser Institute, 1994).

43. Christopher Serres, "All Trade Routes Lead South," *Western Report,* 27 June 1994.

44. See John J. Barr and Owen Anderson, eds., *The Unfinished Revolt: Some Views on Western Independence* (Toronto: McClelland and Stewart, 1971); Larry Pratt and Garth Stevenson, eds., *Western Separatism: The Myths, Realities, and Dangers* (Edmonton: Hurtig, 1981). Also see David E. Smith, *The Regional Decline of a National Party: Liberals on the Prairies* (Toronto: University of Toronto Press, 1981).

45. For a review of the Quebec position on free trade during the last decade, see Pierre Martin, "Free Trade and Party Politics in Quebec," in Charles F. Doran and Gregory P. Marchildon, eds., *The NAFTA Puzzle: Political Parties and Trade in North America* (Boulder: Westview Press, 1994).

46. On the current limits of incremental tax reform, see Richard M. Bird, "Federal-Provincial Taxation in Turbulent Times," *Canadian Public Administration* 36:4 (Winter 1993).

47. Jeffrey Simpson, "Ontario Begins to Wonder about a Better Deal within Confederation," Toronto *Globe and Mail,* 1 December 1994, p. A22.

·8·

The Transformation
of the Belgian State

Erik Jones

The death of King Baudouin in August 1993 brought thousands of mourners to the streets of Belgium. For many, the massive public display of grief was as unexpected as the demise of the King himself. The institutions of the Belgian state are so often heaped with scorn, ridiculed for inefficiency, and preyed upon by political opportunists that many doubted whether Belgians could unite around any one issue, even their love for the King. Yet Belgium is not Great Britain, and King Baudouin's untimely death revealed the monarchy to be a powerful bond amid the internal divisions of the country. Reflecting on Baudouin's last address to the nation, the King looked healthy but was not, while the state he ruled appeared more stricken than it actually was.

Belgium-baiting is a sport played perhaps too often by newspaper columnists and media pundits. While there is much truth to assertions that Belgium is beset by domestic conflicts and external constraints, the Belgian state has shown a remarkable ability to adapt itself to changes both within the country and without. The metamorphosis of King Baudouin from a silent, brooding youth to an open, compassionate, and much beloved monarch is only one manifestation of the Belgian state transformed.

The purpose of this chapter is to examine the crisis of the state in Belgium, to assess the importance of recent economic and political developments, and to suggest possible future transformations. The organizing principle for my discussion is the concept of legitimacy referred to in chapter 1. To be legitimate, a state must be sensitive to the changing wants, desires, and aspirations of its citizenry and it must be effective in the provision of public goods. My assumption is that if there is a crisis of the state in Belgium, the Belgian state must be unresponsive, ineffective, or both.

A strong case can be made that the Belgian state is no longer responsive to the will of the people. The old system of consociational democracy, within which Belgian social life was organized around ideologically determined subnational cultures, has given way to a more competitive political marketplace. Meanwhile, elites from trade unions and employers associations retain influence and control over important aspects of government. The power of these elites is no longer commensurate with their ability to deal with an ever broadening range of political problems and interest group aspirations, and so a gap has developed between state officials and the citizenry.

Within this gap, right- and left-wing populists have flourished, using nationalist, ethnic, and even linguistic grievances to consolidate their influence. More than one in four Antwerp voters lent support to the right-wing Flemish Bloc in the October 1994 regional elections. In the June 1994 European elections, the right-wing francophone National Front gained almost eight percent of the vote in Wallonia, and the left-wing populist José Happart received a record number of preference ballots in the francophone Socialist Party. The obvious strength of such movements reinforces the centrifugal tendencies in Belgium, exacerbating tensions between the country's regions and linguistic groups. For the state, this poses the danger that federalism will give way to national disintegration.

The case can also be made that the Belgian state is no longer effective in its governance of the country. More than 14 percent of the labor force is unemployed, and government debt amounts to over 140 percent of domestic production.[1] Such performance, coming as it does after more than a decade of intermittent price-wage restraint and fiscal austerity, seems to indicate that the government has little influence on job creation and almost no control over its spending.

Moreover, the European Union has set highly visible standards for effective governance through the convergence criteria for economic and monetary union (EMU). To be a viable candidate for EMU, a member state must have a deficit less than or equal to 3 percent of gross domestic product (GDP), and a government debt converging on or below 60 percent of GDP. Belgium clearly fails on both counts. At the same time, the Union has set itself up as a potentially viable alternative to the nation-state. With the Union's pretensions to centralized authority and even, perhaps, to fiscal federalism, it is not clear what role the state will retain in managing the national economy. Thus for many in Belgium, and particularly those who aspire to a Europe of the Regions, the state is not only ineffective, it is also unnecessary.

Certainly it would be impossible to say that these arguments lack merit. Indeed, in many ways the two claims are complementary. A "Europe of Regions," with Wallonia and Flanders as charter members, can be more or less xenophobic—although more is perhaps likely. What is important in this context is that Wallonia and Flanders will not be Belgian, and that the Belgian national state will have ceased to exist. My contention is that both arguments underestimate the adaptive powers of the Belgian state. By taking each argument in turn, it is possible to suggest that, while important, neither supports an easy prediction of Belgian disintegration.

TENSIONS WITHIN THE CONSENSUS STATE

The Belgian state no longer possesses the ability to generate national consensus. Although the center-left Dehaene government has been able to negotiate impressive agreements within the coalition and with representatives of industry and labor, it has failed to create a feeling of national solidarity. Few admire the government in Belgium, and any respect for Jean-Luc Dehaene is limited to his prowess as a political operator.[2] The average voter no longer feels secure in the hands of politicians and often complains of having little basis on which to choose between the political parties. Moreover, political activism is not a strong trait among the Belgians. Having spent several generations tied to one political ideology or another, the people lack the confidence to speak for themselves. Thus, in the words of sociologist Lucien Huyse, the voters are caught "between exit and voice," drowning the state in their apathy and frustration.[3]

It was not always this way. The linkage between the citizenry and the state in Belgium once relied on a complex network of political parties, trade unions, and employers associations. The country was divided less by class or language than by faith or ideology. In the 1950s, for example, the three main political parties—the Catholics, Socialists, and Liberals—accounted for over 90 percent of the votes at election time. The issues that they debated centered on the continuation of the monarchy, the relationship between church and state, and the concept of worker democracy. At times the ideological fragmentation of the country threatened to tear Belgium apart, as with the massive demonstrations following the return of King Leopold III in 1950 or a second set of demonstrations coinciding with the implementation of Gaston Eyskens's economic modernization program in 1960. Alternately, the ideological pillars of Belgian society were able to forge agreements on the grand issues of the day, as during the School Pact of 1958 or the wage-price moderation of the 1960s.

Whatever the circumstances, the watchwords for Belgian democracy were consociationalism and corporatism. Consociationalism meant that Belgians were content to follow the leadership of their ideological elites—politicians, trade unionists, or employers who had risen through the ranks of purely Catholic, Socialist, or Liberal organizations. The existence of comprehensive ideologies made elite actions predictable and encouraged followers in their deference to elite authority. For example, when Catholic politicians negotiated compromises with their counterparts from the Socialist and Liberal camps, they could be trusted to remain true to the faith and to defend the beliefs of the church and its followers.[4]

Corporatism functioned in much the same way, but relied on interests more than ideologies.[5] Elites from trade unions and employers associations bargained with each other over the direction of economic policy and the provision of social welfare. Workers relied on trade union leaders to remain true to the interests of the laboring classes, and employers counted on their own representatives to safeguard the interests of capital. The government, when it chose to participate, upheld the interests of the rest of society—most often by restricting the use of corporatism to those issues best handled by industry and labor, and by ensuring that the trade unions and employers associations ultimately got along.

From the standpoint of state-society relations, the two different processes, consociationalism in politics and corporatism in economics, reinforced each other within the overarching ideological framework. The Catholic and Socialist parties had their working-class unions to mobilize electoral support, while the Liberal party had its white-collar union and business links to mobilize financial resources. When negotiations between political and economic elites went smoothly, in other words when consociationalism and corporatism functioned, Belgium was ruled by consensus. The center-left government that presided over the onset of the "golden" 1960s commanded almost 85 percent of the parliamentary seats. However, when negotiations broke down and when elites could not agree to work together, consensus dissolved in strife. The Catholic Duvieusart government that sparked the protest of 1950 was based on a majority of less than 1 percent; and the Center-Right Eyskens government that confronted the strikes of 1960 faced important defections from the prime minister's own Catholic party.

Elite relations determined the stability of the consociational system because electoral behavior was ideologically constrained. Rather than choosing between political parties, Belgian voters were born into ideological "families"; subnational political cultures that dominated (or permeated) virtually every aspect of life from primary school through university, employment and trade union affiliation, and to health care and old-age retirement. Thus the Belgians of the 1950s were often described as being grouped in comprehensive ideological social pillars—living separate lives while sharing the same geographic space. The elite level was the point of intersection for the various ideological pillars and so elite cooperation translated into social consensus, elite conflict into social strife.

Enter the Political Market

Political reform, however, has taken Belgium beyond its traditional system for consociational democracy. It may also have taken Belgium "beyond politics" as the term is conventionally understood in that country. The pillarized organization for society did not hold up very well with the passage of time. Because the pillars relied on ideology for self-distinction and internal solidarity, they could not survive the declining importance of ideology in everyday life. Today, consociationalism no longer describes the form of political and social organization in Belgium, and it is an open question whether consociational democracy continued to function after the late 1960s. Belgians are still Catholic in name but few go regularly to Church. Moreover, the end of the Cold War has undermined much of the distinction between Christian democrats and social democrats, even as the near collapse of the welfare state and the explosion of public deficits clustered everyone around the liberal, free market economy.

A host of "new" or "post-materialist" political issues have captured much of the popular attention—many of which, such as environmental protection or immigration, do not fit comfortably within either of the three principal ideologies; Catholicism, Socialism, or Liberalism. At the same time, the one issue that does appeal to traditional materialist concerns—the high rate of unemployment—consistently denies resolution. Consequently, whatever deference the Belgians may have expressed during the 1950s has dissolved, and political elites are either ignored or they are coming under close and sometimes even personal scrutiny. Consider, for example, the contrasting fates of former Prime Minister Wilfried Martens, who vanished into a Europarliamentary netherworld, and former francophone Socialist party leader Guy Spitaels, who had to resign from the government after being implicated in the notorious Augusta Scandal.

Following this line of argument, it is possible to suggest that the numerous scandals that have cropped up recently derive more from the attitudes of the voters than from the behavior of politicians. Belgian politicians have long been forgiven their petty corruptions. During the 1950s, however, at least politicians were able to provide satisfactory and predictable responses to the pressing problems of the day. Now, politicians are corrupt *and*—to all appearances—incompetent. Consequently voters are far less forgiving and more likely to transfer their support to any party that offers either a solution to some pressing concern (for example, the environment) or a forum for voters to have a voice in policy. Arguably, a combination of the two factors, a problem solved and a more direct style of voter participation, is preferred. This explains, perhaps, why the Belgian party system is ranged, on the one hand, with left-wing activist parties possessing strong environmental agendas and, on the other hand, with right-wing populist parties offering simple-minded solutions to immigration.

Traditional political parties—like the traditional ideological families—are losing favor among voters because they assume a deference of followers to elites. An extreme example of such behavior can be seen in the February 1993 election of Philippe Busquin as party leader for the francophone Socialists: Busquin won 521 of 523 votes. Numbers such as these reveal that not only was he selected long before the election, but also by whom he was selected—the party elites. Small wonder, then, that Busquin's alleged involvement in the "Uniop" party financing scandal cast dispersions on the entire socialist political class. In March 1994, Busquin resigned as party chairman and was subsequently reelected, again by an overwhelming majority. Meanwhile the party experienced a dramatic loss of support, dropping nationally by 3 percentage points and two seats in the June 1994 European elections and by almost 8 percentage points in the October 1994 regional elections in the party's Liège stronghold.

The appropriate contrast to the Walloon Socialists is with the Flemish Liberals and Democrats (VLD). Where the francophone Socialists have held strongly to their consociational past, the Flemish Liberals have been eager to push for political reform—going so far as to change their name in a symbolic act of transformation. When Guy Verhofstadt ran for election as leader of the renamed Liberal party in June 1993, he faced strong opposition from Herman De Croo. Both contestants believed in roughly the same economic program, but they disagreed on relations between elites and followers within the party. As De Croo himself admitted before the vote:

> Verhofstadt rides bicycles while I ride horses. . . . [Your] senses should go along with whatever you choose to ride. In politics that is . . . the Flemish voter. Verhofstadt believes that the voter can be radicalized. I do not. A Fleming has a grocer's mentality, and prefers agreements and compromises. . . .[6]

De Croo lost, and Verhofstadt garnered an impressive 68.5 percent of the vote—not from the hundreds of party militants, but from the entire membership, numbering in the thousands. Verhofstadt's repeated calls for more participatory democracy put him in very good stead with the voters, and enabled him to increase the popular approval rating of the Flemish Liberals by more than 10 percent from 1991 to 1993.

Verhofstadt's success was not, however, without limits. In the June 1994 European elections, the VLD suffered a stunning upset, gaining less than percentage point in comparison with its 1989 Europarliamentary performance. Political analysts read this defeat in two ways: either voters were unconvinced by Verhofstadt's repeated calls for greater activism or they were frightened by the stark imagery of a neo-liberal, market-based society.[7] Whatever the reason, the traditional Catholic and Socialist parties were not the prime beneficiaries of the VLD's poorer-than-expected performance. Aside from the modest gains made by the Liberals, only the far Right and a range of minor parties succeeded increasing support from the electorate. Trapped between exit and voice, Belgian voters appear to have chosen both at once, abandoning the traditional consociational parties for a pot-pourri of new political groups.

As Belgians grow increasingly fed up with their assumed deference, the traditional political parties are undergoing a dramatic shake-up. This is neither something new to Belgium, nor it is something unique. Traditional parties also fared poorly during the 1970s, and the plight of Belgian elites is shared in almost every advanced industrial democracy. The real difference from times past is the growing intensity of popular aspirations for what has come to be called "political renewal"—a changeover from assumed deference to popular participation or at least popular choice.

Here again it is useful to focus on the Flemish Liberals and Democrats. In spite of his recent electoral setbacks, Verhofstadt has succeeded in doing something that no politician in Belgium has ever done before. He has transformed one of the traditional ideological families, creating a flexible catch-all party from a more rigid programmatic organization. In doing so, Verhofstadt has declared war on the rules of the game for inter-party relations. He has broken the bonds between party officials and interest groups, and, most important, between ideology, political power, and everyday life.[8] Should the other political parties choose to follow his example, we can expect to see a far more competitive and a far less cooperative system of Belgian political parties.

Life after Corporatism

Corporatism seems also to have outlived its usefulness in supporting the government or its economic policy. The social "partnership"—meaning generally cooperative relations between representatives of employers and trade unions—is a second cornerstone of the Belgian consensus state. To appreciate this point it is necessary to consider that modern Belgium was born in the early 1960s and only after a massive series of strikes that threatened to tear the country apart. In total, almost 700,000 workers took place in more than 300 manifestations over a five week period.[9]

The strikes were in response to Gaston Eyskens's "Single Act," which was intended to modernize the economy while stabilizing government accounts. Belgium of the 1950s was the slow student in Europe's economic miracle. However, Gaston Eyskens had already tried and failed to induce a Keynesian deficit- and demand-led expansion. Therefore, his coalition of Christian Democrats and Liberals thought to encourage economic modernization through manipulation of the supply-side of the Belgian economy using fiscal reforms, investment subsidies, and—most important—concerted wage restraint. Syndicalist elements in the Belgian labor movement refused to moderate their demands for higher pay, and levered off the Single Act to attempt to wrest control over the economy. The putsch was ultimately unsuccessful and Eyskens was able to implement his Single Act shortly before tendering his resignation.[10]

The fall of the Eyskens center-right cabinet did not lead to a reversal of his supply-side policies. With the collapse of the syndicalist opposition, the balance of power within the trade union movement shifted decisively in favor of the advocates of social partnership. The trade unions agreed to concerted wage restraint in exchange for investment in job creation. Labor costs fell, investment rose, and Belgium moved into a period of unprecedented growth in output and productivity. At the same time, the trade unions were brought into virtually every aspect of economic policymaking.

Indeed, it is the inclusion of the trade unions which distinguishes the modern Belgium from the premodern. Though it is not fair to say that relations between the social partners have always been amicable, there has been no repeat performance of the winter of 1960. Concerted wage restraint broke down for much of the 1970s and Belgian competitiveness suffered accordingly. Nevertheless, the social partnership remained. Cooperation between representatives of labor and industry was never again as smooth as during the 1960s, but it was still widely evident.[11]

A turning point came in the early 1980s with the formation of a center-right government under Wilfried Martens. For Martens, it was a fifth government in fewer than as many years, and its success was clearly contingent upon his ability to gain control over the economy. Much like Gaston Eyskens before him, Martens called for concerted wage restraint. Socialist trade union leader Georges Debunne refused and threatened to break off the social partnership. However, Christian Democratic trade union leader Jef Houthuys conceded and once again accepted the trade off between concerted wage restraint and investment in job creation. His concession to Martens was essential to the functioning of the economic recovery program and probably also to the stability of the center-right cabinet. In spite of social science commentaries arguing that Martens ran roughshod over the unions, it is likely that Houthuys could have brought down Martens' fifth government as easily as he witnessed the demise of numbers one through four.[12]

Houthuys, by his own admission, was a devoted corporatist.[13] He believed that the social partnership was a natural state of affairs and he detested syndicalist pretensions to class struggle. When Houthuys left the trade union movement in 1987, however, he had no means of ensuring that his corporatist preferences would continue to predominate. Perhaps more important, popular recognition that Houthuys colluded with Martens throughout the economic recovery programs of the 1980s exacted a high price from the leadership of the Christian Democratic Trade Unions (ACV). Only a few months after Willy Pierens—the present leader of the ACV—concluded a difficult national collective agreement in the Autumn of 1992, he was attacked for supposedly trying to sell out to the government on indexation. The comparison with Houthuys was explicit and derogatory.[14]

Corporatism has become a dirty word in the lexicon of Belgian politics, and the social partnership has grown more difficult to manage with each passing day. Flemish Christian Democratic party chairman Johan van Hecke, for example, took great pains to distinguish the government's ill-fated 1993 social pact from "traditional Belgian paktology" and then went on to argue that the Christian Democrats were not a "corporatist party."[15] Sociologists and political scientists would certainly debate the historical accuracy of his assertion. Nevertheless, it was a strong indication of the difficulties that Dehaene would experience trying to implement this latest round of "crisis legislation."

When national bank governor Fons Verplaetse called for wage restraint in combination with a range of fiscal measures, he was met with the united resistance of the Christian Democratic and Socialist trade unions. Pierens initially held out, preferring to keep his Christian Democratic trade unionists at the negotiation table. Quickly, however, Pierens joined with the Socialists to call for a series of warning strikes. When the crisis plan was announced, the situation reversed itself: The Socialists backed down from direct action while the Christian Democrats held to their proposed schedule for strikes. This time, though, it was the Socialists who had to give way, and Socialist trade union leader François Janssens bowed to pressure to make a common front with Pierens and the ACV.

The trade unions ultimately capitulated to government pressure, and accepted a face-saving maneuver from Dehaene. Nevertheless, the structure and functioning of the social partnership has been fundamentally altered by the experience of that Autumn. The balance of power has shifted within the national labor organizations from central control to constituent trade unions. At the same time, the confidence of employers associations in trade union discipline has worn thin.

Through all of this, the Belgian state perseveres. However, if it is true that the Belgian state stepped into modernity only through the collaboration of the social partners, the future looks decidedly postmodern. Links between political parties and trade unions are slowly but surely dissolving, even as the rising structural component of Belgian unemployment leaves little room for the social partners to maneuver. Belgians will continue to trade off wage discipline for productive investment, but it will be the market—and perhaps also the government—that will dictate terms.

A House Divided?

Regional tension is perhaps the best-known aspect of the Belgian state in crisis. And the inability of the state to generate broad national consensus aggravates this tension. Thus it is easy to imagine a vicious circle, where the state's inability to generate consensus exacerbates interregional conflict that further undermines the consensus-building efforts of the state. In a worst-case scenario, the state succumbs to the forces of regional "nation-building" and Belgium simply ceases to exist. However, while this scenario may seem possible, it is unlikely.

The Belgian state has always had to contend with internal opposition. When Belgium declared its independence from the Netherlands in 1830, there was little strong feeling of Belgian nationalism. The revolution, according to historian Els Witte, grew not out of nationalist sentiment but rather out of a temporary union of interests in opposition to Dutch rule. Landowners sought to preserve their feudal rights, Catholics their religious beliefs, and the liberal bourgeoisie their economic independence. Only the small industrial class of mine- and mill-owners—from the Walloon regions of Hainaut and Liège—actually supported the Dutch monarchy (and its generous subsidies), and yet they lacked the political clout to ensure a continuation of the United Low Countries.[16]

Thus, to borrow a phrase form Val Lorwin, the Belgian state was born a "union of opposition."[17] However, once Dutch rule was removed, Belgium benefitted from little internal solidarity. The state, as many of the chapters in the volume argue, has to foster a sense of national identity. On this count, the Belgian state had only modest success. Witte contends that during the first 18 years of Belgian history the state had yet to have a strong impact on popular attitudes.[18] Even after 1848, Belgium had to compete for popular allegiance with the Catholic, Liberal, and (later) Socialist movements. Well into the twentieth century, to be Belgian was only as important as to be part of a particular ideological community.

The consociational system described above provided an important support to "Belgian" as an identity, at least to the extent that ideology could repair the absence of a strong sense of Belgian nationalism. In a similar way, the institutions of the Belgian state strengthened the ideological building blocks of consociationalism. The Belgian social welfare system channeled money from the state to ideologically affiliated trade unions and health mutuals, gave patronage to political parties, and (during the 1950s) even began to subsidize secular and nonsecular education.

However, once ideology began to lose importance in the late 1950s and early 1960s, the weaknesses of Belgian nationalism became apparent. Regional "nationalism" emerged, not to supplant the state but rather to fill the vacuum created by the "End of Ideology." Hence, regional identities began to claim their own support from the state even as the national ideological families began to divide across regional and linguistic boundaries.

Successive rounds of decentralization have been the result of the changeover from ideological to regional identification.

And yet the state remains. It is a federal rather than a consociational state, but it is still Belgian. This is apparent not only during the passage from one monarch to the next, but also in the international sporting arena,[19] in the provision of peacekeepers to the United Nations, and in the pride associated with Belgian "international" diplomats: During 1994, all Belgium wondered whether Prime Minister Dehaene would become president of the European Commission, if former Prime Minister Marc Eyskens would become Secretary General of the West European Union, or if Socialist Foreign Minister Willy Claes would become Secretary General of NATO. Only Claes ultimately succeeded, and yet somehow that was enough.

Still regional conflict is an annoying distraction from more pressing issues. Francophone Socialist José Happart's repeated attempts to become mayor of the Flemish town of Voeren—in French, Fourons—without bothering to learn to speak Dutch are but one set of examples. And yet there is nothing in these conflicts to indicate that either Wallonia or Flanders seriously wants to do away with the Belgian state. Rather, they have more the appearance of an attempt to rationalize (*ex post*) the powers won by regional political authorities. To paraphrase Flemish journalist Marc Reynebeau, regional politicians stir up the forces of regional "nationalism" in order to give political legitimacy to the nation-building at work within the institutional and territorial boundaries created by the newly federalized Belgium.[20] With luck they will succeed in creating a federal system that is more durable than its consociational predecessor. It may not be as consensual, but that is no reason to believe it will be less Belgian.

CONSTRAINTS ON THE BARGAINING STATE

But if Belgium is no longer a consensus state, wherein lies its future? Chapter 1 of this volume asserts that modern states have become "bargaining states," trading off their autonomy in the hopes of achieving greater effectiveness through collective effort. This notion of the state is often used by students of European integration, where intergovernmental bargains are an essential ingredient to policy effectiveness.[21] The same understanding of the state can be applied to corporatist intermediation as well. Corporatism means that the state bargains with domestic actors, usually trade unions and employers associations (the social partners), in the hope that the "state and groups [can] borrow from each other the authority to do what they cannot do alone."[22]

In his study *Small States in World Markets,* Peter Katzenstein characterizes the smaller West European states as relying on the combination of domestic compensation and international liberalization.[23] Moreover, he makes the strong argument that this combination is the key to small country success, both politically and economically. In a sense, his analysis implicates the smaller countries as bargaining states on both levels, the domestic and the European. Each of the countries in Katzenstein's study relies on domestic corporatism to a greater or lesser extent, and each participates in the some part of the process of European integration—either the European Economic Area (Switzerland and Norway) or the European Union.

Belgium is no exception to Katzenstein's argument. Rather, it is a case in point. Since the early 1960s, Belgium has engaged the social partners in economic policymaking and particularly major economic adjustment programs. Belgium is also a long-time participant in the process of European integration. Much of the state's effectiveness in economic policymaking is dependent upon its ability to bargain successfully, whether at home or within Europe. When the social partners come into conflict or the process of European integration slows down, the effectiveness of the Belgian state typically suffers.

Given the demise of Belgian consensus-building, its prowess as a bargaining state increases in importance. At some point the state must be able to negotiate a contract between regional political authorities—the linguistic communities and regional governments of Brussels, Wallonia, and Flanders—placing definitive limits on what is federal and what is to be handled elsewhere. Such an agreement will rely on the state's being able to demonstrate that some issues are best handled at the Belgian level, that all three regions have an interest in common action, and that none of the three will be unduly burdened by federal policy.

However, for Belgium as a bargaining state, the problems of persistent unemployment, excessive indebtedness, and European encroachment take on a double meaning. Not only do such problems represent a visible display of state ineffectiveness, they also impose harsh constraints on the state's ability to bargain. Actual ineffectiveness runs parallel to perceived ineffectiveness, creating a vicious circle from which there is little chance of escape.

The Disappearance of Work

Persistent unemployment is perhaps the most obvious example of this type of circularity. High levels of unemployment are damaging to the state in and of themselves: they place a strain on popular morale and public coffers, provide fodder for right- and left-wing extremism, and sacrifice a large percentage of the very people the state is meant to serve. In Europe today, unemployment has become almost a litmus test for effective governance, and one that forces many European to ask uncomfortable questions about why they seem to suffer while the non-European countries of the OECD do not.[24]

However, the constraint that high levels of unemployment place on the state's ability to bargain at the industrial and regional levels is perhaps even more important to Belgium than the simple existence of joblessness. At the industrial level, for example, persistent unemployment adds an important complication to Dehaene's use of corporatism, even if it is only corporatism in decline. Trade union representatives are often forced to take contradictory positions—calling for more money and more jobs—in order to placate an increasingly disgruntled workforce. This phenomenon is particularly evident in the debate over working-time reductions. Trade unions have repeatedly asked for take-home wages to remain the same even if working hours decrease. Employers respond that the net effect of such a policy would be to increase fixed-time labor costs and is therefore unacceptable. Dehaene, who favors both working time reductions and lower fixed-time labor costs, is caught in the middle. As of this writing (May 1995) a resolution of this conflict remains unclear.

At the regional level, the skewed distribution of unemployment has sparked a competition between the regions to provide jobs and preserve incomes. In April 1992, for example, the 10.6 percent of the Walloon labor force was unemployed compared to only 5.6 percent in Flanders. The figures for male unemployment were even more impressive: 7.6 percent in Wallonia and only 3.3 percent in Flanders.[25] Not surprisingly, some Flemish politicians have taken note of this disparity to call for a "federalization" of social insurance—claiming that Flanders, as a region, is a net contributor while Wallonia is a net recipient. Also not surprisingly, the Walloon and Flemish regional governments have launched a battle for scarce public procurement resources and lucrative public procurement contracts. This struggle reached the height of irony when the Flemish regional government charged its Walloon counterpart with violating European competition legislation in awarding a contract for public buses.[26] Thus Dehaene is constrained to try and placate both regions, all the while asserting that the state can manage the jobs crisis.[27]

A Question of Excess

Public indebtedness represents a second major constraint on Belgium as a bargaining state. Economists often point out that public debts and deficits are not in themselves bad; it all depends on what the money is used for.

Nevertheless, few would deny that a debt-to-GDP ratio in excess of 140 percent represents an important problem:[28] debt servicing requirements reach deeply into the public purse; interest payments out of current revenues transfer resources from the poor to the rich; government borrowing squeezes private investors out of domestic capital markets; et cetera. The essential question remains the same: what was the money used for? But any assessment of the "merits" of the debt is complicated by the many adverse symptoms of over-indebtedness.

Excessive public indebtedness places particular constraints on Belgium as a bargaining state. If we accept Katzenstein's argument that Belgium—as a small state in world markets—responds to economic change in part through domestic compensation, then it is necessary to ask what kind of compensation Belgium has to offer. Tax relief and transfer payments become increasingly difficult as the debt continues to grow. Moreover, how can the government compensate its citizens for austerity measures? Thus Belgium's debt problem can be understood only by answering three questions: (again) what was the money used for; can Belgium survive without overspending; and does Belgium have the political discipline and economic resources to pay down its debt?

The high level of Belgian public debt does not have Keynesian origins. At no time, with the temporary exception of the late 1950s and the mid-1970s, did Belgian policymakers *choose* to stimulate the economy through deficit spending.[29] The reason for this is simple: they never believed that a deficit-led expansion would work. And they were right. During the deep recession of 1975, for example, the net impact of Belgium's modest fiscal stimulus was to dampen, and not inflate, domestic demand.[30]

Belgian policymakers also did not *choose* to become actively involved in the provision of social welfare until late in this century, and then only with respect to pensions.[31] Although there were early proponents of a Beveridge-style welfare state in Belgium—meaning one financed out of general taxation—these were resoundingly defeated by the joint efforts of trade unions and employers associations. The trade unions advocated a system where they would retain control over welfare provision, and the employers insisted that welfare payments be funded through payroll contributions rather than income taxation. Consequently, the Belgian welfare state has its origins in nineteenth-century notions of social insurance rather than in twentieth-century aspirations for general social welfare.[32]

A pre-Keynesian, pre-Beveridge welfare state should never have accumulated such a massive public debt. And yet it did. The "insurance" aspects of Belgian social welfare ran into difficulty because of the soaring numbers of unemployed and due to skyrocketing health-care costs during the 1970s and 1980s. Trade unions and health care mutuals did not have the financial resources to carry the burden, and employers were not internationally competitive enough to accept an increase in payroll contributions. Consequently the state, as financier of last resort, was called upon to fill the gap. From a 1975 low of 39.9 percent of GDP, Belgian public debt ballooned to 102.9 percent of GDP in 1985.[33] Government transfers grew by 36 percent—twice the rate of expenditure on consumption or employment—and interest payments on the debt more than doubled.[34]

During the first half of the 1980s, the Martens V government succeeded in implementing an impressive austerity program. Measured as a share of domestic production, government outlays for consumption, employment and transfers stabilized and even declined. However, the ultimate costs for rescuing the Belgian social welfare system showed up in the least controllable part of government outlays, debt servicing. Throughout the 1980s, interest payments on public debt were the fastest growing part of the budget, forcing the government to run ever more impressive deficits in spite of rigid austerity.[35] The 1985 Martens VI cabinet responded with successively deeper cuts in, particularly, welfare transfers and public sector employment, but was nevertheless unable to launch a massive overhaul of the social welfare system.[36] By the end of the decade, the successive Martens cabinets finally stabilized the growth of the debt-to-GDP ratio, but only with the help of strong economic performance. When the Belgian economy turned down again at the start of the 1990s, debt growth accelerated anew. Interest payments again led the way, forcing the government to implement ever tighter forms of austerity.

The interest–rate–snowball effect of excessive public borrowing is the tragic part of the story. As commentators often point out, no other state in Western Europe is in as desperate a position as Belgium.[37] The explanation, they suggest, is that government officials in Belgium were too weak in the face of pressure from special interest groups. Rather than fight irresponsible increases in government spending, public officials bowed to interest group pressure. The balance on government accounts suffered as a result.

However, while the argument that Belgian officials were somehow exceptionally profligate is supported by impressive debt and deficit figures, it fails to note that most other West European states were initially more Keynesian, and had more direct control over the institutions for social welfare. Consequently, while the conservative revolution in those countries represented a dramatic break with previous policies, neo-liberal state retrench-ment benefitted from greater effectiveness. State officials converted to mon-etarist beliefs had direct control over the social welfare institutions they wanted to reform.

In Belgium the "conservative revolution" (if that is the correct term) was at the same time less dramatic and less effective than elsewhere. It was less dramatic because Belgium had never been a "happy" Keynesian state. Elites from labor and business long accepted the principles of the monetarist state and even planned for the shift to the Center-Right along traditional cor-poratist lines. And it was less effective because efforts to increase business competitiveness relied on the state's assuming (temporarily) a greater bur-den in the provision of social welfare. One of the mainstays of Martens's center-right adjustment strategy was a program to cut business payroll contributions and instead substitute state financing for social insurance.

In order to alleviate the lack of competitiveness, the new "neo-liberal" state had to involve itself further in the provision of social welfare. This involvement relied on a transition from the nineteenth-century philosophy of social insurance through a more Beveridge-style welfare state simultane-ous to (if not even before) attempts at welfare reform. A dramatic explosion of government indebtedness was the result. Belgian officials were not more profligate than politicians elsewhere. They simply had less direct control over the institutions providing for social welfare system. This explains, perhaps, why Belgium's pension system—the first major institution for social welfare to fall under direct state control—is no more generous or financially unstable than the systems run in most other European countries. The institutions responsible for health and unemployment insurance, however, are excep-tionally prone to abuse in comparison with other countries.[38]

Thus, in spite of the state's failure to gain effective control over public borrowing, the experience of the 1980s gives significant cause for opti-mism with respect to the future. To begin with, trade union elites played a leading role in the shift to the Center-Right and in the design of austerity measures. Economists from the Christian Democratic labor movement designed the initial recovery program and the leadership of the Christian Democratic trade union federation ensured the program's implementa-tion.[39] Secondly, the electorate demonstrated a willingness to accept short-term sacrifices in the interests of long-term prosperity. The Martens center-right cabinet was reelected in 1985 with a modest increase in its par-liamentary majority, and in spite of promises from the leadership of the Liberal and Christian Democratic parties that they would continue to enforce austerity measures for the (then) foreseeable future.[40] Finally, the government did assume a greater role in the provision of social welfare, and thereby gained greater leverage over welfare institutions. Once the government became a primary financial resource for social support schemes, the management of those schemes became more directly a matter of public policy. Cuts in social welfare spending under the Martens VI cabinet were not as dramatic as some would have liked, but they were nevertheless an improvement over the past.

This line of analysis makes it possible to interpret the Belgian debt problem as follows: The debt was incurred when the state attempted to bail out a social insurance system that had been designed and managed by trade unions, medical mutuals, and employers associations. Therefore if the state is to extricate itself from the debt crisis it will have to withdraw from the provision of excessively generous welfare support schemes. The examples of other West European countries during the 1980s suggests that such a retrenchment of the state is possible, albeit difficult. Moreover, the Belgian people have shown themselves willing to accept short-term sacrifices in the interests of longer-term prosperity. They also have little tradition of massive state provision of social services. Thus, welfare reform should be possible without changing the basic popular perception of the state and without undue social unrest.

The major losers in the process of welfare reform will be the elites from trade unions, health mutuals, and employers associations. It is these elites who bear the traditional responsibility for welfare provision and so it is they who will be held accountable for the implications of welfare reform. Thus it is hardly surprising that the same Christian Democratic labor movement that supported austerity measures under Martens V, became more activist as Martens VI began to implement deeper cuts in welfare outlays. An austere Thatcherite state would have had few qualms about undermining the position of these functional interest elites during the 1980s. The Belgian state (under the stewardship of the successive Martens cabinets) was too dependent on them to take drastic measures. Given the decreasing role of corporatism in Belgian economic policy making, that may not be the case in the future.

The European Problem

Ironically, the European Union has also emerged as a constraint on Belgium as a bargaining state. This is ironic because Belgium traditionally relied on European integration to increase its ability to bargain domestically. By joining the European Coal and Steel Community, for example, Belgium gained access to German financial support for subsidies to unproductive coal mines in Wallonia. Thus the Catholic governments of the early 1950s did not have to attack the economic mainstay of their Socialist and Liberal opponents during a period already rife with tension over the return of King Leopold III and over the church-state divide.[41]

The European Economic Community increased the bargaining powers of the Belgian state as well, by making possible the foreign-investment led expansion of the 1960s. Access to foreign investment was the cornerstone of the government's plan to reduce public spending, restructure the mature industries of Wallonia, and industrialize the Flemish economy. Once the plan was implemented, Belgium's central location in Europe's fledgling common market was the key to its success. Gross fixed capital formation increased to an average 21.9 percent of GDP during the 1960s from an average of 16.5 percent in the 1950s.[42] And, foreign investment accounted for fully one-half of the total net investment in manufacturing between 1960 and 1972.[43]

Finally, the European Monetary System stabilized Belgian exchange rates with its major trading partners during the early 1980s and particularly after 1983.[44] This enabled the Martens V government to pursue an export-led growth strategy based on nominal wage restraint. Had France been free to pursue its own strategy of competitive devaluations, Belgian nominal wage restraint would have had significantly less impact on Belgian real (labor cost adjusted) effective exchange rates within Europe. Martens would have had to call for ever greater nominal wage restraint in order to get a meaningful increase in cost competitiveness, and it is unlikely that the trade unions would have complied. With the support of the EMS, Martens was able to generate a 2 percent real depreciation of Belgian effective exchange rates during the period from 1982 to 1985, and Belgium moved into a period of export-led growth.[45]

During the early 1990s, however, European integration failed to provide additional room for maneuver to Belgian policymakers. The coal and steel pool no longer served as an essential support to the Belgian coal industry as the government closed the country's last operational mine in 1991. Foreign investment did not flock to Belgium as during the 1960s. And, perhaps most damaging of all, the EMS ceased to stabilize nominal exchange rates during the currency crises in September 1992 and August 1993. The successive devaluations of the pound, the lire, the peseta, et cetera have had an important negative impact on Belgian competitiveness that has increased the need for both austerity and wage restraint.[46]

Finally, the present drive for monetary integration threatens to place Belgium between the Scylla of economic depression and the Charybdis of exclusion from Europe's hard core. If Belgium struggles mightily to achieve the Maastricht targets for deficit and debt reductions, this will likely have a strong negative impact on domestic demand and place upward pressure on unemployment. If Belgium tries to convince its European partners to make an exception and allow it to participate in EMU without meeting the Maastricht norms, the Italians, the British, and even the Germans are likely to resist. Such a possibility has forced at least one Belgian economist to ponder what will happen in "an EMU without Belgium."[47]

CONCLUSION

Belgium cannot deny its role as a bargaining state. And, as a bargaining state, its future looks decidedly unclear. Nevertheless, that should not be interpreted to mean that Belgium has no future. If we return to the notion of political legitimacy posed from the outset, it is possible to chart the broad outlines of the Belgian state transformed.

The new Belgium will be representative, but through a more pluralist than consociational political formula. Political parties will have to contend in a competitive political environment, where the electorate no longer adheres to strict ideological attachment. Rather voters will move in the margins between parties offering what they believe to be a sound vision of society and a reasonable economic program. Verhofstadt's Flemish Liberals and Democrats will continue to lead the way, at least until the other traditional parties—particularly the Christian Democrats—can convince the electorate that they too have a sensible program for political renewal. Examples of such behavior can be found in Flemish Christian Democratic Party Chairman Johan van Hecke's *Appeal to a Responsible Fleming*, in the still nebulous discussions of progressive front-forming between the Christian Democratic labor movement and the Socialist trade unions, and in the reconsolidation of the Flemish Socialists at the level of local government.[48] The Walloon parties—and particularly the francophone Socialists—have been slower to respond to the call for political renewal. However, perhaps the recent gains made by the right-wing *Agir* and *Front Nationale* will provide a sufficient shock to the Socialists to enable them to overcome their ideological inertia.

The new Belgium will also be less corporatist, and more open to market liberalism. This is true in spite of the continued dominance of economic ministerial portfolios by former members of the labor movement for the simple reason that the labor movement is too diverse in character to present coherent centralized negotiating positions. Thus the tension between the labor movement and the government is more evolutionary than incidental, and Belgian politicians will have to accept the limitations of policy-making without united labor support.[49]

Finally, the new Belgium will be federal. This almost goes without saying, and yet the point to note is that federalism can be representative without being centrifugal.[50] If, as Prime Minister Dehaene hopes, the regions can get used to their new competencies without pushing for further institutional reform, they are likely to find that geographic and linguistic attachment are more stable than ideology as sources of identity. Thus, a federal Belgium is likely to enjoy more solid foundations than did consociational Belgium. At the same time, Flemings and Walloons will be able to identify more, rather than less, with their national state. Here it may be useful to consider Dehaene's recent proposal for the creation of political groups at the federal level—not a return to the consociationalism of times past, but a new level of political representation commensurate with the changed nature of federal governance.[51]

The question of effectiveness is, however, more problematic. While it is possible to suggest that Belgium will succeed in its fiscal reforms, the outlook is less bright with respect to unemployment. There is no silver bullet, no magic formula. Indeed, there are strong reasons to believe that even work-sharing will do little to address the fundamental structural problems.[52] But Belgium is not alone in its unemployment dilemma, and while the company of Europe offers cold consolation it also offers hope. At the recent summit in Essen (December 1994), the European Council listed the fight against unemployment as its number one objective. And, a year before that, it was Dehaene who held the European presidency that brought forth the Delors White Paper on "Growth, Competitiveness, Employment." Certainly neither pronouncement holds the key to a solution. Both, however, indicate the willingness to succeed.

That leaves only the question of Europe and, more specifically, EMU. Will the strict requirements for monetary union undermine confidence in the Belgian state? If the federal government chooses to abandon its attempts at fiscal reform the answer is probably yes. However, after more than a decade of austerity measures, the Belgian people still show a surprising willingness to accept short-term sacrifice for long-term benefit. For its own part, the Dehaene government is firmly committed to bring public spending under control, albeit at a pace dictated more by the requirements of political viability than by the criteria set down in the Maastricht Treaty.

As long as Dehaene continues to make progress in reining in the deficit, Belgium is unlikely to be excluded from Europe's monetary "hard core." And it is likely that Belgium will be ready to join the EMU in 1999. According to at least some estimates, Belgium will be able to meet the 3 percent deficit criteria by that time.[53] Such an accomplishment will hardly be ignored by the rest of Europe, or indeed by the Belgians themselves.

◆ NOTES TO CHAPTER 8 ◆

1. These are the figures reported in the Belgian press, and may not be comparable internationally. Certainly they do not look the same as those reported by the European Commission.
2. This assessment is perhaps too strong. However, it is an impression that is likely to be shared by the self-effacing Dehaene. See Paul Goosens and Hubert van Humbeeck, "Er is nog leven na Korfu," *Knack* 24:27 (July 6-12, 1994), pp. 18-21.
3. Lucien Huyse, *De politiek voorbij: Een blik op de jaren negentig* (Leuven: Kritak, 1994), p. 17. Huyse is referring to Albert Hirschman's classic discussion of exit, voice and loyalty.
4. Arend Lijphart, "Consociational Democracy," *World Politics* 21:2 (1969), pp. 207-25; Lucien Huyse, *Passiviteit, pacificatie en verzuiling in de belgische politiek: Een sociologische studie* (Antwerp: Standaard Wetenschappelijke Uitgeverij, 1970).
5. For a discussion of the relationship between consociationalism and corporatism, see Ilja Scholten, "Introduction: Corporatist and Consociational Arrangements," in Ilja Scholten, ed., *Political Stability and Neo-corporatism: Corporatist Integration and Societal Cleavages in Western Europe* (London: Sage, 1987), pp. 1-38.
6. Veerle Beel, "Een kwestie van karakter," *De Standaard Magazine,* May 28, 1993, p. 13.
7. Marc Reynebeau, "Zwarte zondag bis," *Knack* 24:24 (June 15-21, 1994), pp. 14-17.
8. For an overview of Verhofstadt's renovation of the Flemish Liberals, see Jos Bouveroux, *De partij van de burger: De verruiming van de Vlaamse liberalen* (Antewerp: Standaard Uitgeverij, 1992).
9. See Gustaaf Durant, *Gaston Eyskens: Minister van Staat* (Zele: Reinaert Uitgaverij, 1983), pp. 161-70; Alain Meynen, "De economische en sociale politiek sinds de jaren 1950," in Els Witte, et al., eds., *Politieke geschiedenis van België: Van 1830 to heden,* (Brussels: VUB Press, 1990), pp. 286-88.
10. Alain Meynen, "De grote werkstaking 1960-1961: Een inleiden overzicht van de ekonomische en socio-politieke achtergronden van de grote werkstaking 1960-1961," *Belgische tijdschrift voor nieuwste geschiedenis* 9:3/4 (1978), pp. 481-515.
11. See A. Van Den Brande, "Neo-corporatism and Functional-integral Power in Belgium," in Ilja Scholten, ed., *Political Stability and Neo-corporatism,* pp. 95-119, especially p. 115.
12. Hugo De Ridder, *Omtrent Wilfried Martens* (Tielt: Lannoo, 1991).
13. Hugo De Ridder, "De vier van Poupehan," *Knack* 21:12 (March 20-26, 1991), pp. 10-13.
14. "ACV centraal in zoektocht naar akkoord," *De Standaard,* (March 26, 1993), p. 1.
15. "CVP-voorzitter wil snellere verjonging na Martens-incident," *De Standaard* (September 24, 1993), p. 1.

16. See Els Witte, "De doorbraak van een burgerlijke parlementair-constitutionele staat (1830-1848)," in Witte, et al., eds., *Politieke Geschiedenis van België*, pp. 17-61.
17. Val R. Lorwin, "Belgium: Religion, Class, and Language in National Politics," in Robert A. Dahl, ed., *Political Opposition in Western Democracies* (New Haven: Yale University Press, 1966), pp. 147-87. The paraphrase is from page 149.
18. Again, see Witte, "De doorbraak."
19. See Marc Reynebeau, "Elf dagen in Vlaanderen," *Knack* 24:27 (July 6-12, 1994), p. 12.
20. Reynebeau, "Elf dagen in Vlaanderen," p. 13.
21. Robert O. Keohane and Stanley Hoffmann, "Institutional Change in Europe in the 1980s," in Robert O. Keohane and Stanley Hoffmann, eds., *The New European Community: Decisionmaking and Institutional Change* (Boulder: Westview, 1991), pp. 1-39.
22. Peter Gourevitch, *Politics in Hard Times: Comparative Responses to Economic Crises* (Ithaca: Cornell University Press, 1986), p. 230.
23. Peter Katzenstein, *Small States in World Markets: Industrial Policy in Europe* (Ithaca: Cornell University Press, 1985).
24. Consider, for example, the Delors White Paper. European Commission, *Growth, Competitiveness, Employment: The Challenges and Ways Forward into the 21st Century* (Luxembourg: Office for Official Publications of the European Communities, 1993).
25. Eurostat, *Statististiques de base de la Communauté* 30 (1993), p. 153.
26. Guido Despiegelaere, "De prijs van een bus," *Knack* 23:48 (December 1-7, 1993), pp. 14-17.
27. See the interview with Dehaene published in the maiden issue of *Alter Ego*, a slim monthly newspaper that bills itself as a "pluralist, independent and federal monthly": Paul Goosens, "Interview met premier Jean-Luc Dehaene," *Alter Ego* 1 (April 1994), pp. 1-2.
28. Such high debt levels are a problem even if incurred for the national defense in wartime. See Michael Wickens, "There is No Substitute for Real Growth," *European Brief* 2:2 (November 1994), pp. 59-60.
29. The Keynesian deficit-led expansion of the late 1950s was modest in international terms. See Wayne Snyder, "Measuring the Effects of Belgian Budget Policies," *Cahiers économiques de Bruxelles* 44 (4th quarter 1969), pp. 527-48.
30. Robert W. R. Price and Patrice Muller, "Structural Budget Indicators and the Interpretation of Fiscal Policy Stance in OECD Economies," *OECD Economic Studies* 4 (Autumn 1984), pp. 27-72.
31. Public sector pensions date back to the 1840s. Private-sector pensions were subsidized by the state as of 1926 and then incorporated into an unfunded pension system in 1967. Finally, the standard minimum old-age pension was adopted in 1969. See Organization for Economic Cooperation and Development, *Economic Surveys: Belgium - Luxembourg* (Paris: OECD, 1994), pp. 89-90.
32. The argument from the employers's side probably seems hard to believe, since payroll contributions result in increased labor costs. However, during the 1940s, Belgian employers argued that higher labor costs and lower income taxes would lead to productivity gains, while lower labor costs and higher income taxes would lead to the full employment of an unproductive workforce. Higher taxation would also strengthen the power of the state while diminishing the sense of responsibility (which comes from participating in an insurance scheme) felt by the workers. Thus, while employers were disturbed the increase in labor costs, they felt that payroll contributions were the lesser of two evils. See Guy Vanthemsche, *De beginjaren van de sociale zekerheid in België: 1944-1963* (Brussels: VUB Press, 1994), particularly pages 76, 87, and 92-103.
33. Belgian Ministry of Finance, *Public Debt: Annual Report 1989* (1989), p. 103.
34. Calculations based on data from the European Commission.

35. This effect can be seen by comparing the deficit on total accounts to the deficit less interest payments, also known as the "primary" balance. During the period from 1984 to 1990, the total deficit averaged 7.8 percent of GDP while the primary accounts ran a surplus equal to, on average, 2.9 percent of GDP. Data provided by the European Commission.

36. André Leysens, *De naakte Staat* (Tielt: Lannoo, 1994), pp. 87-96.

37. See, for example, Paul De Grauwe, *Onze schuld: Ontstaan en toekomst van werkloosheid en staatschuld* (Tielt: Lannoo, 1994).

38. OECD, *Economic Surveys: Belgium - Luxembourg* (Paris: OECD, 1994), pp. 65-74.

39. See Hugo De Ridder "De vier van Poupehan" and *Omtrent Wilfried Martens*.

40. Josef Smits, "Belgian Politics in 1985: 'No Turning Back'," *Res Publica* 28:3 (1986), pp. 441-74.

41. Alan S. Milward, *The European Rescue of the Nation-state* (London: Routledge, 1992).

42. Milward, *European Rescue* (1992), p. 156. Data provided by the European Commission.

43. Willy Van Rijckeghem, "Benelux," in Andrea Boltho, ed., *The European Economy: Growth and Crisis* (Oxford: Oxford University Press, 1980), pp. 592-93.

44. Other commentators have made a decisively different interpretation of the role of the EMS in the recovery strategy of the Martens V government. Focussing on the events leading up to the February 1982 devaluation, they argue that the EMS strengthened Marten's position vis-à-vis the trade unions by limiting his room for maneuver. The essence of their claim is that participation in the EMS lent strength to the Belgian central bank and credibility to neo-liberal adjustment strategies. See Paulette Kurzer, *Business and Banking: Political Change and Economic Integration in Western Europe* (Ithaca: Cornell University Press, 1993) and Göran Therborn, *Why Some Peoples Are More Unemployed Than Others* (London: Verso, 1986). However, a closer look at the historical record casts doubt on the validity of that argument. To begin with, neither business nor the Christian labor movement would support a shift to the center-right under Mark Eyskens in 1981 because both groups feared this would result in speculation against the Belgian frank. Secondly, the impetus for devaluation came from the IMF (not the trade unions) and was initially resisted by central bank president Cecil De Strycker. However, once Martens was able to form a government on the center-right, economists from the Christian labor movement lobbied strongly in favor of a modest devaluation (equal to about 10 percent) against the opposition of the Liberal party. De Strycker was never consulted, and neither was the European "monetary committee" of central bankers and finance ministers. Rather, Martens went first to the IMF. Third and finally, Liberal Vice-Prime Minister Willy De Clercq agreed to accept the devaluation only on the condition that it be deepened to 14 percent. The Christian labor movement economists close to Martens were reluctant to accept such a deep devaluation, but agreed in the interest of harmony within the center-right coalition. In the end, the Germans permitted only a 8.5 percent devaluation of the frank and this was accepted as sufficient by Martens and his advisors from the Christian labor movement. The point to note is that neither the Liberal party, nor the Belgian central bank was satisfied with the outcome. See Hugo De Ridder, *Geen Winnaars in de Wetstraat* (Leuven: Davidsfonds, 1986) and *Omtrent Wilfried Martens* (1991) for detailed journalistic accounts of these events. See also Wilfried Martens, *Een gegeven woord* (Tielt: Lannoo, 1985) for the prime minister's own account of the events, as transcribed by *Knack* editor Frans Verleyen.

45. The real depreciation is measured in terms of employee compensation vis-à-vis Belgium's EMS trading partners. If it were measured against only Germany, the amount of the depreciation would be much higher. Calculations based on data from the European Commission. This interpretation of the Martens V recovery strategy is inspired by Paul De Grauwe and Wim Vanhaverbeke, "Exchange Rate Experience of

Small EMS Countries: Belgium, Denmark, and the Netherlands," in Victor Argy and Paul De Grauwe, eds., *Choosing an Exchange Rate Regime: The Challenge for Smaller Industrial Countries* (Washington, DC: International Monetary Fund, 1989), pp. 135-55 as well as the accompanying comments by Daniel Gros, pp. 156-62.

46. See E. Buyst, "De Belgische economie in een periode van internationale laagconjunctuur," *Maandschrift economie* 57:1 (1993), pp. 17-25. The need for austerity increases with a drop in competitiveness because of the slower growth of exports, and therefore GDP. The need for increased wage restraint derives from the nominal appreciation of the Belgian frank.

47. Paul De Grauwe, "De EMU zonder België?" *Leuvense Economische Standpunten* 78 (January 27, 1995).

48. See Johan Van Hecke, *De slogans voorbij: Appèl aan de verantwoordelijke Vlaming* (Tielt: Lannoo, 1994); Peter Renard, "Dichter bij elkaar," *Knack* 24:21 (May 25-31, 1994), pp. 14-19; Hubert van Humbeeck and Jos Grobben, "Leuven in de brouwerij," *Knack* 24:42 (October 19-25, 1994), pp. 12-15. The last of these is an interview with former interior minister Louis Tobback, who left his ministerial post to become mayor of the town of Leuven as well as leader of the Flemish Socialist party (SP). Tobback's predecessor as SP leader, Frank Vandenbroucke, also had mayoral ambitions. However, when he failed to form a coalition in the small community of Scherpenheuvel he had little choice but to accept the post of Belgian foreign minister as second prize. Soon thereafter, Vandenbroucke was implicated in the Augusta Scandal and forced to resign.

49. Indeed, Dehaene has already indicated his acceptance of such a fate. See Marc Reynebeau and Rik Ban Cauwelaert, "De premier doet voort," *Knack* 24:43 (October 26 - November 1, 1994), pp. 12-17.

50. For students of European integration, who tend to regard federalism as centripedal and not centrifugal, this statement must seem bizarre. However, in the Belgian context federalism is associated with the devolution—and not the centralization—of political authority.

51. Reynebeau and Cauwelaert, "De premier doet voort," p. 17.

52. De Grauwe, *Onze schuld*, pp. 71-80.

53. Paul De Grauwe, "The Black Hole in the Hard Core," *Europe Briefs* 2:2 (November 1994), p. 61. Professor De Grauwe, a senator for the Flemish Liberals and Democrats, would probably not agree with my citing him in this conclusion. His own article suggests that even meeting the 3 percent deficit to GDP ratio will hardly be enough to bring Belgium into EMU. And he has gone on record suggesting that Belgium should try to do better than only 3 percent. Personally, however, I believe even a three percent deficit to GDP ratio would be sufficient—both for Belgium and for Europe.

·9·

Britain:
The Melancholy Pleasure of Decline

Patrick McCarthy

To write an essay about the state in Britain is a very different matter from writing about the state in France or Italy. Until recently the word was barely used in normal British discourse. Frenchmen have long spoken about *l'état français* and Italians about *lo stato italiano,* but even today the "British state" sounds odd to all but those who study it. The reason why it seems odd might furnish the starting point of a discussion; in turn this could lead to the suggestion that the "British state" sounds less foreign since Margaret Thatcher's domination of it. This essay will then have five sections. The first two will present the historical problem of the state in Britain, while the third deals briefly with the British version of the Keynesian state. Thatcher's attempt to resolve the historical problem of the state merits as much space as we can afford. Finally we shall consider the contemporary situation in the British state and speculate about its future development.

"LE MAL ANGLAIS"

No other European country is as convinced of its woes as Britain. The irony that pervades culture and conversation reveals rather than masks the aware-ness of decline. Variations on when decline began and what caused it fill many volumes. Occasionally an intrepid, inevitably foreign observer questions whether Britain is declining, but the British do not heed him.[1] I shall accept the general concept of decline, noting only that each of the major European countries considers itself specially flawed. France feels that it has lagged behind first Britain and then Germany; Britain feels that it is lagging behind itself.

Even Thatcher tried to lead the country backward toward a lost Victorian splendor. A television series like *Jewel in the Crown* depicts a glorious, if already melancholic Raj; intellectuals write books about Bloomsbury because it was the silver age when a still great Britain began to contemplate decadence; formerly industrial towns have turned their factories into museums; and cricket captains such as Michael Atherton merely rub dirt on the ball, whereas Douglas Jardin nearly drove Australia out of the Empire by bowling bodyline. Melancholy breeds defiance: soccer supporters lay to waste foreign cities in order to prove their team is still the best, while Tory politicians refuse to yield to Brussels an autonomy that the Westminster parliament has long ceased to possess. Some of the decadence, however, is feigned: the revelations about the Prince and Princess of Wales merely put to rest the myth of a Royal Family that lived by moral standards that other Britains were no longer prepared to accept.

If we must begin with decline, we do not need to indulge ourselves in the many refinements of the theme. At the risk of oversimplification, I shall argue that the principal explanations overlap. Aside from a few heretics,[2] most economic historians agree with Eric Hobsbawm that decline began in the late-nineteenth century. Britain had led the world through the first two phases of the Industrial Revolution—the cotton and railway cycles—but it fell behind during the third phase, which was dominated by the electrical and chemical industries. In *Industry and Empire* Hobsbawm argues that the reasons were purely economic: British entrepreneurs continued to make money selling traditional products to colonial buyers, so they had no stimulus to develop new modes of production. Similarly foreign investment, which in the pre-1914 years accounted for three quarters of gross domestic capital formation, drew resources from domestic industry because the return on capital was higher outside Britain.

A neo-Marxist argument pushes the cause of decline back further. Britain drew ahead of France in the eighteenth century because, instead of a court aristocracy, it possessed a ruling class that farmed in a capitalist manner and traded as well. These were the younger sons who so impressed Voltaire when he visited England. However their very success meant that, while Britain could industrialize first, it could not complete the transition and create a bourgeois, capitalist ruling class. The mill owners and iron masters were absorbed into a mercantile aristocracy that held back further industrialization.[3]

Neither this nor the sociocultural interpretation of decline is incompatible with Hobsbawm. Indeed he argues that the surplus wealth created by trade was the trigger of industrialization. Moreover the Empire (whether it was the organic creation of a ruling class that had long looked abroad or the logical market of a capitalist seeking to maximize profit) was bound to change British society.

The Empire needed civil servants to govern it, missionaries to Christianize it, and soldiers to deal with indigenous populations that did not wish to be governed and Christianized. By providing outlets for capital investment— there were many others like the United States—it strengthened a financial class that was closer to the mercantile aristocracy than to the mill owners. "You could only make money, if at all," Orwell writes of the pre-1914 years, "by a mysterious operation called going into the City."[4]

Thus, argues Martin Wiener, there developed in Britain a culture that was resolutely anti-industrial and glorified rural England. Wiener gives priority to culture over economics and also traces the origin of decline back to the 1851 Exhibition, which marked the triumph and the swan song of British engineering.[5] Wiener does not help his own cause by exaggerating and oversimplifying. Culture does not directly reflect—much less shape— society and a century of British writing cannot be reduced to a plea for green fields and smiling peasants. *Tess of the d'Urbervilles* depicts the class tensions and the hardships of rural life, and at least some people read it in this way. Evelyn Waugh, who was sympathetic to Tory squires, wrote about them with fierce lucidity in *A Handful of Dust*. Yet Wiener is right to point out that Oxbridge and the great public schools awarded engineering a low priority, and that there was no British equivalent of the Ecole Polytechnique or the German Technische Hochschule.

So there survived in Britain a curious mixture of the ancient and the modern whose successes took away the impetus to radical change. Britain fell behind Germany in chemicals, but still produced in ICI one of Europe's largest chemical companies. Britain fared well in shipbuilding, which was the last of the nineteenth-century industries. Britain remained a military power. The young public-school educated officers enabled their country to play its part in the First World War victory, and British military technology continued to equal that of Germany's. In 1940 the Spitfires and Hurricanes were a match for the Messerschmidts. Indeed the habit of winning wars and attributing the triumphs to the superiority of British institutions was the most serious barrier against reform. Yet economic decline was inexorable: in the interwar years unemployment began earlier and lasted longer than in other European countries: for example, the cotton industry lost half its labor force.

A NON-STATE

Politically the pre-1914 British state was the admiration of Conservative Europe.[6] It was so harmonious that it could scarcely be called a state. One might generalize that, whereas in France the state had always provided the impetus to modernize, in Britain its original role had been to protect a dynamic civil society against tyranny. In the Nineteenth century the nation had been confirmed in its liberalism because its brief period as "workshop of the world" had taken place when simple industries such as cotton required scant help from the state, whereas the chemical industry was too complex to dispense—at least in Europe—with public intervention. This liberalism, which allowed great freedom to a civil society that was no longer as dynamic, unfolded within the context of a few institutions that were felt to represent and inspire the people.

At the center of these institutions was a constitutional but hereditary monarchy, whose rise to popularity coincided with the start of economic decline. Parliament and common law enjoyed a legitimacy (if one ignores Ireland) which the French Third Republic did not possess. Much freedom had been given to the working-class, which had suffered great hardship during the Industrial Revolution. By 1914 its institutions, the trade unions and the Labour Party, were accepted.

The Taff Vale dispute had the paradoxical effect of driving the unions deeper into politics in order to obtain the passage of the Trade Disputes Act, which reestablished free collective bargaining outside the aegis of the government. State violence was mostly reserved for the colonies: the Irish had been starved into emigration, while the Boers were placed in concentration camps. However, in England the Labour Party, far from being banned like the German Socialists, was ushered by the Liberals into the tradition of parliamentarianism. Tolerance was extended to Methodists, Catholics, and atheists by an Anglican Church, itself legitimized as much by the nation as by Christ. National identity was securely rooted in the sacred institutions.

These institutions were presented as ancient even when they were recent. Queen Victoria revamped the monarchy, turning it into a model of middle-class rectitude. Even then it was not until the closing years of her reign that she appeared more frequently in public and became well-liked. The cult of the countryside was born of the opposition to further industrialization. The obvious defects of Britain's institutions were masked by this spurious traditionalism. The second chamber was gutted of power in 1911 but retained prestige because it was a club for hereditary peers. The medieval spires of Oxford hid the fact that in 1914 Britain had nine thousand university students and Germany sixty thousand.

In this seemingly "idyllic"[7] setting the two political parties that would dominate most of the twentieth century took their places. The Conservatives were not merely and not sufficiently the party of capitalism. Industrialists moved over to them as the Liberals grew ever more ambiguous about economic issues, but the Conservatives were the party of the ruling class as a whole and hence also the party of Britain's world role. Two generations of Chamberlains tried to change this to a protectionist imperial bloc in which domestic industry could be rebuilt. But Neville Chamberlain's appeasement meant that in the aftermath of the Second World War Winston Churchill's version of internationalism, which took scant account of industry, would win out.

The Labour Party was little more than the political arm of the Trade Unions. Dispatched to Westminster to reverse the Taff Vale decision, it was the voice of a working class that was eager, with clear reservations, and allowed, subject to understood conditions, to take its place in the grand order. An ambitious program of social reform was enacted before 1914. Of course there were conflicts of interest. The return to the Gold Standard, undertaken to further the financial interests of the City of London, precipitated the 1926 General Strike that left the coal miners bitter, and that helps explain the 1984 clash between the miners and the government.

Such conflicts fostered change: the memory of the Depression helped produce the Labour landslide in 1945. But the basic settlement that had emerged before 1914 endured into the 1970s. A minimalist but sacred state, in which very different social actors agreed to cohabit, produced stagnation. One might, for example, have imagined an alliance between labor and domestic industry against finance capital. None developed, which may vindicate Hobsbawm's thesis. In Germany, the dynamic Bismarckian state had forced the cohabiting partners to modernize, but the British state envisioned no such role.

Meanwhile the unions were interested in redistribution, but not in production. They were belligerent toward industrialists, but they did not seek to replace them. Nor did they think that economic decline was their concern. In the depths of the Depression, Orwell complained with some exaggeration that there was no turbulence left in England.[8] Class distinctions were ossified. They were sharper in Italy, but in no country was the awareness of class so pervasive and so caste-like as in Britain. It was the reverse side of the early acceptance of the industrial proletariat.

King, Parliament and Empire were protected by rituals that the escapades of an Edward Vlll barely marred. The Conservatives felt themselves to be the high priests of the temple and hence the natural party of government. Labour offered no more than perfunctory challenges to institutions such as the public schools and a mandarin civil service blessed with a classical education. Such deference explains why "the very notion of the state . . . is alien to the British political tradition."[9] Economic liberalism, the strength of civil society but above all this premodern reverence explain the distrust of the state as a rational, organizing force.

One returns to the key difference between Britain and most of continental Europe. In Italy, the state was ubiquitous because the new nation was playing catch-up and the industrial bourgeoisie, like every other segment of society, wanted help. The formula did not work: the overworked state was inefficient and corrupt. In France, the Third Republic feared the might of the state and limited its power, but after the Second World War the dirigist state became the motor of economic modernization. The British state had no such resources. However, at least until 1945 the Britain looked far more stable and even more democratic than continental Europe.

Still the miners' bitterness showed there was more, albeit suppressed, turbulence than Orwell imagined. In Britain the lack of a rationalizing state left the social actors—the City, the unions, the civil service, the Anglican bishops—holding power in an uneasy alliance. None was strong enough to defeat the others but each held the others back. The debate about whether Britain's international role lay in maintaining free trade or in creating an imperial, protectionist bloc racked the Conservatives. So the rituals of unity hid conflicts and fragmentation.

However, acquiescence in the rituals came easily to a deferential population. In return it received a civic freedom (except in Northern Ireland) that entranced visitors from continental Europe. Of these some, like Sigmund Freud, were fleeing appalling dictatorships. Others merely disliked having to carry identity cards. This group joined forces with Americans in quest of tradition to produce a weird hybrid called the Anglophile, who admired in Britain precisely those things which made for stagnation.[10] Other foreigners had been more perceptive: the best French observer of pre-1914 Britain, Valery Larbaud, chronicled the end of the grand Victorian nation.[11]

In 1940, this ancient-modern Britain had its greatest but also its most disastrous hour. When continental Europe fell to Adolph Hitler, it held. It would not of course have won the war without the United States and the Soviet Union, but it mobilized its population with a success that demonstrated how well its non-state could work. Alas, it also exhausted its reserves and ushered onto the world stage its successor, the United States. Worst of all, its victory blinded it to the need for fundamental change, which the defeated French recognized.

THE KEYNESIAN ILLUSION

It seems grossly unfair to argue that Britain did not change. The Labour government has been depicted as the cutting edge of reformism, the maintainer of the market while correcting it with nationalizations and planning, and the creator of the welfare state.[12] In the context of economic decline Labour's achievement was more narrow, but even here Stafford Cripps's policy of freeing resources for production by an effort of austerity has won praise. However, Labour continued the choice of seeking a world role, both military and financial, although it meant playing junior partner to the United States. In particular it meant exposing the pound as a reserve currency to buttress the dollar. The option of a different international role as the leader of a European bloc was barely considered. By the time Labour left office in 1951 economic planning had been virtually abandoned. Nor had the nationalization of the Bank of England given the government real power over financial matters.

The Conservatives had even less inclination to reconsider Britain's international role, which they backed with high military spending: in 1952 it stood at 10.5 percent of gross national product (GNP).[13] They spoke the rhetoric of free enterprise and did little to help domestic industry. Nor, still shell-shocked by their 1945 defeat, did they dare challenge the power of the trade unions. Thus the forces that had presided over "pluralistic stagnation" remained in place.[14]

Two contradictory changes distinguished the postwar from the prewar. The first was Keynesianism, which was adopted by both the major parties. Demand management seemed to resolve the problem of unemployment and to stimulate growth. It lent itself to a centrist brand of politics that allowed the uneasy alliance of very different classes and interest groups to continue.

Although interventionist, Keynesian methods militated against tougher forms of intervention, whether of the Left (planning) or of the Right (anti-union legislation). It thus removed the need to make hard choices. Adapted to a stop-go cycle it reconciled domestic industry's demand for cheap credit and the City's demand for a strong pound, while achieving neither goal over a sustained period.

In the context of the U.S.-led postwar boom Keynesianism enabled Britain to achieve higher standards of living and higher levels of consumption than ever before. Combined with the residual prestige of the Second World War victory (itself nurtured by a flood of popular war films), the new prosperity cast a glow of shiny cars, domestic appliances, and televisions over the 1950s. However, observers noted that British growth levels were well below those in continental Europe: between 1951 and 1964 production increased by 40 percent, compared with 150 percent in Italy and West Germany. British exports grew by 29 percent and French exports by 86 percent.[15]

The comparisons may be unfair because postwar Britain was starting from a higher level, but British decline was showing through the Keynesian façade. It found its clearest expression in foreign policy. The Suez fiasco demonstrated that Britain could not act alone in the world and that the United States—quite naturally—would not offer automatic support. The solution was to join the nascent European Community (EC) but Harold Macmillan's bid was belated and botched. Charles de Gaulle might have vetoed Britain anyway but Macmillan made it easy for him by opting for a nuclear deterrent that was autonomous (of Europe but not of the United States). Before that, the British campaign for entry was unenthusiastic because it was encumbered with a concept of national sovereignty that ascribed a unique value to institutions like the Westminster Parliament. Parliament had emerged from the victory over totalitarian Germany with renewed renown, as had the monarchy that was strengthened by George VI's decision to remain in London during the bombing.

At home Britain needed to be finished with pluralistic stagnation, but the compromises were carved in stone. The unions continued to let management manage but exacted wage increases that the companies passed on in the form of higher prices. Anachronisms abounded as the civil service was still better suited to running an empire than a modern economy; engineers were not promoted in business, and businessmen were excluded from the ruling group of the Conservative Party. It was necessary for one actor to break out of this charmed but condemned circle and the obvious candidate was the state.

Like all other modern states, the British state had acquired new responsibilities. Moreover Britain ran the welfare services with an honesty and an efficiency that were unthinkable in Italy. But welfare was meant to patch up the old compromises and to stabilize relations among the social classes. It exacted no sacrifices from anyone. By contrast, modernizing the economy meant shaking up the working and middle classes, as well as the educational and bureaucratic elites. The British state lacked the instruments which the French state possessed.

The old political actors remained locked in this conflictual alliance. The Labour Party could persuade the unions to modify their wage demands for a short time, but it could not alter their decentralized structure, which left the Trade Unions Council (TUC) unable to play a corporatist role. The Conservatives continued to straddle domestic industry and the City, which invested worldwide. Since, elections were closely contested throughout the 1950s and 1960s, neither party could afford to alienate a large block of voters. Economic intervention served to preserve the existing order rather than promote innovation. Regional aid and lame ducks took precedence over seed money for new technology. The contrast with the French state, detached and hence able to direct and to arbitrate, was striking.

Both parties attempted planning. The Conservative bid foundered in the chaos of Macmillan's last years, while Labour floundered between defending the pound and battling the unions. Planning would have been no panacea. Indeed its value might have lain less in the intelligent allocation of resources than in jolting the various actors out of their frozen postures. It might have forced management and labor to cooperate or increased the prestige of the engineer.

A long overdue crisis came in the 1970s. Both major parties were discredited and in the Spring 1974 election they gained only 74.9 percent of the vote, whereas the figure for the 1955 elections had been 96.1 percent. Fragmentation rather than the rise of a coherent new party accounted for the lost votes: Scottish nationalism reflected dissatisfaction with English rule rather than a convinced demand for self-rule, while the Liberals and later the Social Democrats represented an odd lament for the lost, failed centrism.

The lament arose because the major parties were deserting their long held positions. The 1974 oil crisis removed the illusion of Keynesianism, and the 1976 recourse to the International Monetary Fund (IMF) was yet another blow to national pride. The Irish question returned as the North ceased to simmer and instead boiled over; Britain began a twenty-five year struggle against the Irish Republican Army (IRA). The Labour Party went in two directions, each disastrous. In power from 1974 to 1979, the Labour party attempted a long period of wage restraint, alienated the unions, and went down to defeat after the Winter of Discontent. In opposition after 1979, Labour lurched unconvincingly to the Left, it lost around 25 percent of its electorate in the 1983 elections, and it aroused among voters a distrust that has lasted until today and was a factor in its 1992 defeat.[16]

In the 1950s awareness that Britain was not participating fully in the postwar boom was limited to an elite. Now the sense of crisis was everywhere. Novelist Margaret Drabble captured national sentiment well in 1977: "over the country depression lay like fog . . . people blamed other people for all the things that were going wrong—the trade unions, the present government, the miners, the car workers, the seamen, the Arabs, their own husbands. . . . A huge, icy fist with large cold fingers was squeezing and chilling the people of Britain, that great and puissant nation, slowing down their blood, locking them into immobility."[17] No generic depiction of decadence, this passage reveals the stagnation and fragmentation of British society, as well as a certain self-indulgence, a frustrated search for explanations and a tendency to blame working-class actors. The way was open for Margaret Thatcher.

A STRONG STATE TO DO WHAT?

Thatcher's supposed dislike of statism is a red herring.[18] The Conservative Party reiterated its distrust of the rational, inevitably overbearing state and its preference for a web of local communities of which the state is a mere handmaiden.[19] Thatcher herself described a social chain of individual, family, market, and nation. But when she attacked the state she concentrated her fire on the Keynesian state, and her criticism was that it was too weak. The Heath government's supposed defeat at the hands of the coal miners in 1974 was the example to be avoided. In general Thatcher felt that, coddled by universal social services and subsidies for inefficient industries, the individual lost the urge for wealth-creation and autonomy. Similarly the state lost its capacity to choose and to command. It was a moral rather than an economic crisis, and it must be resolved by the creation of a different and stronger state. One might call it the monetarist state.

Thatcher was acutely aware of British decline, but to what extent did she understand that the real problem was the old non-state and not its Keynesian mask? In part she did. Several of the institutions linked with the Conservatives—Oxbridge and the Church of England—incurred her wrath.

To the extent that she was able to break out of pluralistic stagnation Thatcher was successful. But her monetarist state was too one-sided and too negative to transform Britain as she sought.

The New Right thought that she injected into Conservatism had taught Thatcher that the state had lost its prestige by attempting to do too much. Ideally it should limit itself to making the market operate efficiently by supplying external security, internal order, competition and price stability. But in practice decades of Keynesianism had choked the market and only state power could liberate it. That in itself was sufficient reason to strengthen the state. Since in fact the problem lay deeper, the state would have to undo nearly a century of history.

Throughout her years in office Thatcher added to the state's coercive power. In 1984 she passed the Police and Criminal Evidence Act, which allowed the police greater freedom to stop and search people, while in 1986 came the Public Order Act granting the police more leeway in the control of crowds. The Protection of Privacy Bill (1988) limited investigative journalism, while an Official Secrets Bill (1989) excluded public interest as a defense of civil servants who disclosed evidence of crimes. Thatcher conducted an extraordinary campaign to prevent the publication of *Spycatcher*, the memoirs of an ex-Secret Service Agent, Peter Wright. Inevitably Northern Ireland bore the brunt of this restriction of civil liberties: Sinn Féin spokesmen were denied access to the media (although in this Thatcher was following legislation introduced by the Irish government) and trial without jury was widely used.

Still more important was Thatcher's campaign to concentrate state power in her own eager hands. Over the years she weeded out from the Cabinet and other positions of power in her party members of the "wet" tendency like James Prior, Ian Gilmour, or Peter Walker. They were replaced by "harder" men like Norman Tebbit and the culture of the Conservative Party was changed. Even as she increased her own power, Thatcher set out to gain a reputation as a tough leader who did not flinch from difficult decisions. Thus she allowed a group of IRA hunger strikers to die in 1981, persisted (at least officially) with deflationary policies in the face of escalating unemployment in the same year and then went off to war against General Leopoldo Galtieri.

Foreign policy allowed Thatcher the opportunity to demonstrate that hers was a new brand of government. It is unlikely that previous governments, whether Labour or Conservative, would have sent a fleet to recover the Falklands. Certainly no earlier government had been as rude to the other

EC leaders or as crude in its anticommunism. Ironically the substance of most of her foreign policy was not new. Indeed it continued the bid for a world role, based on the special relationship, which was an integral part of *le mal anglais*. The chance to turn the Franco-German leadership of Europe into a troika was toyed with from 1984 to 1987 and then missed.

Continuity of content was combined with a more rhetorical style that emphasized to domestic groups that they might receive the same treatment as Galtieri. For the reconciling, Keynesian state Thatcher substituted her fierce brand of nationalism, which tended to exclude internal enemies like the Toxteth or Brixton rioters, immigrants, and striking coal miners. When Thatcher talked of Britain it seemed a *Gemeinschaft* rather than a *Gesellschaft*. At its head was a state that had at last become an active force in itself: deliberately conflictual and divisive.[20]

For the old forms of the sacred like the monarchy, Thatcher, whose relations with Queen Elizabeth were supposedly tense, substituted her own Methodist vision of the British people as uniquely democratic because they are steeped in the Bible (finally the nonconformist children really would go marching through the land!). A limitation on the new state was that, unlike de Gaulle's Fifth Republic, it spawned no new institutions. Thatcher had partially changed her party so that much would depend on her successor; for the rest her influence would be her own. She was the state.

The task of reviving its authority was a prerequisite to using it to destroy its Keynesian predecessor. This aspect of the Thatcher state is demonstrated by its dealings with local government. The Conservative Party admired local administration in which it saw a genuine community at work. Although she paid lip service to this view, Thatcher at once clashed with local authorities because their extravagance in the years after she took office made it more difficult for her to reduce total public spending. She tried various tactics like capping the rates and cutting the central government subsidy to local councils that overspent. However, Labour-dominated authorities, like the Greater London Council (GLC), persisted in overspending therefore in 1986 Thatcher abolished the GLC along with the six regional councils.

Even this exercise of central government might did not satisfy her. She disliked the local authorities' reliance on the rates or property tax because it worked against home owners, whom she considered—rather dubiously— her natural supporters in her struggle to promote the values of self-reliant capitalism. Once more the Thatcherian state went to battle on their behalf. After the 1987 elections she abolished the rates and introduced a flat-rate poll tax to be paid by all adults. Such a class-based use of the state aroused intense opposition and had—admittedly for its clumsiness as much as for its social bias—to be withdrawn.

Similarly Thatcher attacked left-wing local education authorities for their wasteful ways and their attempt to impose an egalitarian school system. She encouraged schools to drop out of the local network and made provision for parents to exert greater influence in running them. However, parent-teacher associations, while once more a kind of neighborhood community, could not run the schools without help from the Ministry of Education.

The monetarist state had to specialize in saying no if it was to win the struggle against inflation, restore the values of the market and end British decline. Thatcher publicly stood firm in 1981 as unemployment rose sharply, and her remark "the lady's not for turning" became part of her legend. She stopped pumping money into smokestack industries to preserve employment. Steel, subsidized by the previous Labour government, was restructured and made profitable at the cost of massive lay-offs. Work practices changed as management regained control of the shop floor.

Thatcher's greatest struggle was against the unions because they were not just a creation of the Keynesian state, but an integral part of the underlying pre-1914 settlement. Thatcher used three methods: legislation, which ran from restrictions on picketing to making unions liable for damages unless they had consulted their members before calling an official strike; allowing unemployment to rise, which weakened militancy; and frontal clashes such as the year-long pit stoppage. Arthur Scargill proved as good an ally as General Galtieri in helping Thatcher demonstrate her might and avenge the defeat suffered by the Conservatives in 1974.

Removing the unions from the group of actors responsible for pluralistic stagnation was probably a lasting achievement. Exploiting and increasing union unpopularity, Thatcher also forced the Labour Party to distance itself from them and slowly to modernize its culture. However, she did less to force changes in the other actors. It seems remarkable that wage levels continued to rise faster than inflation despite union weakness. Between 1982 and 1989 the annual growth of earnings was between 7.5 percent and 9.5 percent, even when inflation ran at around 4 percent.[21] At least one reason was the ingrained complacency of British employers. Similarly Thatcher helped the City with the 1986 Big Bang deregulation, but the City demonstrated that it was unable to run its own affairs by indulging in a series of scandals that ran from the takeover of Guinness Distilleries to the huge losses suffered by Lloyds Insurance Companies.

Conversely one might argue that Thatcher did nothing for the City nor for industry except deregulate. Stable exchange rates would have suited bankers better but Thatcher held Nigel Lawson back from joining the European Monetary System (EMS). Industry suffered from a shortage of skilled labour but the government was inefficient in improving job training.[22] Nonintervention was a key tenet of the monetarist state, but it is hard to see how British economic actors, accustomed to decline, could improve their performance without assistance. Under Thatcher the manufacturing sector lost 2.1 million workers. Not until 1987 did production return to the 1979 level and, although output per head increased by 4.2 percent per annum, much of that was the result of labor shedding. Services did better and yet non-manufacturing trade was in deficit by 1990. Real GDP per head increased by 2.1 percent per annum, which was average for Western Europe.[23] But other countries have come down to the British level rather than Britain's rising to theirs.

It has been argued that Britain simply became less democratic under Thatcher.[24] But judgement on the state she created will probably be based on the more complex question of whether it halted or merely slowed a decline which, although most visibly economic, had by 1979 embraced many features of British life. The soaring inflation of her last years—it stood at 11 percent in September 1990—and the depth of the recession that followed indicate that the recovery of the mid-1980s was fragile. The South East, which had gained most under Thatcher, who had increased inequality among the regions, was now worst hit, while many of her beloved small businessmen went bankrupt. However, by the end of 1994 recovery got underway, and there are signs that industry is more flexible. Underlying attitudes may not have changed much: only 32 percent of people think entrepreneurs make a real contribution to society, whereas in Germany the figure is 60 percent.[25]

My opinion, which can be no more than provisional, is that, although occasionally iconoclastic, Thatcher left too much of the old England intact. Imbued with hatred for the Left, which to her meant radical trade union leaders, countercyclical government spending, and the EC Commission, she knew intuitively that there were other reasons for Britain's decline but she did not give priority to changing them. The public schools, the House of Lords, and the legal system were spared because they were on the Right. Second the monetarist state was aggressive, but it did not nurture. True the 1980s was no period for dirigism, but Thatcher did not see that civil society needs what has been called the "infrastructural" presence of the state:[26] the state's capacity to provide services like education and communications.

Heedless of the quiet (hardly a Thatcherian adjective) dialogue between the state and its citizens, Thatcher was also poor at bargaining for Britain abroad. Her antipathy to the EC was important not because the EC offered instant solutions to *le mal anglais,* as Heath had hoped, but because her Methodist fervor encouraged a narrow nationalism that was the debased form assumed by the pre–1914 settlement. Pride in Empire and in the Victorian achievements had shrunk to a desperate defiance of the powerful Franco–German-led EC, which found expression in outbursts like Nicholas Ridley's hysterical anti-German harangue. In this sense Thatcher's state was as much a part of, as a cure for, British decline.

AN EMPTY SHELL

In the years since her departure the British state has remained intact, but without Thatcher's activism it is empty. Power is still centralized in the Conservative Party leadership or at least in the parliamentary group. Indeed after Labour's fourth successive election defeat in 1992 Britain seemed to be becoming a one-party state. Under John Major the cabinet has become more collegial, but local government has not been revived. Much of the work it did has been taken over by quangos responsible to ministers.[27] But the government seems not to know what to do with this and its other powers.

Conventional wisdom holds that the vacuum at the center stems from Major's inability to lead, but in the context of this book and this essay the problems lie deeper. The "monetarist" state, which was Thatcher's creation, has run its course. The government has backed off from privatizing the Post Office and, while further denationalizations are possible, they are unlikely to make great economic impact. The limits of popular shareownership as a form of participation in an advanced society are clear: big companies are run by their management and the dominant, mostly institutional investors. The number of people who want to buy their own council houses is finite. Most important, the welfare state has retained its legitimacy. Major's attempt to move toward the political center shows he has understood this process.

Yet the problems which stem from the global economy and are exacerbated by the historical deficiencies of the British state remain. Three are important, and all were bequeathed to Major by Thatcher. The first is political corruption, which is caused at least partly by parties' declining sense of mission and is revealed at least partly because of the electorate's declining trust in its parties. Tales of Members of Parliament taking money to ask parliamentary questions are trivial by Italian standards, but they strike a blow at the "Mother of Parliaments." Meanwhile the retrospective revelations about aid to Malaysia and about Mark Thatcher's possible abuse of his mother's position throw a searchlight on the Thatcher years as well as on the recent history of British institutions. That the legality of using Overseas Development Funds for the dam should be challenged in court by a watchdog group shows a healthy disregard for deference.

More serious are the economic difficulties. Although the economy is recovering, this is partly cyclical, and traditional weaknesses such as the shortage of skilled labor have returned. Moreover the government has not so far been credited with creating the revival, whereas it was greatly discredited by the September 1992 withdrawal from the EMS. This hints at the conclusion that people do not believe the British state has any control over the global economy.

Still more serious is the split within the Conservative Party over the EU. Major's Maastricht compromise did not spare him a Eurorebellion that began in June 1992 and has continued ever since. It is all the more damaging because the perils of federalism, which the anti-Europeans denounce, are mostly imaginary. Outbursts like Patrick Nicholls's dismissal of the French as collaborators and the Germans as warmongers (shades of Ridley) can hardly not be interpreted as a sign that the party of government has no idea what Britain's international role might be. Meanwhile clinging to the autonomy of the Westminister parliament seems just one more refusal of the contemporary world. It is an ironic counterpoint to the electorate's lack of faith in its politicians and it weakens the government's bargaining position in Europe.

In this moment of public disaffection the daily delving into the most intimate details of the heir to the throne's marriage take on a special meaning. It is not enough to dismiss them by arguing that the monarchy plays in Britain the role played in the United States by Hollywood stars. As we have argued the monarchy was part of the premodern structure of British institutions. It was to be public, but an object of admiration and not of scandal. It is hard to see how Prince Charles can regain his subjects' admiration, and the most significant of his revelations is the criticism he has leveled at his parents. Their failings cannot be attributed to youthful irresponsibility or the temptations of modernity but are part of the institution of the monarchy.

Moreover the crisis of the royal family is accompanied by growing public skepticism about other institutions such as the police and the legal system. Both emerge discredited from the affair of the Birmingham Six, where the police appeared to have manufactured evidence and extorted confessions and the judges to have accepted both with scant pretense of impartiality.[28] Nor is this an isolated case. As an answer to the skepticism Major's Citizen's Charter seems only slightly more useful than the *Private Eye* parodies of it.

It appears to me that there are three broad scenarios of what the future of the British state might be. The first is that the loss of faith in public institutions should be lived as a positive process, which would lead to less deference, secrecy, and reliance on the provenly dubious virtue of elites. The monarchy may indeed be "an idea whose time has passed,"[29] and along with it the notions of an established church and a hereditary second chamber. An elected second chamber could be a more useful complement to, and check on, the House of Commons. Local government would be revived in harmony with the trend toward decentralization in other European countries.

In this less sacred and more secular state a written Bill of Rights would replace the reliance on the traditions of Common Law. Economic ramifications might be improved provision for information and consultation of workers, which would be a better long-term gamble than the present reliance on attracting foreign investors by offering them cheap, passive labour. Reducing the power of unions has been confused with demoralizing the workforce. Engineers and entrepreneurs might actually gain public esteem. Politically the secular state would be less reluctant to perceive its chief role as bargaining in international fora. In particular it would abandon its minimalist attitude towards the EU. Finally it would be desirable that a Labour election victory should reestablish the alternation of parties in power.

If this is utopia, then the nightmare might be another round of disillusionment akin to that of the 1970s, but all the worse for that reason. The Conservatives would rule indefinitely with less than 50 percent of the vote. Abroad Britain would be left behind by a Franco–German-led EU core, while the more inward-looking stance of U.S. leaders would make yet another mockery of the special relationship. At home the unhealthy domination of national life by London would go unchallenged. There would be periodic bouts of violence by and against immigrants, as divisions between inner city areas and suburbs would grow deeper. For the monarchy the nightmare might simply be more of the same.

The most likely scenario lies somewhere between the two. Tony Blair has created at least the possibility of an alternative government, and his talk of community, while vague, hints at some infrastructural role for the state. Civil service reform is underway. A small opportunity is being offered finally to resolve the "Irish question." However, serious institutional reform is as unlikely as improved worker consultation. Moreover it is hard to believe that the British can or even wish to shake off a sense of decline, which has become an integral, cherished part of national life.[30]

◆ NOTES TO CHAPTER 9 ◆

1. See *The Economist* review—July 17, 1993, p. 87—of W. D. Rubinstein, *Capitalism, Culture and Decline in Britain* (London: Routledge, 1993).

2. Sidney Pollard, *The Wasting of the British Economy* (London: Croom Helm, 1982). Pollard dates decline from 1945.

3. Perry Anderson, *English Questions* (London: Verso, 1992).

4. George Orwell, "Such, Such Were the Joys," *Collected Essays, Journalism and Letters,* Volume 4 (London: Penguin Books, 1970), p. 379.

5. Martin J. Wieser, *English Culture and the Decline of the Industrial Spirit* (Cambridge: Cambridge University Press, 1988).

6. In 1871 the French traveler, Hipolyte Taine, admired in Britain the combination of industrial success and stable government. The ex-Communard, Jules Vallès, saw oppression not stability but agreed about industrial might.

7. Ralf Dahrendorf, *On Britain* (Chicago: University of Chicago Press, 1982), p. 74.

8. Orwell, *Collected Essays,* Volume 1, p. 296.

9. David Marquand, "The Decline of the Post-War Consensus," in A. Gorst, L. Johnman and W. S. Lucas, eds., *Post-War Britain 1945–64* (London: Pinter, 1989), p. 9.

10. A good example of anglophilia is Bernard Nossiter, *Britain, a Future that Works* (London: André Deutsch, 1978). Ralf Dahrendorf's *On Britain* is a long struggle between his critical judgement and his anglophilia: he knows the sovereignty of the Westminister parliament is a "fiction" but still considers it "pleasing," p. 104.

11. See Larbaud's review of Vallès's *La rue à Londres* in Valery Larbaud, *Oeuvres complètes,* Volume 3 (Paris: Gallimard, 1950-55), pp. 417-21.

12. Leonardo Paggi, "Prefazione" to his edited *Americanismo e riformismo* (Turin: Einaudi, 1989).

13. Peter Oppenheimer "Muddling through: the Economy 1951-1964" in Vernon Bogdanov and Robert Skidelsky, eds., *The Age of Affluence* (London: Macmillan, 1970), p. 121.

14. Samuel Beer, *Britain Against Itself* (New York: Norton, 1982), p. 25.

15. Michael Pinto-Duschinsky, "Bread and Circuses: the Conservatives in Office," in Bogdanov and Skidelsky, eds., *The Age of Affluence,* p. 57.

16. A. Heath, R. Jowell, J. Curtice, "Can Labour win?" in their edited *Labour's Last Chance: the 1992 Elections and Beyond* (Aldershot: Dartmouth,' 1994), p. 288.

17. Margaret Drabble, *The Ice Age* (London: Weidenfeld and Nicolson, 1977), p. 59. Drabble became a leader in the intellectual opposition to Thatcher. But her novels about the Thatcher years, such as *The Radiant Way,* depict university-educated, usually anti-Thatcher characters from a puritan viewpoint that stresses their flimsiness.

18. Andrew Gamble, *The Free Economy and the Strong State: the Politics of Thatcherism* (London: Macmillan, 1994). I have drawn heavily on this excellent study.

19. David Willetts, *Modern Conservatism* (London: Penguin, 1992), p. 105.

20. For Thatcher's use of language see my "Il linguaggio di Margaret Thatcher," *Europa/Europe* 2 (1993), pp. 151-70.

21. Andrea Bolto, "Has Mrs Thatcher changed the British economy," *Rivista di politica economica* (April 1989), p. 275.

22. Leslie Hannah, "Mrs Thatcher, Capital-Basher?" in Denis Kavanaugh and Anthony Seldon, eds., *The Thatcher Effect* (Oxford: Oxford University Press, 1989), p. 47.

23. Samuel Brittan, "The Government's Economy Policy" in Kavanaugh and Seldon, eds., *The Thatcher Effect*, p. 12. Brittan's judgement is positive.
24. Anthony Sampson, *The Essential Anatomy of Britain* (London: Hodder and Staughton, 1992).
25. *The Economist*, May 28, 1994, p. 72. For a negative judgement on Thatcher's economic policy see John Wells, "The Economy After Ten Years" in Nigel M. Healey, ed., *Britain's Economic Miracle: Myth or Reality?* (London: Routledge, 1993), pp. 91-108.
26. John A. Hall, "The State and Economic Development," in his edited *States in History* (Oxford: Basil Blackwell, 1986), p. 174.
27. *The Economist*, August 6, 1994, p. 31.
28. Chris Mullin, *Error of Judgement: The Birmingham Bombings* (London: Chatto and Windus, 1986).
29. *The Economist*, October 22, 1994, p. 13.
30. I wish to thank Karaca Mestci who worked as my research assistant on this essay.

C O N T R I B U T O R S

DANA H. ALLIN

is Deputy Director of the Aspen Institute Berlin. He has written a number of articles on Germany, and his most recent book is *Cold War Illusions: America, Europe and Soviet Power, 1969–1989*.

DAVID P. CALLEO

is Dean Acheson Professor and Director of European Studies, Paul H. Nitze School of Advanced International Studies of the Johns Hopkins University. His most recent books include *The Imperious Economy*, *Beyond American Hegemony*, and *The Bankrupting of America*.

SERGIO FABBRINI

is Associate Professor of International Relations at the Instituto Universario Orientale of Naples and Professor of Comparative Politics at the University of Trento. His most recent book is *Quale democrazia, l'Italia e gli altri*.

JULIUS W. FRIEND

has been lecturer on French Politics and History at the Paul H. Nitze School of Advanced International Studies of the Johns Hopkins University, and is adjunct Professor of European History at the George Washington University. He was also chairman for Area Studies on Francophone Europe at the Foreign Service Institute. He retired in 1979 from the Central Intelligence Agency as a senior analyst in European Affairs. His major publications include *The Linchpin: French-German Relations 1950-1990* and *Seven Years in France: François Mitterrand and the Unintended Revolution*. He is now preparing a history of the Mitterrand period, 1981-1995.

MICHAEL J. GREEN

is a member of the research staff for the Institute for Defense Analyses, and he is a senior research associate at the MIT–Japan Program, and a professorial Lecturer in Japanese Studies at the Paul H. Nitze School of Advanced International Studies of the Johns Hopkins University.

ERIK JONES

is a Research Fellow at the Centre for European Policy Studies (Brussels) and an Assistant Professor of International Relations and European Studies at the Central European University (Prague).

GREGORY P. MARCHILDON

is an adjunct Professor in the Canadian Studies Program at the Paul H. Nitze School of Advanced International Studies of the Johns Hopkins University.

PATRICK MCCARTHY

is a Professor of European Studies at the Bologna Center of the Johns Hopkins University. He is author of *Céline, Camus* and *The Crisis of The Italian State* and has edited *The French Socialists in Power 1981–1989* and *France-Germany 1983–1993: The Struggle to Cooperate.*

I N D E X